P9-CQS-171

The President Speaks
Annual Addresses Delivered
To The National Baptist Convention of America
1898–1986

Edited By
Marvin C. Griffin, Historian
National Baptist Convention of America

Copyright © 1989 National Baptist Convention of America, Inc.
Library of Congress CIP Number 89-9830
ISBN 1-55513-085-2

Table of Contents

Preface

Presidential addresses of the National Baptist Convention of America in this book cover the evolution of the Black Baptist National Organization and the struggle for unity from 1898 to 1986.

Two addresses appear in 1916, delivered by Dr. E. C. Morris (National Baptist Convention, Incorporated) and Dr. E. P. Jones (National Baptist Convention of America). These two addresses enable the reader to see the separation from the viewpoint of each Convention President, following the "split" in 1915.

This has been a labor of love which stems from my election as historian of the National Baptist Convention in Detroit, Michigan in 1958. In the absence of a historical depository by the Convention, the task has been difficult, challenging, and rewarding.

Grateful acknowledgment is made to the following:

American Baptist Historical Collection, Rochester, New York; Southern Baptist Historical Society, Nashville, Tennessee; and Moorland-Spingarn Research Center, Howard University, Washington, D.C.

President E. Edward Jones assisted by prodding, encouraging, and supporting the goal to research and publicize historical information concerning the National Baptist Convention of America.

Clerical assistance in typing and reading of the manuscript by Irene H. Thompson, Bettye H. Johnson, and Dawne Thompson-Washington.

This book is a result of the guiding hand of my mother, Beulah Griffin, who introduced me to the Baptist family. It would not have reached publication without the patience and loving concern of my wife, Lois.

My hope is that this historical project will help keep alive the praiseworthy traditions of Black Baptists in America.

Marvin C. Griffin
Austin, Texas
December, 1987

Elias C. Morris

Elias C. Morris (1855-1921) was born May 7, 1855, of slave parents in Murray County, Georgia, on a plantation. After the Civil War, his parents moved to Chattanooga, Tennessee. Eighteen months later, they moved to Alabama. There, he received common school training. He learned the trade of a shoemaker under Rev. Robert Caver, who rewarded his diligence be placing him in charge of his business.

In 1874, he was baptized in Star Baptist Church, Stevenson, Alabama. He was granted license to preach in 1875. He attempted to establish a church, but before the work was completed, he was persuaded to go west. He arrived in Helena, Arkansas, March 7, 1877, and joined the Centennial Baptist Church. In 1879, he was called to the pastorate. For many years, he pastored First Baptist Church, Helena, Arkansas, one of the largest churches in the state.

He was elected Secretary of the Arkansas Baptist State Convention in 1880 and became President in 1882. He served six months as an agent of the American Baptist Home Mission Society. He assisted in organizing the Baptist Foreign Mission Convention of the United States. He organized the *Arkansas Times*, the first denominational paper in the state, which later became the *Baptist Vanguard*. He founded the *People's Friend*, a weekly newspaper circulated in the South and Southwest.

In 1884, he founded Arkansas Baptist College, which was supported and controlled by Black Baptists. He was President for two years and thereafter served for many years as Chairman of the Board of Trustees.

He was Vice-President of the American National Baptist Convention; President of the Baptist Foreign Mission Convention of the United States; and President of the Publishing Committee of the Baptist Magazine.

He was honored by the people of Arkansas as a delegate to the National Convention of Colored Men in 1881; the National Republican Convention, 1884; and trustee of the Helena School Board.

Dr. Morris was President of the National Baptist Convention (U.S.A., Incorporated) for twenty-eight years (1893-1921). He was eloquent as a preacher, mighty in debate, cool and clear-headed in business, genial in disposition, and unswerving in loyalty to Baptist principles.

Annual Address of Dr. E. C. Morris
President of the National Baptist Convention of America
In Session at Kansas City, Missouri, September, 1898

Brethren of the Convention, Ladies, and Gentlemen:

It is by the grace of God that we are again permitted to meet in another annual Convention. Our purposes in gathering here as the representatives of a great church organization are manifold, and are of vital interest to a struggling race of people as well as to our own denomination. We are here to review the past with the hope of better planning for effectual work in the future. Words are inadequate to express the very high appreciation which I have for the privilege of addressing the most prominent representatives of my people, persons upon whose shoulders rest in a great degree, the weal or woe of ten millions of Negroes.

In the outset I want to thank you sincerely for the repeated honors which you have thrust upon me in choosing me for your President. I have endeavored to serve honestly and faithfully the trust reposed in me, and have at no time been unmindful of the fact that no greater honor lies within the gift of a people than the leadership of their denominational interests. This organization represents the largest and most invincible army of Negro Christians in the world, as well as a sisterhood of churches which have done more toward lifting up the masses of an emancipated race than any other denomination among our people.

Our presence in this great Western city is to serve notice upon the world that we are yet in the field, eighteen-hundred-thousand strong, to renew the conflict and to press the battle for right principles an uncompromising gospel into all the world for a witness unto all people.

The difficulties of the past year have been many and the obstacles very great. The clouds have at times been so very thick that nearly every great leader was hidden from view, but when those clouds would break away and the smoke of battle would rise from the field, we could look out and see them, as Jackson, "standing like a stone wall." The most serious difficulties which we have encountered the past year have been from within. In a great organization like ours we have "many men of many minds," and in a denomination which grants to every man the right to think, act, and interpret for himself, since he does not transcend the authority of the Bible, it is expected that some disagreements will arise, but we count such as light afflictions and console ourselves with the thought that "they will endure only for a season."

A very grave misunderstanding—and, I may add, misrepresentation—grew out of our meetings held in Boston one year ago. I do not charge that any one with willful intent has tried to disrupt our National Convention, but it is known to every man who attended that meeting that it has been held before the world in a false light by some of our brethren who ought to have known better. I am charitable enough, however to say that the brethren doubtless were honest in the publications made and believed they were right.

The people of our country have been told that the Boston meeting was a "mob," that "the right of free speech was suppressed," and that "visiting white brethren were treated with the utmost discourtesy." These statements have had some effect upon the work, but have not prevented its success, for Truth, crushed to earth, shall rise again. The truth of the matter is that the greatest, grandest, most enjoyable, and most orderly meeting ever held by our National Convention was the one held at Boston. The people of that grand city, without regard to race, color or condition, united in helping to make the meeting a complete success, opening to us the most historic halls and grandest churches, and turning out in large numbers and mingling freely with the members of the Convention; and they were a unit in their praise of the meeting. As to there being the slightest discourtesy toward any class of our visitors, it can be said that such a statement is entirely without foundation. So far as the charge that the color line was drawn is concerned, I would say that it, too, is without the semblance of truth. The fact is generally known that the National Baptist Convention is an organization composed of messengers from regular Baptist Churches, Associations, Conventions, etc., and while our constitution does not mention the fact, it is understood that all these are organizations among the Negro Baptists. Our white brethren recognize it thus, and, therefore, none of their Churches or Conventions send any messengers to our meetings. However, I venture to say that, should they do so, such messengers would be received on perfect equality with our own. At most of our meetings we have had fraternal messengers from the great societies among our white brethren, and it is useless for me to say that in every case they have been cordially received and given a most hearty welcome, and I hope the day will never come when we will not have the fraternal visits of these brethren. Moreover, I wish to assure you that there is no desire on the part of the management of the Convention to widen the breach or to encourage further separation between the "white" and "colored" Christians in this country, but the management is not blind to the fact that the white and colored people in this country are as separate in nearly every profession and calling in life as if they lived in different worlds. We verily believe that the time will come when there will be no separate Christian institutions, and would gladly welcome such today; but as the day has not yet come and the "strong," who "should bear the infirmities of the weak," are not yet ready to obliterate those lines, the thing for us to do is to go forward, do something, get something, so that when the day shall come around to unite the Baptist forces of America in one great society we will have something to offer as a separate and distinct race of people.

Another thing which has, perhaps, somewhat hindered our progress is the fact that our country has been engaged in war with another nation. While some of the wisest and greatest men of our country deprecate war and did all in their power to prevent it; nevertheless, there was no way out of having an armed conflict with Spain and maintain our honor as a Christian nation. When our Chief Magistrate had done all in his power to prevent active hostility, and at the same time bring about a peaceable settlement of the inhuman, uncivilized Cuban war; and when he saw that his own and other Christian charities that were being extended to the starving women and children, whose husbands and fathers were fighting for freedom, had been challenged and resisted by Spanish arms, his great heart, which met with quick vibration from seventy-million other hearts, rose up and said that Spanish barbarity and misrule must cease. You know the results up to this time.

But the war is not yet ended, notwithstanding the fact that peace negotiations are now pending and actual hostilities have ceased. Through the mists that rise over the battlefield and in the ragged ranks of the poor and oppressed slaves of Spanish tyranny, the Church of God sees an opportunity to plant the banner of the Cross in places made more accessible by the triumphant victory of the American flag. Wherever the flag of our country has been borne in triumph the principles of religious liberty have also been carried.

The American Flag A Symbol

That grand old flag is a significant symbol to every patriotic American. Its colors and peculiar arrangement are object lessons, and inspire love for home and native land. To me it is an emblem of resplendent beauty. Not only do the stars represent the sisterhood of the States, but they recall the beautiful sentiment spoken by Job when he says, "Canst thou bind the sweet influences of Pleiades, or loose the bands of Orion?" while the beautiful colors recall the bow of promise which God has placed in the clouds, and inspire confidence that the principles which our flag represents shall be extended to every nation.

Our race in this country, for many years held as slaves, and not now enjoying the full and complete protection of that flag, challenges the whole country to find a class of people more loyal. Wherever and whenever it has been placed in the hands of the ebony-hued sons of America, its folds have not been allowed to trail in the dust. The American Negro can look through the "reign of terror" to which has has been subjected, and from which he now suffers and see the ultimate triumph of those principles which lie at the very foundation of our government—that "all men are created free and equal," etc. He believed that the success of this flag in the Revolutionary War would bring a better day, and followed it then. He followed it under Jackson without the hope of reward, and he saved it from dishonor in the Civil War; he also bravely led the charge under those colors at Santiago, and will ever remain loyal to it until this is indeed in truth the land of the free and the home of the brave.

Mob Violence

One of the most serious menaces of our country today is the unbridled spirit of mob violence, which, I am sorry to say seems to be on the increase. There seems to be an unholy alliance between some of the officers of the law and the mob to overturn the very foundation on which our government rests. This condition of affairs cannot long exist without seriously affecting the whole country. The causes which have in many instances led to the taking of human life without judge or jury are held up as excuses for the mob's shameful work. While I insist that our ministers should speak out in no unmistakable terms against every class of crime, and especially the most heinous of all crimes—rape—at the same time I insist that the men who gather for no other purpose than to empty their revolvers into the body of a helpless criminal are themselves guilty of a crime which shall cry out from the ground, and God will, if the people do not repent and turn from this sin, overthrow the government; and I call to the Church today in the words of another, "To your knees, to your knees, O Church," and let us move this blight from our land. Bear in mind that God has said, "Vengeance is mine."

Our Foreign Work

The Foreign Mission Board has labored against great odds during the past year, greater odds than any which have confronted it in any year of its existence, and yet with perhaps greater success. It was thought that the apparent differences which existed between the Board and the ex-members of the Richmond Board had been satisfactorily settled when the chairman of the Louisville Board agreed at Boston to yield every point and accept whatever plan the brethren at Richmond might suggest; and it was not known that a portion of the brethren were bent on splitting the Convention until after the adjournment of the meeting. When the questions of dividing the country into districts for more effectually doing foreign mission work was raised by the Virginia delegation at Boston, the attention of the Convention was called to the fact that such an order had been made one year previous, and the Secretary informed the Convention that the work of districting the country was then in progress. It was thought that this fact would give general satisfaction, and the Board was advised to proceed at once to form said districts. This the Board proceeded to do; but it developed that this was not satisfactory to some of the brethren, and nothing short of an independent organization would be acceptable. Just what success the District Convention has had I am unable to say, but I am sure that no cause has ever existed in this body which would in any way justify the action of the brethren in an attempt to divide our forces in this great work.

The Work of the Two Boards Compared

From the organization of the Foreign Mission Convention, in 1880, to the consolidation of the three Conventions, in 1895, the Foreign Mission Board was located at Richmond, Virginia. Since that time the Board has been located at Louisville, Kentucky. It has been my pleasure to be an ardent supporter of the foreign mission work under both of these Boards, and I have an unbiased knowledge of the work accomplished by each of them. For years the Board at Richmond labored through its missionaries to maintain mission stations on the West Coast of Africa among the Vey tribes. I need not tell you the sad story of how we were driven out of that country, and that Brother Coles, who was the last to preach there, and Sister Coles barely escaped with their lives. I do not attach any blame to the Board at

Richmond for the misfortunes which befell the work under its charge. They did the best they could, and all that they did has been destroyed; and when the Board at Louisville took charge of the work; they had but little more than the name with which to commence. Brother Jackson, who had gone out to Africa of his own account, was subsequently taken up; and an effort was made through him to establish a mission station at CapeTown, South Africa. The present Board has been on the field for only three years, and has fourteen missionaries actively engaged. While it has had some reverses, it is too magnanimous to charge any Christians in this country with it.

That you may know of some of the things with which Baptists have to contend, I give you here an exact quotation from a letter received from Brother John Tule, who went to Africa since the adjournment of our meeting at Boston:

> I reached here in May last, and from that time I have preached, and have baptized twenty-one precious souls, and went to the Petty Chief for a mission site. After his consent, we went to work and made three thousand bricks with our own hands; and, in spite of that, the Wesleyan (Methodist) missionaries went to the chief and offered him money to drive us out of his locality, and then came he and his tribe, armed, and broke all our bricks; and we went to the magistrate of that district, who demanded the contract of our Board as their authorized agent, but were unable to produce one, and then and there were warned not to preach in that district.

The fact that these missionaries were forced to leave the country has caused some of our brethren to accuse the Board of not giving them the proper support. "Consistency, thou are a jewel."

The Foreign Mission Board has not been as aggressive as I think it might have been; but when I consider the unwarranted attacks made by our own brethren and the effort of some to lead the people away from the Convention, I wonder how it has done so well.

Home Mission Board

This is the Board whose work has caused so much comment and which has caused many of our good brethren to criticize severely the action of the National Baptist Convention in authorizing the Board to begin the publication of Sunday school periodicals; but the wisdom of that act will be seen in the success which has crowned the efforts of the Home Mission Board in this special line of work. It is needless now that I say a single word in defense of this great undertaking on the part of the Negro Baptists, but it is necessary that something be said concerning the charges which have been brought against the project and against its friends. It has been said that those of us who have fostered this enterprise and have contended that it was a necessity in order to show to the world that we are worthy of the sacrifices made for our race, and also for the purpose of training ourselves in the management of great concerns, are ungrateful creatures, and are drawing the color line by endeavoring to have a business of our own and then attending to it. The charge is a grave one, and should be given more than a passing notice; for if it be true that we have suffered more on account of that thing called the "color line" than any other people in the country, and if it be true that in less than forty years we have forgotten the wonderful sacrifices of men and means for the elevation of our race, which had been driven to the lowest depths of degradation by slavery, then such miserable wretches as we are unfit for the association of good people; but I wish today that the charge is without foundation, and we challenge the whole country to find a set of men who have done more to obliterate the "color line" in our religious societies or who have shown by their acts more of the true spirit of gratitude than those who are the friends to this enterprise. Before the enterprise had a beginning those who now foster it endeavored in every honorable way to secure a proper recognition of our leading men in the publication house which had for thirty years been our benefactor and was at the time receiving ninety percent of our patronage. No undue haste was taken in the matter, but for years the question was discussed in our meetings and brought to the attention of the Board of the Publication Society; and when "patience ceased to be a virtue," we then set about laying a foundation for ourselves.

I sincerely believe, my brethren, that God, who is now carrying the race through a period of transition without a parallel in its history, has permitted this to come upon us for our own good. There can be no comparison between our Publication Board's work and that of other societies in a like work. It required many years for some of these to even reach the place to publish a paper to accompany a few tracts which they issued; others began with a borrowed capital; but we commenced with nothing but faith in God and the justice of our cause.

I am glad to say to you that, notwithstanding, we were accused of issuing "backs with covered white men's brains." In less than two years from the date of our first issue we are turning out more than

200,000 periodicals each quarter, and that the entire work, from the janitor in the printing office to the editor at his desk, is done by our own people, and that the machinery on which the work is done and the building in which it is done are the property of this Convention, and I may add that this Board has in its employ thirty men and women of our race, all of whom are paid regularly from the Secretary's office once every quarter. The Board's report will show the financial standing of the Publication Department, and I need not enlarge upon that, but shall I not ask you to share with us the joy we have in the fact that we can no longer be regarded as mere consumers in the literary world, but that we may be justly termed producers, and that five thousand of the best Negro Sunday schools in this land buy that literature from the counter made by this Convention and from the hands of the very men you appointed to stand behind it?

> Praise God, from whom all blessings flow;
> Praise Him, all creatures here below.

Educational Board

You will recall the fact that I recommended the consolidation of the Home Mission Board and the Educational Board in my report at Boston one year ago. Since no action was taken upon the recommendation, I will say that, aside from the publication of the magazine, nothing has been done. Dr. Johnson has endeavored to get his Board together to plan for assisting in the educational work of the denomination, but to no avail. There is a broader and greater opportunity before this Board than before either of the other Boards. However, I am still of the opinion that the work of the two Boards should be consolidated. The magazine has been allowed to fall upon the hands of a few, and yet it has been a success—not as great a success as it deserves, for it must be made to represent in the highest degree the best thought and best literary talent in the denomination, and this can be done by the Convention's giving to it the support it deserves.

Cooperation

Much has been said during the past year on the matter of cooperation between the white and colored Baptists along educational lines in the South. I have been free, as an individual, to express myself in favor of cooperation which indeed cooperates. The work of the

National Baptist Convention has been held up as an obstacle to the cooperation of the Baptist societies in the work of missions and education among the Negroes in the South. Neither the Convention nor its officers, at any time, in any way, desired or attempted to discourage the plan, nor has the Board or the Convention ever been asked to consider or in any way advise in the matter; and until the other Baptist societies recognize that there is in existence such a thing as a National Baptist Convention, no official notice will be taken of the cooperative plan. Personally, I would welcome the day when a plan could be entered into that would not only obliterate the color line, but at the same time wipe out all sectional lines, but the burden of this great undertaking will fall first and heaviest upon the shoulders of our white brethren, who must open the way for cooperation in all the branches of work carried on by the Baptists in this country.

A Plea For Unity

Many well-disposed, devout, Christian brethren who desire no doubt to see the very best things done for the race and the denomination have deemed it expedient, in order to secure the aid and cooperation of our stronger brethren to play neutral upon the work of this Convention and some have said we should surrender all and let other societies do the work we are endeavoring to do. Such an action would be without precedent, and, if followed, would destroy every atom of manhood there is in the members of our churches. Brethren, what we need, and what we must have if we are ever to command the respect of our white brother, is unity. "Behold, how good and how pleasant it is for brethren to dwell together in unity!" is as applicable today as it was in the days of the Psalmist. We have 1,600,000 people who are as loyal to their churches as any that ever lived, and if we can succeed in getting the 14,000 Baptist ministers united in the great work before us, no power on earth can prevent our carrying to success every object of this Convention. If you will indulge the speculation, I will say that I believe that an all-wise Providence has the matter in hand, and that He is effectually using the other race to drive ours together; for those who yesterday were the most bitter opponents of Negro enterprises—Negro Convention, Negro Churches, Negro Associations, Negro papers, Negro magazines, Negro song books, etc.—are today loudest in their claim for such organizations. I need not give the reasons, for every daily paper in the land furnishes the reason why we should be united, but let us hope that the day will come, and that by our unanimity of action, we will help to bring it on, when there will be "neither Jew nor Greek."

As I come to consider the discussion in our own ranks, I am constrained to say, in the words of Hosea: "My people are destroyed for lack of knowledge: because thou has rejected knowledge, I will also reject thee, that thou shalt be no priest to me: seeing thou has forgotten the law of thy God, I will also forget thy children." My brethren, will you hear me for my people's sake, for the generations that are to follow us? Is there no way by which we can prevent the systematic methods used to keep our people divided and to make them war against each other in everything, from a small grocery store to the greatest religious society among us? Wherever and whenever an honest effort is made to do anything for the race, persons can be found who, like Catiline, sit in counsel with us, and, on going out, immediately seek to overthrow every plan laid. When I look at these things, I am in full sympathy with Paul when he says: "I have great heaviness and continual sorrow in my heart. For I could wish that myself were accursed from Christ for my brethren, my kinsmen according to the flesh."

Help us to build each other up,
Our little stock improve:
Increase our faith, confirm our hope,
And perfect us in love.

Do not think me pessimistic. I have faith in God and in the ultimate unity and triumph of our churches in this work, for I think I can see through the dim vista of time, as we go forward and grasp the problems of life and keep pace in the steady march of civilization. One Grand Army of Christian Believers; and I can hear the tramp of an unnumbered throng, like the voice of many waters, and, listening still, I can hear the voice of that multitude as they raise the old battle cry of "One Lord, one faith, and one baptism;" and in that grand procession, as they march against the powers of darkness, I can see the Galilean Jew sitting in the chariot with the Ethiopian eunuch, and their song is: "The kingdoms of this world are become the kingdoms of our Lord, and of His Christ; and He shall reign forever and ever."

Annual Address of Dr. E. C. Morris
President of the National Baptist Convention of America in Session at Nashville, Tennessee, September, 1899

Brethren of the Convention, Ladies, and Gentlemen:

Again, by permission of a kind Providence, I have the honor of coming before you to deliver my annual address as president of your great Convention. I congratulate you upon the wonderful record and unparalleled progress made by the Baptists since the organization of this Convention. It came into existence at the right time and for the very purposes it has so ably served, viz, to save this wing of our great and invincible denomination from disgrace, to show that in the onward movement of the Great Army of God in the world, Negro Baptists are a potent factor. Until thrown into separate organization, such as this, it was not known what part those of our race in Baptist churches bear in the mighty conquest against the kingdom of darkness and in the upbuilding of the Master's kingdom on earth.

The wisdom which dictated such an organization was, in my opinion, divine. Had it not been divine, the strong and well-organized forces which have conspired to overthrow every enterprise put on foot by this Convention would have succeeded. But I am glad to say that instead of being overthrown, the Convention and its enterprises are stronger today than at any time before, and it has by its peerless record, drawn to it many who once stood in open rebellion against its objects. It has been my opinion for some time that the leaders in this Convention have been for many years misunderstood and, therefore, misrepresented, and that when the real objects and policy of the leaders are fully known, all opposition will cease, and we will have the encouragement and cooperation of all the great Baptist societies in the country.

I wish to repeat what I have said on several occasions: that this society entertains no ill will toward any other Christian organization in the world. It seeks to be on friendly terms with all, and the charge that this organization means to draw the color line, and thereby create prejudice in "Negro" Christians against "White" Christians, is without foundation. We admit, however, that practically, and not constitutionally, the color line has been drawn by the establishment of churches and schools for the "colored people" and the employment of missionaries, colporters, etc., to the colored people, which has resulted in the organization of associations and conventions by the Negroes in more than half of the states in the union. And since these organizations exist, it is the duty of all to do everything in their power to build up the cause of Christ in and through these agencies.

But if these separate organizations did not exist, there is a reason for the existence of a National Baptist Convention, because, owing to the agitation of the slavery question, the white Baptists of the North and South had divided into two societies, represented respectively by Northern Baptists and Southern Baptists, and when the cause of the division had been removed, the Northern Baptists went immediately to work to educate and evangelize the emancipated. The Southern white people soon fell in line and began by a system of taxation to aid the emancipated in acquiring a common school education, and many of the Southern white ministers lent their aid in church work. But their organizations remained separate and are separate today. Hence, it was one of the prime objects of the promoters of this Convention of obliterate all sectional lines among Baptists and have one grand, national society which would know no North, no South, no East, no West; and in this we have been successful. From Maine to California, we are one, notwithstanding the efforts of designing men to disrupt the Convention by making false publications concerning it. If you will pardon the particular reference, I will say that one of our number who for three years held official position in this convention had published in a little paper out in North Carolina, the startling statement that the "Convention has departed from the New Testament standard and has turned into an ecclesiastical body; and that it exists for political purposes, the president exercising his power the year round, attempting to dictate the policy of 1,700,000 Baptists." Others of our ranks have styled us ingrates—all because we

> Dare to be a Daniel,
> Dare to stand alone!
> Dare to have a purpose firm!
> Dare to make it known.

But against all we have marched steadily on and disproved all that has been said, until we have enlisted the cooperation of the most thoughtful Negro Baptists throughout the civilized world. We have endeavored to avoid any entangling alliances with other Baptist organizations, but have prayed for and sought to maintain friendly relations with all. I cannot account for the apparent disposition of some of our Baptist societies to ignore utterly the existence of the

National Baptist Convention. Since the Negro Baptists in all the states of this great Union are in harmony with the work of this Convention and are contributors to its objects, there can be no good reason why any organization should attempt to form alliances with the respective states to do the very work which the Convention is endeavoring to do. In the matter of Cuban missions, notwithstanding the fact that this Convention had declared its purpose to do mission work in Cuba, other Baptist societies which had similar purpose in view, consulted and even had correspondence with persons not officially connected with the National Convention upon the matter of cooperation. This breach of fraternal courtesy is not understood, except it be that others think that they can more easily handle our people by having them divided, than by recognizing an organization with an official Board or Boards empowered by the Constitution to act for the whole body. That the time will come when all the Baptist societies in America will recognize the existence of this Society, I have not the slightest doubt; but for reasons known only to themselves, they have not done so yet.

A prominent minister of our denomination told me a few weeks ago at Greenville, Mississippi, that he had opposed the work of the National Baptist Convention because he did not think it possible to get the Negro Baptists of this country organized, and that their notions of church independence and church sovereignty were such as to preclude any such thing as a national organization. "But," says he, "I see you are about to get them together." I was a bit modest in giving a reply at that time, but I will assure you, my brethren, that the time is not far away when our organization will be so systematic that at the pressing of a button, the Baptists from Maine to California, and from the Canadian border to the Gulf of Mexico, will spring to action as one man, and there will be a oneness of faith, a oneness of purpose in holding forth the truths of that Book which teaches that there is but one God.

I stated that the Convention had declared its purpose to do mission work in Cuba. And it did, at the meeting held in Kansas City, one year ago, appoint a commission to visit the island with a view of ascertaining the moral, religious, and educational status of the Cuban people. An appeal was made to the churches to send up money to pay the expenses of the commissioners, and I am glad to say that many churches responded to the appeal and sent money to the Treasurer of our Convention. The commission, owing to the unsettled state of affairs, thought it would be a useless expenditure of money to go there at the time designated by the Convention. Hence, the money sent is now in the Treasury, subject to the orders of the Convention. The principal points in Cuba had been entered through the agency of our Foreign Mission Board and other Baptist societies before the time had come for the committee to go out, so that we may say, Baptist missions are already under way in Cuba. Providence seems to have favored us in that Rev. Campbell and wife were secured by our Board and that Dr. C. T. Walker and Rev. Richard Carroll were given chaplaincies in the Army. Dr. Walker succeeded in gaining 100 conversions while there, and you may surmise the rest. We are in duty bound to aid in carrying the Gospel to the Cuban people. Like the black troopers who went up El Caney and saved the lives of their white comrades from destruction, so must the Negro Baptists of this country join their white brethren in carrying the Gospel of the Son of God to that people.

The Philippine Affair

Before the Cuban question had been settled and Spain had been forced to take her barbarous hand off those people, a war broke out in the Philippine Islands, and our country is one of the principals in that conflict. The United States, having given Spain $20,000,000 for the Spanish possessions in the Archipelago, attempted to secure those rights and was met by all the force the Filipinos could command. While the scene of operation is a great way off, the situation is far more serious than is generally thought. More than 40,000 Americans are there, exposed to the malarial conditions of the country and the determined spirit of a relentless foe.

The policy of our government in the prosecution of the Philippine war has been severely criticized, and even now, many are opposing the further prosecution of the war. Necessarily, Christians are opposed to armed conflicts and bloodshed. And we contend that all international questions can and should be settled by arbitration. The war which is not upon us has divided our country into two strong factions, *viz*: Expansionists and Anti-Expansionists; and the contention growing out of the points of this division makes the horizon dark with commotion, and calls to Christians everywhere to appeal to that God who holds the reins of governments, that He might intervene and establish peace among the nations.

Law and Order Versus A Race Problem

In our domestic relations to this country, many of our people feel that they have a just cause to complain of the treatment they receive at the hands of the people among whom they live. And the man is indeed blind who cannot see that the race feeling in this country has grown continually for the last two decades. But since the organic law of the land stands unimpeached, there is no room left to inquire, "Is it only race hatred, or is it not the outgrowth of a lawless spirit which has taken possession of many of the people in this country?" Perhaps it appeared when this spirit of anarchy first took hold in this country that it was directed to a particular class or race of people. But that can no longer be said. For, indeed, it is evident that those who will forget themselves so far as to take the laws into their own hands and hang, shoot down, and burn helpless Negroes, will ere long turn and slaughter one another. Indeed, such is the case now. Mob violence is not confined to any particular section of our country. The same disregard for law and order which exists in the South when a Negro is involved, exists in the North when the miners or other laborers are involved. The people have become crazed and have lost their respect for the law and the administrators of the law, and unless there is a speedy change no man will be secure in life or property. The apologies which are being given for the mob's shameful work, by no means remove the fact that there is a growing disregard for the laws of our country. I would counsel by people everywhere to be law-abiding, no matter how much they may suffer thereby. It does not stand to reason that the whole race is a set of cowards because the inhuman treatment administered to members of our race is not resented. But one thing is true: the men who will take the laws in their own hands and thereby prevent the piercing rays of the letter and spirit of the law from shining through the courts upon the crimes committed, are themselves a set of cowards. Ministers of the Gospel and good people everywhere should lift their voices against all classes of crime which is blackening the record of our country. The man who will not lift his voice in defense of the sacredness of the home and the chastity of the women of this country, is unworthy to be called "a man." It is but right that the man who breaks over the sacred precincts of the home and perpetrates a dastardly deed—it is but right that he be made to pay the penalty of the inhuman act. But let all such be done by and through the law. The wisest and most prudent men of our country foresee the evils which threaten the perpetuity of our republican institutions, if the present disregard for law and order be kept up. The agitations which are going on will soon bring a reaction. Reason will again be enthroned; the laws of the country, like the laws of God, will be supreme; and from the least to the greatest, the people will "submit to every ordinance of man, for the Lord's sake." Those who are inclined to the opinion that there is a great "Race Problem" confronting us, are asked to look beyond racial lines for a moment and behold the civil strife in many of the states in the Union where the state militia, United States marshalls, and sheriffs with strong guard, are called upon to protect lives and property, to stand and guarantee the moving of the wheels of commerce, while the cries of hungry women and children force husbands, fathers, and brothers to wage open conflict with the administrators of the law, and then they will modify their opinion as to a race problem and agree that a serious law and order problem confronts the people of this country.

Local Dissension

The work of the National Baptist Convention has been somewhat hindered by local dissensions, most notably in Georgia and Virginia. The National Convention officers have endeavored to steer clear of local disturbances which have divided our brethren in several of the states, notwithstanding the fact that in one state (Virginia), the contention was made that the National Convention was responsible for the opposition to the cooperative plan as carried on by the Home Mission Society. The charge was made without reason. No men regret more than the officers of this Convention that our people should divide into factions in their state and national work; nor have the officers of the Convention at any time interfered with the cooperative plans adopted in any of the states. We have frequently expressed ourselves in favor of cooperation in all line of Christian work, and have not changed our opinion in the matter. But when I say this, I mean to be understood as favoring that the plans to be drawn and the conditions to be met and followed should be mutually agreed upon by all the parties concerned in the work; that the plans should be such as not to lift up one and humiliate the other; but to place all upon absolute equality in Christian work, making fitness the only essential in promotion of one above the other. But recent developments go to show that this country is not yet ready for the kind of cooperation I have in mind. I insist, however, that cooperation in any of the states which will force a division of the Baptists in their organizations of long standing, should be discontinued and the plans so changed as to meet the reunited body. The National Baptist Convention does not hope to gain anything by reason of these divisions, but pleads for unity in every state, even though, for the time being, the Convention should lose all its support in those states.

District Convention

Much has been said concerning the utility of a District Convention. At first, it was said that the organization was to antagonize the National Baptist Convention in Foreign Mission work. But the leaders of the movement insisted that they had no such purpose, and made the representation at the Kansas City meeting that they proposed to work in harmony with the National Baptist Convention; but recent developments go to show that the leaders of the District Convention have endeavored to induce some of our missionaries to resign work under the Foreign Mission Board and accept work under the District Convention Board. If this be true, and the issues are thus drawn, without any words of abuse or ill-feeling toward the promoters of the District Convention, the National Baptist Convention will proceed to occupy the entire field in so far as our representatives are received by the churches. There can be no doubt of the people being in favor of one grand national society among the colored Baptists, and any effort or scheme to defeat that object will be repudiated.

Foreign Missions

The all-important questions of the hour is that of Foreign Missions. The Foreign Mission Society is the oldest of our national organizations and has a greater claim upon our people than any other, for it indeed represents the spirit and mission of the Master, as well as His church. No man can be true to Christ and refuse to support the cause of missions. And, yet, I am sorry to say, that many of our churches have turned a deaf ear to the urgent appeals of the Board for means to support our missionaries, and have really joined in with our enemies to deride the Board when it failed to pay the salaries promptly.

While there has not been as much adverse criticism during the present year as in the past, there has been some. Our Baptist papers have been more considerate of the Board's responsibilities, and have not permitted so many things which are intended to impede the progress of the Foreign Mission work, to find circulation through them.

It has been difficult for the Board to keep in harmony with some of the workers in South Africa. The Board deemed it wise and expedient that Rev. R. A. Jackson be dropped from the list of missionaries, and I am informed that he was paid up in full. I am of the opinion that the Board should place a ticket at the disposal of Brother Jackson in case he desires to return to this country. Brother and Sister Tule have resigned, and I am told that their salaries were paid in full. This leaves only eleven workers on the field at this time. I am of the opinion that much of the dissatisfaction arose on account of the fact that our tireless and earnest Corresponding Secretary does not give enough personal attention to the duties of his office. No man can give satisfaction in that office who attempts to traverse the country from one end to the other. If the churches of this country are to be reached and stirred up to their duty in the work of Missions, it must be done by a system different from the one followed for the last five or six years. I have not the slightest doubt that the Foreign Mission Board has done the best it could, under the circumstances. But with a little more aggressiveness on the part of the officers of that Board, many of the circumstances which hinder the work very materially will be removed. A new impetus must be given to this department of our work. We can no longer hope to retain the confidence and respect of other peoples of the world, unless we do more for the redemption of the heathen, and especially those of our fatherland. If it should appear that we are a little selfish in our missionary operations, we can offer the just apology that the heathen of Africa are by far the most neglected of any on the globe—less money is being given for their evangelization than for any others. This Convention will not rise to the full dignity of a great missionary organization until it has at least fifty active workers on the field. This can and should be done. As the Foreign Mission Board will give a full report of its work for the year, I shall not say more on this theme just now, but will ask you to consider some recommendations respecting the work of the Board which I will mention later.

Home Mission Board

The Home Mission Board was constitutionally established in September, 1895. But in 1896, it brought into existence one of the most notable heritages the Negro Baptist ever did, or ever will have, in that our Publishing House was then established. This enterprise was started with nothing save faith in God and the justice of the cause, backed by Negro brain and ambition. And today, $10,000 worth of real property, $16,000 worth of printing material and machinery, an average monthly distribution of nearly $2,000 worth of periodicals, sixty-eight ardent workers and writers of our own race, causing a payroll amounting to one-hundred dollars ($100.00) per day, speak out in one tremendous voice and tell whether or not we have made progress. The sun has forever gone down on any race of people who will not encourage and employ their literary talent. How could the Negro Baptists ever hope to be or do anything while they were committing literary suicide? From year to year, scores of our young men and women were graduating from school without the slightest hope or encouragement, in a land where the color of their skin debars them from a liberal or equal chance with others. Were we to stand still and do nothing? No. Our Home Mission Board put forth an effort to remedy this condition to some extent, and it has been successful so far.

The Baptists have read a little history, and are endeavoring to profit by the mistakes and useful deeds of others. They find that the literary standing of the Greeks and Romans keeps them before the world as a vivid example of ancient progress, and they are quoted with pride the world over by many of the ripest scholars of the day. Furthermore, we will find by reflection, that although the former were the slaves of the latter, by the excellent reputation of Grecian philosophers, teachers, etc., the Romans were only too glad to bow at the Grecians' feet to learn from them the secret of that higher power which intellect wields over mere brute force. The Greeks were able to give this knowledge, and never would have become slaves had they only watched carefully their true literary standing, and not gone off into skepticism, and the variegated porch of the poets would, no doubt, have still been in use had it not been that "cooks were in as great a demand as philosophers." It has been well said that "no man who persists in thinking can be kept in bondage."

If we mean to improve, why should we not make an attempt at the preparation of our Sunday School literature as well as a few books and papers to which we lay claim? In religion, the key to which comes from the Bible, we must not, as a great Christian society, be found wanting. Then, we must not agree for others to take all the advantage of studying and then writing the Bible lessons as presented to our Sunday Schools. If the Negro had no chance to study and interpret the Holy Scriptures, he could only be expected to stand off and talk about what has been prepared by somebody else, and never be able to give authority for what he holds. If we are to preach and teach, we must have some personal, unbridled knowledge of our subjects, and the interest which is at the bottom of this knowledge is caused by the taking on of responsibility. If we have to go through the same test as others (and we do), why not have the same advantages?

The progressive Negro Baptists deliberated on all these things for four or five years, and have consequently given some of their business managers a chance to manage business, their bookkeepers opportunity to keep books, their printers and binders a chance to print and bind, their Bible students and writers impetus to study and write, and their thousands of anxious Sunday School students, both young and old, opportunity to get their lessons from books made by their own brothers in color.

Although the publication of Sunday School periodicals had proved to be an expedient work of Home Missions, this has not been the only work of our Home Board. It is doing no small amount of missionary work in supplying needy stations and in the support of missionary workers. In this latter work, the Board hopes to enlarge its operations in the near future.

Educational Board

The progress made by this Board has been very slow, but the plans which have been laid are well laid. It has continued the publication of the magazine under very stringent circumstances. Through the efforts of the Corresponding Secretary, arrangements have been made which will insure the regular and permanent issuance of the magazine from the Publishing House at Nashville. I regret very much that the Board has not yet undertaken the formation of a federation of the schools owned by our people, with a view to aiding them through means solicited by the Board. It is quite evident to me that these institutions cannot become the beneficiaries of philanthropic people until a proper channel is created through which their gifts may be conveyed.

Our B. Y. P. U.

Too much cannot be said in commendation of the movement of our Baptist young people. We have a vast army in our churches who are yet to be developed into practical, useful Christians, and the effort to form a national organization should meet with the encouragement of all lovers of our grand old Church. Thousands of the best and most highly cultivated young men and women of the race are in our churches, and are capable of performing any and all the duties necessary to lead our young people to success. There is no reason why all the literature used by our B. Y. P. U.'s should not be produced by our own folks. For the first time in the history of our Convention, one session will be devoted to the young people's work.

A Look Ahead

Thirty-six years have passed since the shackles of slavery were broken from the limbs of our people in this country. And these have been years of trial and conflict in which the Negro Baptists have borne no little part. In this brief period, they have succeeded in building more schools and colleges than any other denomination of Negro Christians, and have enrolled as members of their churches more than all the rest combined. For this glorious heritage, we sincerely thank God, and have a heart full of love for all who have aided in any way to bring about such a condition. But the fact that such a vast army has volunteered to follow the lead of those who contend for the principles enunciated at Olivet and for which the Apostles suffered and died; for which Bunyan, Hall, Roger Williams, Spurgeon, and an innumerable host of others battled to uphold, it is but meet that we pause to ask: What of the future? A very large number of the 1,700,000 Negro Baptists are crude and undeveloped. They know but little of the practical side of Christianity. The work of developing these that they may become the safe guardians of the undying principles which have distinguished our Church in all ages of the Christian era, is no small task. But I assure you, my brethren, that we have the men and means to keep our organization abreast of the times. And we will keep them so if we will only be united and submit to proper leadership. I have no doubt that the census of 1900 will show nearly 2,000,000 Negro Baptists in this country. Can you as leaders trust that host to support the present and future enterprises as you trusted them in the past to build and support churches all over this land? The charge of mutiny seldom ever comes against a Baptist; and as they have been loyal and true to their local organizations, so will they be to this Convention and every enterprise put in motion by it.

We are nearing the close of the present century, the most remarkable in many respects of all the centuries since the dawn of creation. And, without reference to the wonderful achievements in steam, printing, and electricity, and many more unparalleled discoveries and inventions, I come to say that when the light from the eternal hills announced the birth of the nineteenth century, our race—our fathers and mothers—groaned in the grasp of slavery, and held the place of goods and chattels. But by the direction of an unerring

Providence, when a little past the meridian of the century, a decree was handed down that the "slaves are and henceforth shall be free." Hence, I conclude that one of the marvels of the century will be that although it opened and looked for sixty-three years on a race of slaves, it closes with that same race a happy, free people, having built more churches and school houses, in proportion to their numbers, than any people dwelling beneath the sun. While the flickering light and agonizing groans of the nineteenth century are being lost in the misty and retreating past, let us look ahead. A little less than four months from now, that tireless steed, Time, will come forth and announce the birth of the twentieth century. Already in the distance can be heard the thunder of his neck and the fury of his nostrils, and the inhabitants of the world are preparing to greet his coming. Many of the great Christian societies are planning to make the opening year the most important and aggressive in Christian missions since the beginning of the New Dispensation. Some are asking for a million dollars, some for half a million, and some for still less. And as I see these great societies line up as if on dress parade and call for more men and means to go more strongly against the power of darkness, I am forced to ask: What is the duty of the Negro Baptists? The answer comes back that as the nineteenth century opened upon us as slaves and closed upon us as freemen, so may the Gospel, borne on the tongues of the liberated, set at liberty during the twentieth century, the millions bound in heathen darkness.

Annual Address of Dr. E. C. Morris
President of the National Baptist Convention of America
In Session at Richmond, Virginia, September, 1900

Brethren of the Convention, Ladies, and Gentlemen:

In the name of Jesus our Redeemer, and by the guidance of His kind providence, we meet in this historic city in another annual session of our Convention, to hand in our reports as servants in the Master's vineyard and to gather inspiration and means to push forward His cause into all the world. I confess that I feel a special joy at meeting so many of you at this time and place—in this grand old State which bears the honor of being the "Mother of Presidents," and which has the distinction of being one of the foremost in the Union in point of loyalty to Baptist principles. We are also reminded of our nearness to the place where the first of our race, so far as history gives account, were landed upon these shores two-hundred and eighty years ago, not as men, but as goods and chattels. It is quite appropriate that we, the descendants of that few who were landed at Jamestown, should meet here as men, having been lifted up by our contact with other peoples of this nature, and look back upon the scenes of the past to behold "what wonders God hath wrought."

Permit me to congratulate you, in the first place, upon the extraordinary prosperity enjoyed by the people in every part of this great country, and especially the success which has been achieved by the heralds of the Cross who are enlisted under that banner of which you are the representatives. As a great church organization, we can share in the unprecedented prosperity that, like a tidal wave, has swept over our country, and the successful conquests which our nation has waged against error abroad, setting before us an open door which no man can shut. Notwithstanding our nation has been engaged in bloody conflicts with foreign foes, there has been no period in the history of our organization that has been more prosperous than that of the present year. We have maintained our record of making steady increase both in numbers and property throughout the country. Perhaps the most notable evidence of this is found among the colored Baptists of the North and East, where there has been considerable emigration from the South, and where there is a large number of honest, earnest, devoted, consecrated ministers endeavoring to bring the people of their respective fields to a proper acceptance of the Word of God; and we may say also, that our organizations are not sectional, but in the language of the poet

Jesus shall reign where'er the sun
Doth his successive journeys run.

This exalted sentiment impels the leaders of the National Baptist Convention. In our effort to carry forward the work of the Convention, we have endeavored to keep in friendly touch with all the Baptist societies in the world. We recognize that while we have separate organizations, our cause is one—that we have one great aim in view, viz, the giving of the Gospel of the Son of God to the world, without apology. In this we are glad to say that our relation has been fraternal and pleasant so far, and I think it is growing warmer each year. It is only when irresponsible bigots attempt to espouse the cause of the older societies that misunderstandings gain circulation and prominence. It is, indeed, unfortunate both for the societies and for us that these apparent differences gain circulation. Quite a lengthy article was given to the public in the *Biblical Recorder*, published at Raleigh, N.C., on August 1st, and given further circulation by the *Florida Evangelist*, under the caption "Questionable Methods of Colored Baptists." The article was a severe arraignment of the Secretary of our Publishing Board. If the friends of the National Baptist Convention had not possessed a personal knowledge of the method and work of that department, they, perhaps, would have been influenced by it. We like criticism when it comes from friends having a view to correcting errors for the good of our race and denomination. But so far as this one is concerned, we are in a serious quandary as to whether the editor wrote it from a spirit prompted to benefit the colored Baptists, or whether he was influenced by some one who is an inveterate enemy of our publishing concern. We venture to say that, when the truth is known, some man of our own race, who ought to be rejoicing at its progress, will be found at the bottom of the whole affair. But be the matter as it may, I am glad to say that the reports of the respective Boards to the National Convention have met the hearty approval of the Convention, and convinced all the world not too biased to believe it, that the Negro Baptists are doing work now which gives opportunities and successes to the race which did not come to them when all their contributions went to, and all their work was being done by, the societies operated by the white brethren.

This has been a very busy year with the officers of the Convention. We have spared neither time nor money in a protracted effort to get every part of our respective Boards in their great campaign against sin and error. We have put behind us the mutterings and contentions of those who would seek to stir up strife, and have endeavored to have harmony and unanimity in the work of the Convention. We have endeavored to exercise great patience and charity toward those who seemed to think a National Convention of Negro Baptists unnecessary, as we are sure that time and environment will be sufficient to convince them of the necessity of such an organization. To me, as the "heavens declare the glory of God," so do the signs of the times in church and in state point to the fact for the Negro to ever be received and given the place of a man in religion, in politics, in business, etc., he must accumulate, he must own, control, or manage enterprises for the development of the race and the blessing of mankind. And this condition of affairs will not give offense to any except those who would prefer to be agents, rather than owners, of such concerns.

You will permit me here to repeat what I have said on former occasions: that the conditions in this country have forced the Negroes to be separate in their churches, associations, and conventions, from their white brethren, and these smaller organizations have, by reason of the same conditions, been forced to form this national society. And since we have this National Baptist Convention, it is imperative that it have a high and noble object; and as this object has been clearly defined, it is unnecessary that I should again attempt to bring it before you.

The man or men who cannot see the wisdom displayed in effecting this organization is indeed blind. Before the organization of the National Baptist Convention at St. Louis, Missouri, in 1886, our denominational strength as to men and means was a thing unknown. But in the few years we have maintained the principles of our society, there has sprung into activity a spirit to do mission work, educational work, publication work, and the like which is without a parallel in the history of our race, and which at the same time has developed an army of practical businessmen as well as inspired others to become great and useful as writers, bookkeepers, typographers, managers, theologians, etc. Since these things are true—and no one will doubt them—we would not entertain, by any means, even a suggestion to cease this onward march.

We cannot afford to sit idly by for fear of criticism and permit other organizations among Negroes in this country to show the possibilities of the race by undertaking to do something in a way separate from their white brethren, and not do something ourselves in that way. When we can point to the fact that a Board representing Negro Baptists in this country is successfully operating and supporting mission stations and missionaries in far-off Africa, in Cuba, and in South America, and that our Home Mission Board is supporting missionaries far out in the West, and at the same time operating a publishing plant which is now doing a business of $50,000 a year, supplying fully nine-thousand of our Sunday Schools with a literature which is acceptable to the very best; and then that we have as a result of separate effort, supplemented by the aid of friends at the North, such institutions as Selma University, Selma, Ala.; State University, Louisville, Ky.; Natchez College, Natchez, Miss.; Guadalupe College, Seguin, Texas; Central City College, Macon, Ga., Howe Institute, Memphis, Tenn.; Arkansas Baptist College, Little Rock, Ark.; Virginia Seminary, Lynchburg, Va.; and many others of equal importance to our people, we can say, "The Lord hath done great things for us; whereof we are glad." Already we lead all the other denominations among our people in the matter of progressive enterprise; only one thing remains to be done to place the Convention where is properly belongs before the world, and that is to establish and successfully maintain a great National University such as will command the support and respect of all peoples and races—a University which will be to the Negro Baptists what Brown University is to the white Baptists, or Wilberforce is to the African Methodists.

A Step In The Right Direction

For the first time in the history of our Convention, a step has been taken by the Foreign Mission Board toward cooperation with one of our great Baptist societies of the North. You will recall the fact that when we met one year ago at Nashville, Tenn., great enthusiasm was created by the reception of a letter from Rev. C. S. Morris, who was at that time in South Africa. He had been sent out by an organization of white Baptists in the North in cooperation with our Foreign Mission Board, for the purpose of considering the advisability of establishing industrial missions in South Africa, and also, if possible, to settle the differences that existed between our Board and some of the missionaries in South Africa. On Brother Morris' return to this country, he at once set out to create a sentiment in favor of the mission work which he had planned to do before he left. I shall not speak of the work of that peerless ambassador, as he will come before you in person. But it was upon his suggestion that a conference was held in New York last April between the representatives of the Missionary Union and our Foreign Mission Board, which conference resulted in an agreement to cooperate in the support of Brother Morris while he traveled in this country with a view to creating a wider sentiment and a greater desire to help in foreign missions. This is the beginning of systematic cooperating between the Northern societies and our Convention, and I think it will prove to be a wise project. As to this agreement, the Foreign Mission Board will report in detail, but enough is in evidence to show that our Convention is not hostile to Christian cooperation with other societies.

Retrospect

A brief review of the past as relates to our race and denomination would not be out of place at this time. To look back to the days when our people had just been delivered from a cruel bondage, clothed with ignorance and superstition, having crude, unpolished ideas of religion, no schools or churches, no leaders—nothing but a helpless mass of humanity—it is revolting in the extreme. In those days of misery and extreme necessity, among the many agencies which God sent to redeem and lift up these people, was the American Baptist Home Mission Society. I speak of it particularly because of the fact that in this city, the old Lumpkin Jail, which held so many of the slaves for sale, became the seat of the first school for the training of our people under the auspices of that magnificent society. From that feeble beginning has come to us the beautiful Union University, which is, doubtless, the pride of every loyal Baptist in the land. Notwithstanding that it has been but a few years since the emancipation of our race, the distance which we have traveled is very great. We could not have made the journey or the marvelous progress which we have made, had we not been given the aid of such friends as those who foster the work of the Home Mission Society. I cannot refrain from referring in this connection to the much revered and greatly lamented Dr. Corey, who spent many years of his noble life in this city, as President of the Richmond Theological Seminary. He was a prince of good men, and perhaps looks from his spiritual abode today, with glorious satisfaction, upon this gathering, and into the faces of many whom he trained or gave their first lessons in theology; and his noble spirit, like that of John Brown, is still "marching on." The work of these grand and noble men is immortal, and if there were a disposition or effort on the part of any to destroy it, it would prove futile.

But I can say without fear of successful contradiction that there is not the slightest enmity in the leaders of the National Baptist Convention against any of these good and great men or the work which they have done for the elevation of this race. But our method of showing our deep and abiding appreciation for what has been done for us has been misunderstood and misrepresented. The manly, cultivated, God-like ministers and laymen among us believe that the best method of showing their gratitude to those who have helped them is to do something to help themselves and others who are in need. We believe that every effort made for our people during the thirty-five years of the past by the friends of our race is an unanswerable argument that for every school, university, or other enterprise planted and supported by others for the benefit of the Negro Baptists, there should be one, as a supplement, planted and operated by ourselves. How else can we show our appreciation for the help we have received? Words alone will not do it. Deeds are immortal. As we look over the long list of the noble-hearted philanthropists, the hundreds of consecrated teachers and preachers who arose above social caste and associated themselves with our fathers in the days of their early trials in order that such a scene as I have before me be made possible, our hearts go out to them in loving remembrance, notwithstanding most of them have been gathered to their final reward. And so deep is my confidence in the Word of God, I am reminded to repeat the words of Paul, when he said, "Wherefore seeing we also are encompassed about with so great a cloud of witnesses, let us lay aside every weight, and the sin which doth so easily beset us, and let us run with patience the race that is set before us."

But allow me to say that the supplementary institutions planted by the colored Baptists do not seek to supplant those formed by our friends, but rather to augment and enlarge the opportunities of and for our race. It is necessary that there be mission boards, publication boards, educational boards, colleges, seminaries, academies, etc., owned and operated by the Negroes, as it is for them to own the houses they live in or to have newspapers, dry goods stores, grocery stores, farms, factories, or any other enterprise necessary to develop the business side of the race. The National Baptist Convention, in this connection, stands for the complete development of the Negro as a man along all lines, beginning first with his religious life, and ending with the material, or business life. In these laudable objects, we expect to have the sympathy and cooperation of all true men.

Foreign Mission Boards

The work of modern foreign missions is about a century old; while with us as a separate organization, it is about twenty years old. And yet, the Son of God, who is an embodiment of missions, stood upon Olivet nearly nineteen-hundred years ago and gave orders to His church to go into all the world and preach the Gospel to every creature, giving in connection therewith the blessed promise, "I am with you alway." If any one thing more than another should cause the church to repent, it is the neglect of foreign fields. It is my conviction that in proportion as the command to publish the Gospel to the heathen world has been obeyed, prosperity has been brought into our Christian homes.

We no longer need to apologize for the work being done through our Foreign Mission Board, for in the fact of the many discouragements and unwarranted thrusts made at its methods and plans, it is doing a remarkable work for the Master in South Africa and elsewhere. It appears to be a providential thing that South Africa has been selected as the base of our missionary operations on the dark continent. Rev. R. A. Jackson, who through the mediatorship of Rev. C. S. Morris, has resumed work under our Board, is proving to be an instrument of marvelous results in our African mission work. Even the natives look upon him as a God-sent man and believe him to be the one who is to lift them out of the pit of sin and ignorance. The Foreign Mission Board has been able this year to be more punctual in the payment of salaries than in previous years. This was very fortunate, owning to the fact that prices for food were very high on account of the British-Boer war. The officers of our Board have been faithful to the trust imposed upon them, and not only have sought the cooperations and support of all who believe in the work of missions, but have taken time to study it both as it relates to the heathen and to the people of this country. All the officers of the Board attended the great Ecumenical Conference of Foreign Missions, held in New York City from the 21st of April to the 2nd of May, 1900, which meeting was an inspiration to them as well as to all who had the pleasure of attending it.

The Secretary of the Foreign Mission Board has not ceased at any time to call loud to the Baptists of this country to come up to the help of the Lord against the mighty. He has gone from city to city and from state to state, and has succeeded in creating an interest in foreign missions hitherto unknown to colored Baptists. I must urge, in this connection, that greater respect be given to the appeals sent out by our Foreign Mission Board, for it sometimes occurs that conditions arise on the field that require immediate relief, and as we have no invested funds, we must depend wholly upon the contributions sent up from our churches, associations, and conventions, to meet these conditions. The Board is endeavoring to raise before the close of the century, forty-thousand dollars for its foreign work. This amount has been apportioned to the various States, according to the number of Baptists in them. We sincerely hope that the leaders in the various States will see to it that the amount allotted to be raised by their States, if not sent in already, will be forthcoming.

Home Missions and Publications

I confess that a special pride thrills me when I come to speak of our Home Mission Board, with its marvelous work of publication, partly because of the fact that it has undergone a greater degree of opposition and persecution than any of the Boards, and partly because of the material benefit it has been to the race. We do not conceal the fact that this Board has enjoyed a greater measure of prosperity than any of the rest, notwithstanding it has met with greater opposition. But since it has been so fully demonstrated that such an enterprise was a pressing necessity and the undertaking having proved a great success, we now venture to say that those who were its bitterest opponents will concede the wisdom of its beginning.

It was a hazardous undertaking, made, as it was, at the close of one of the most marvelous centuries since the dawn of creation, at a time when art, science, and literature were at their zenith and when the more advanced races were vying among themselves as to which could produce the best and most acceptable literature for the vast army of Christian readers. For a people only thirty years from slavery to undertake such a project was indeed perilous. As was expected, criticism came thick and fast, but our manager, a man who lays no claim to an education, was well prepared to receive all that came. And permit me to say that to his indomitable courage, coupled with his vast store of common sense, is due much of the success of that enterprise. He has lived to see the time already when many who were his severest critics are glad to acknowledge his superiority. The same may be said of the contributors to our periodicals, none of whom lay claim to perfection; nor do we claim for this Board that it produces a literature equal to the best, but we do claim it to be equal to any produced by our race and superior to that of any other race having only one generation of thirty years of advantages and opportunities in which to prepare for such work. Allow me to say, also, that as our increasing Baptist family sees more and more of this work and falls in to help it on, so will the work improve in literary taste and mechanical construction. When fourteen-thousand Baptist Sunday Schools, instead of nine-thousand, as we now have, are honest, faithful patrons of our Publishing Board, we will be prepared to remove even the little objections which are now raised. In this connection, I wish to say to the Negro Baptists of the world and to those of this State in particular, that if you would occupy a place in the sacred history of today which is to be read by unborn generations, you will have to ally yourselves with these distinct and separate enterprises, fostered and managed by the race; otherwise, the passing of your life will be like the duration of a meteor or shooting star, while your fellows who have endeavored to leave a distinct heritage will be as fixed as stars in the gaze of future generations. Every race must make and write its own history. The work of the Publishing Board stands for all there is in the Negro Baptist family so far as Christian literature is concerned, and we predict that before the close of the first decade of the twentieth century, all will be in line to encourage and support this marvelous undertaking.

In addition to the publication work, the Home Mission Board is supporting in part two missionaries in the extreme West, cooperating with State and district Boards in the employment of fourteen other missionaries and colporters, and aiding other feeble points with gifts of books and Bibles and other literature. I feel sure that the Board's report for the year just closed will show most gratifying results. We must do our part of the work on the Home field, and must not neglect to give the Bible to all who will accept it. To this end we are endeavoring to do a Bible work, which should be supported on Bible Day by the entire Negro Baptist family.

Educational Board

The work allotted to this Board by the National Baptist Convention has been looked upon by many with a somewhat suspicious eye, owning to the fact that the educational work among the Negro Baptists has been largely looked after by the American Baptist Home Mission Society. But I want to say here and now that there need be no apprehension by any that it is the purpose of this Board to antagonize the work of the Home Mission Society. It is, however, the purpose of this Board to seek to strengthen or aid the schools owned and managed by Negroes themselves and to plan for the building and support of a National University by this convention, and to encourage, if allowed to do so, the Home Mission schools. None among us are so ignorant as to think for a moment that the colored Baptists are able to support all the educational work necessary for the religious training of our people. During the past year, this Board has been active in an effort to get the schools owned by the race to associate themselves for mutual protection and benefit. So far it has succeeded in getting quite a number of the best schools to enter into the confederation. These schools are to receive the moral support of the Convention and whatever financial aid it can give them. It is expected that in the next twelve months all the schools owned by the Negroes will join the federation, thereby bringing themselves in the same relation with the National Baptist Convention as they sustain to other societies, that they may receive such aid as the Convention may be able to give.

The National Baptist Young People's Union

This new and heretofore untried department of our Convention work has been carried forward with a commendable degree of satisfaction and success. The work began with practically no money; but with faith in God and confidence in His people, the Secretary of this department has aroused interest in the work and stirred the hosts of young Baptists to such activity as they never had during the progress of our great denomination. He has been loyal to every department of the Convention's work, advertising the same with a measure of success that was marvelous in the eyes of all who bore witness to his labors.

The work of organizing the young people has been pushed with unusual rapidity. Hundreds of local unions have been organized, many districts and States have been put in organic touch with the Board and made acquainted with its system of education and work. An effort has been made to make these societies helpful to the churches. The course of instruction outlined by the Board has been especially helpful in teaching the young people that the special work of their societies is to provide the essential drill ground for the unfolding of Christian doctrines, and to develop the young people of the churches in the responsibilities and activities of Christian life. Signs of the good work being done by this movement are seen and acknowledged by many of the leading pastors. The special effort of the Corresponding Secretary to raise an organizing fund of five-thousand dollars is both timely and commendable. In view of the valuable assistance rendered by pastors by this organization in the training and development of the latent and otherwise dominant forces under them, it is the imperative duty of every pastor to lend a strong helping hand in the effort to more thoroughly organize and systematize the work.

Tribute to the Late Rev. E. K. Love, D.D.

In the midst of this address, you will permit me to pause to say a word concerning one of our fallen heroes, one of the brightest stars in the ministerial galaxy. Rev. E. K. Love, D.D., of Georgia, who was an ardent supporter of our National Convention and its work, and who was preeminently the leader in his State and who also at one time occupied the chief seat in this Convention, passed from labor to reward on the 23rd day of last April. The news of his death was like an earthquake shock to his friends throughout the country. Notwithstanding the fact that he was in ill health at the last meeting of our Convention, and was only able to come in at times and drop a word of advice and encouragement, it was not thought by many of his admirers that he would so soon be taken away. Men die, but principles never. His devotion to the principles of this organization was so strong that nothing but death could separate him from the work undertaken by it. But as his noble spirit looks down from the clouds, we would say to him that the cause which he so ably espoused and for which he laid down his life is still advancing. If I am correctly informed, he was standing at his post when the fatal arrow of death struck him down. "A veteran sleeping on his arms beneath the red cross shield." This Convention will doubtless adopt suitable resolutions and set apart a memorial page in the journal as a mark of the respect and esteem in which he was held.

What of the Future?

As a religious organization representing more than half of the Negro race in this country, and in view of the record the race has made in the past thirty-five years, it is but appropriate to ask, "What of the future?" Before the question can escape from our lips, many discouragements rise up to face us and throw a shadow on the road ahead. But when we consider the past history of our country and the environments of the race, we may reasonably conclude that such things might be expected. Our race and people in America are, like the unwary waters of the mighty deep, impatient, irrepressible, and determined upon the amelioration of their condition. We do not condemn this spirit of anxiety in them, but we should bear in mind that only thirty-five years have passed since the march to a state of cultivated citizenship and high Christian motive was begun. We all deprecate the fact that conditions have arisen to darken the future of the black man in this country. We all regret that racial conflicts have taken place in any part of this glorious land, and that the spirit to disregard the laws of the country has grown in the last decade to marvelous proportions. But such disregard for the law does not represent the best element of our citizens or the true spirit of Americanism. Crime should and must be punished, and I would feel humiliated to hear any member of my race say one word in extenuation of the crimes alleged against persons who belong to the race, but I insist that the strong arm of the law is sufficient to mete out justice to all violators. But there is no doubt as to the fact that the utter disregard for law and order has produced a feeling of unrest all over the country, which has presented a serious problem to both the white and black races in the United States. This problem, however, is being considered in the counsel of both races by their wisest and best men, and it is my firm conviction that it will meet with satisfactory solution before another generation is passed. Many of our good and great men have suggested as a means to the problem rising out of the race conflicts such theories as African emigration, the industrial training of the Negro masses, colonization, etc. But it appears that none of the plans proposed meets the approval of a very large number of our people. The majority of the Negroes believe themselves to be American citizens by every right to which any can lay claim, and cherish the hope that pluck, energy, economy, and accumulation along material lines will eventually solve the problem. Racial prejudice cannot be removed in a single generation, except in those cases where the religious nature dominates all others, and this, as you know, is a rare thing. What the black man cannot understand is that for the first ten years after his emancipation, when he was least prepared for the enjoyment of his civil and political rights, he received these rights and the encouragement and apparent good will of all. But after having come in contact with the schoolhouse and the church, and begun to be more and more a man, there sprang up a unanimous action in the South to deprive him of those rights. There cannot be the slightest doubt that many of the persons today who were born in slavery have improved every opportunity since their emancipation, to show themselves as men, and nothing can come now to make them believe themselves less than men. But having these things to face, is it not well to consider whether or not they are blessings in disguise? Do they not more and more tend to throw the race on its own responsibilities, and thereby establish the fact that it can be a race of resources? My brethren, these things mean to me that the Negroes are to be owners of farms, railroads, steamboats, factories, mills, banks, insurance concerns, dry goods stores, groceries; that we are to have grain dealers, cotton factories, and, in short, are to be actually associated with the business interests of the world. If we are permitted to judge the future by the past, so far as it relates to the race, it seems that nothing can be more hopeful than the future outlook of the Negro. When we take into account the outside agencies which God has at work in our behalf, coupled with the unprecedented efforts being put forth by the race and denomination, we will enter the twentieth century under conditions which to me are most encouraging. Our ministers and churches are far better prepared now than they have been at any time in the past to undertake great things for God. They are seeing the imperative demands being made upon them daily, for better citizenship, a better and more practical Christianity, than they have ever seen before. Better men, better prepared men, in every part of the country, are forging to the front in all our denominational work, and will not leave a stone unturned in convincing the world that while they have brought a majority of the Negro Christians into Baptist churches, they have the ability to utilize this mighty host to the glory of God and the uplift of fallen humanity.

In conclusion, permit me to thank you very sincerely for the hearty and loyal support which you have given to the objects of this Convention, under my administration. And as I go down from the exalted station as President of your great and grand organization, it is with the consciousness that I have striven to do my whole duty. I, perhaps, have not been able to please all the brethren all the time, but I have endeavored to be charitable to those who have differed from me, and am glad to say that my heart goes out in love for one and all with the earnest hope that the time will soon come when there cannot be a single person of prominence found among us that can be used for the disintegration of our Baptist organizations. And finally, permit me to say, if there was ever a time when our race (or perhaps I would better say the people of the world) should draw near to God, and when we should draw near to each other, that time is now. We should bear with patience all the indignities heaped upon us, by those who have apparently lost all respect for the fundamental laws of our great country. And yet, we should contend with manly courage, in a Christian way, for every right enjoyed by any other people under the flag of our nation. But allow me to insist that our greatest hope for the future lies in the fact that "this gospel of the kingdom shall be preached in all the world for a witness unto all nations," for nothing short of the influence of that Gospel which was set in motion by the immaculate Prince of Glory, will bring on that time when there will be neither Jew nor Greek, bond nor free, but all will be one in Christ Jesus.

Annual Address of Dr. E. C. Morris
President of the National Baptist Convention of America
In Session at Austin, Texas, September, 1904

Fellow-workers and Friends:

By the direction of a kind Providence we have been permitted again to assemble in annual meeting of the National Baptist Convention, which is the twenty-fourth milestone in the organized highway of the Negro Baptists as a National Association. As we pause here for a few days to take a retrospect of the perilous journey of the past twenty-four years, and at the same time look forward to the time when we hope to see the Baptists of the United States and of the world reach their ideal, we will, I trust, become inspired to greater effort.

One year ago our meetings were held in the great "City of Brotherly Love." There all the people, it seemed, conspired to give our Convention the most hospitable and enthusiastic reception ever extended to the messengers of a religious society. As to how well they performed that great task thousands of messengers will testify. Notwithstanding the splendid entertainment given by the people of Philadelphia, Dr. Campbell said, in inviting you to meet here, "If you will come to Austin, the people of our city and great State will not only vie with all the cities that have received the Convention, but will surpass them in old-time hospitality."

Quite a while ago I observed through the medium of the press that the citizens of Austin and the good people throughout the State were preparing to redeem the promise made by Dr. Campbell, and now that we are on the ground and see the elaborate arrangements that have been made, we are satisfied that no mistake was made in calling the meeting at this place. We have learned to look at Texas as one of the greatest States in the Union, and especially is this true as to the Baptists, both white and colored, who have made a most enviable record for loyalty to Baptist principles.

The coming together of representative men of the race from all parts of the country will have a twofold effect for good to the race, for it is such gatherings as this that the pessimists among us—men who can see no future for the Negro in America—are convinced of the rapid progress made by the race as a whole, and at the same time see the door of hope opened wider to those who believe that it is the plan of the all wise Creator to have the Negro work out his destiny upon American soil, and that the time will come when the Negro will, under the Constitution, enjoy every right of a citizen.

If the transformation which has taken place in the last forty years is not sufficient to inspire hope in the race, and meanwhile convince the doubting white brother that the hand of the Almighty is visible in the uplift of the Negroes, no argument from me will be convincing. Forty years ago we came from the horrible pit of slavery, bringing with us the cringing fears and dwarfed intellects of those two centuries and more of servitude, and back of that, fifty generations of the darkest superstitions and idolatry. We came forth in time to catch the patriotic spirit and inventive ray of the nineteenth century, which prepared us to enter the twentieth century as men and as citizens, having made greater progress in the same length of time than any people of the world, that had been in similar circumstances. No man who would look upon you without bias or prejudice, you who were either born in slavery or are the children of slave parents, will refuse to confess, that your transformation, is little less than a miracle, a transfiguration. And this wonderful change only waiting for the opportunity of demonstrating to the world the greatness of the civilized, Christianized, educated African.

As we stand upon this mountain of human endeavor and look into the faces of men who came from zero in wealth, learning and religion to occupy places as financiers, professors and ministers of the Gospel, and who, at the same time, have trained a whole race to be the most patient, law-abiding people in the whole country, we can but say in the words of the Psalmist, "The Lord has done great things for us whereof we are glad." It is frequently said that the Negro is not advancing as fast as the opportunities afforded him would warrant. This may be true as to some individual cases, but not true when applied to the race as a whole. Before a verdict should be brought in against the entire race in this particular, it should be considered that the race started forty years ago with nothing, and had to gain whatever is to its credit. It is almost impossible to conceive what the real advancement of the race has been along any given line.

Of course, greater progress has been made in religious affairs than in other respects, and yet the showing made along other lines is creditable. The census reports will show that in 1880, there were more illiterate colored than white in the United States. The census of 1900, just twenty years later, shows that there were 221,423 more illiterate whites than illiterate blacks. Much of the illiteracy of the white people, however, is due to the large number of ignorant white emigrants coming into our country every year. The census of 1890 showed that 57.1 per cent of the Negro race was illiterate, while in 1900 this had been reduced to 44.5, or a decline in the illiteracy of the race of nearly 13 per cent, in one decade. If this same rate of reduction can be kept up for forty years or more, our illiteracy will be practically wiped out. A similar showing can be made as to the accumulation of wealth. A little more than a generation ago, the Negroes were penniless and knew nothing of the value of a dollar. Now, they own a billion dollars' worth of real and personal property, and one-fifth of the race live in homes of their own. The very rapid progress made by the race during these forty years of freedom is due to many causes, the principal one is that God and the good people of the nation have been with us.

Before our emancipation God was preparing Christian Societies at the North to bring to us preachers and teachers and Christian schools, so that there would be no delay in our enlightenment when the chains that bound us in slavery were broken. The work of these societies speaks for itself, and now their efforts are to be supplemented by those of the white people of the whole country, North and South, through educational and missionary boards. Nor have we sat down and depended entirely upon our friends to do all towards our education. We have built and are supporting out of own means more than a hundred high schools and colleges, and the Negro Baptists alone are giving more than two-hundred-thousand dollars a year to the support of their own educational media. I regret to say in this connection, that some of us are disposed to vacillate between the North and the South in the matter of missionary affiliations. Some say that our best friends are in the North, others that the Southern people are our best friends. This comparison should not be made. The truest friends we have are those who are friends for Jesus' sake, whether they be North or South, and there are many such in both sections of our great country. It is ill advised, I think, to give expressions to what is calculated, perhaps to keep up sectional strife.

Perhaps the most potent sign of the progress of the race, and the fact that God is back of it, is the interest that the people of our race in this country manifest for their unfortunate brethren in other parts of the world. Poor, though they may be, and receiving aid from the hands of others, yet we are reaching out our hands to our brethren across the sea, answering as best we can the Macedonian cry that comes from the Isles of the Sea and from the destitute in our land.

So far as I know, no other race has made such a record under like conditions, but, like Paul, the Negro says, "Forgetting those things which are behind, and reaching forth unto those things which are before, I press toward the mark for the prize of the high calling of God."

The efforts of the demagogue politician to create strained relations between the races, especially at the South, have been a menace to us. Our leaders are exceedingly anxious that the very best of feeling shall continue to exist between the two conspicuous races in the United States. Our race has been forced by conditions to bear the unjust criticisms of the unfriendly press in silence. Ere long an impartial sentiment will change this condition of affairs. The world has been told that we are seeking social equality with the white race. Nothing could be more foreign to the truth. Indeed, the Negro is content with separate society and seeks no intermingling with other races.

Intelligent Negroes everywhere deprecate that members of their race are frequently charged with committing outrages against the pure womanhood of the country, and no intelligent Negro would say one word in extenuation of the brute who would fall so low as to even attempt an outrage upon an innocent woman. The men of my race will do as much and go as far as the men of any race to bring to justice any criminal so base. But recent statistical reports go to show that the unnameable crime is not a racial instinct, and in the domain of well ordered governments like those of our states, whatever punishment is inflicted upon a criminal should be according to law, not for the criminals' sake, but for the government's sake.

In 1903, there were forty-four charges made against Negroes for criminal assault in the entire country, while more than that number were charged against white persons in a single city—Chicago. While such criminality seems to be proportionately greater in the great cities, where the number of Negroes is inconsiderable as compared with the white race, yet I would be glad if we could make it impossible for such charges to be alleged against any member of the race. In this connection I would say that an assuring hope that these crimes will cease in the future, so far as our race is concerned, lies in the fact that none of these heinous crimes are positively laid to the intelligent, educated members of the race.

Professor Washington says that he has found but two such cases among the graduates of fifteen reputable schools that he has consulted. So far as I know there is no record in any of the State courts where any Negro graduate of any college was ever convicted of a felony and sentenced to serve in a state prison. Very few of the criminal class of the race have had any school training, hence, it may be seen that as the race advances along educational lines, criminality decreases.

But why take time to reason upon these questions, when it is plainly evident that God and the good people of the whole country are working together for the uplift of the once enslaved race. The General Educational Board, the Southern Educational Board, the general missionary societies of the North, aided by such philanthropic men as John D. Rockefeller, Daniel Hand, Andrew Carnegie and John C. Martin, supplemented by the Christian Societies among the Southern white people, have, it seems, decided to see to it that equal educational advantages shall be enjoyed by all the youths in our country without regard to race or color.

I beg to say again that the Negro is doing no little toward his own elevation and education. This seems to touch upon the surest way of settling the suffrage question to the Negro's edification, for if educational and property qualifications are to be the only barriers to the free exercise of the ballot by the Negro, as seems to be the case now, he will soon surmount the barrier. Even now he owns more than six-hundred-million dollars ($600,000,000) worth of real estate and has advanced to where much more than half of the race can read and write. In all that has been done to uplift the race, none are more deserving of praise than the Negro ministers who have held a balanced mind under the most trying and exciting circumstances, always advising absolute obedience to the laws, even though they had reason to believe that some of the laws were discriminative and unjust. The people have heard them and submitted to their leadership without question.

Turning now to the specific work of the Baptists as carried on by this Convention: The very fact that fully one-half of the Negro Christians in the United States are members of the Negro Baptist churches, emphasizes the responsibility that rests upon you as leaders of this great denomination and lays upon you the duty of looking out for the whole race without regard to sectarian views. Those of you who have been given the prominence to manage the affairs of the denomination in the several departments of this Convention have a double duty to perform. You are to serve both the denomination and to the public from without.

I have endeavored from time to time to convince the public, and especially the members of this Convention, that the affairs of the Convention are in safe, reliable hands. But despite these efforts our Boards are being severely criticized—even the press of the denomination has openly charged extravagance against the officers of the Convention. I beg to assure you that every official act of ours is open to the closest investigation by you. Indeed, we invite you to appoint a committee to carefully examine into all the affairs of the Convention, that the world may know the truth about us.

Our Foreign Mission Work

The Foreign Mission work occupies the first place among Negro Baptists on the principle, "Freely ye have received, freely we give." Nearly a quarter of a century has passed since we first undertook to give the gospel to our brethren in heathen lands. We have not always had easy work in this department and the grand results which have been accomplished cannot be fully realized by the present generation. Rest assured, however, that the seeds sown by Colley, Presley, McKinney, Coles and others are bearing fruit and will yet yield a rich harvest. All sections of Africa are beginning to feel the effect of our Foreign Mission movement. We cannot too strongly put upon you the importance of increased interest in Africa.

While we have not yet attempted any mission work in the Free State of the Congo, I take this opportunity to direct your attention to it as one of the greatest countries in the world. At present the Free State of the Congo is under the protectorate of fourteen of the leading European countries and the United States. The article which is most important to us as a religious organization, in the compact formed by these great governments concerning the Congo is as follows:

> All the powers exercising rights of influence in the aforesaid territory bind themselves to watch over the preservation of the native tribes, and to care for the improvement of the conditions of their mental and moral well-being and to help in suppressing slavery, and especially the slave trade. They shall without distinction or creed or nation protect and favor all religious, scientific and charitable institutions and undertakings created and organized for the above ends, or which aim at instructing the natives and bring home to them the blessings of civilizations.
>
> Christian missionaries, scientists and explorers with their followers, property and collections shall also be objects of special protection. Freedom of conscience and religious toleration are expressly guaranteed to the na-

> tives, no less than to the subjects of the sovereign states and foreigners. The free and public exercise of all forms of divine worship, and the right to build churches, temples and chapels, and to organize religious missions belonging to all creeds shall not be limited or fettered in any ways whatsoever.

As I understand it, this compact limiting the trade of the nations of the world as is related to the Congo, was to continue for twenty years and will expire in December of this year. Unless renewed by the nations referred to, the Congo country will be left open to the greed of the hungry nations of the world, whose only object would be the subjugation of the natives for pillage and spoil.

I cannot close my remarks upon the work of the Foreign Missions without saying a word of commendation of that grand man, who has been chosen as the Secretary of our Foreign Mission Board, Dr. Jordan. When the question was raised one year ago, "Whom shall we send and who will go for us to visit our stations and workers in South Africa?" he came forward and said, "Here am I, send me." He went out, so to speak, without money and without price, and comes back to us with such tidings we cannot fail to move every loyal Baptist to action in support of the work begun by Brother Jackson ten years ago in South Africa.

Home Missions and Publications

The work of Home Missions has grown steadily since the organization of the Home Mission Board nine years ago. This department of our work has been under the efficient management of Dr. R. H. Boyd, who is also Secretary of the Publishing Board. At first, the work was carried on with the little surplus accumulated from the sale of Sunday School literature. This was supplemented by a gift of $1,800 a year from the Home Board of the Southern Baptist Convention, which enabled the Home Mission Board to do an appreciable amount of work on the home field.

You are doubtless glad to know that the cooperative plans entered into by and between the Home Mission Board of the Southern Baptist Convention and the Home Mission Board of the national Baptist Convention in 1900, have been amended so as to provide for the increased appropriation on the part of the Southern Baptist Convention to help us in our Home Mission work. There has been much discussion for the last two months in the National Baptist Union, and are open for your consideration, it is needless that I should take them up. One thing, however, is settled. I think we desire the cooperation of our white brethren in all the work of our Convention and will subscribe to such as soon as the plans of cooperation that will be mutually satisfactory to all can be agreed upon.

It has been said that the present plan of cooperation between the Southern Baptist Convention and our National Baptist Convention to confine its Home Mission work to the field occupied by the Southern Baptist Convention. I have not so construed that agreement and would say that I would not approve of any plan of cooperation that would tend to draw sectional lines between the National Baptists of this great country. Nor would I agree to any cooperation plan that would in any degree prescribe our rights as men and citizens. We see, however, the cooperation of all Baptist societies on the high ground that we are brothers.

The publishing work of the Convention has moved steadily forward. This department has also been under the management of Dr. Boyd from its beginning. It will not be denied by any one who knows the facts that he has proven himself a genius and a master in this special feature of our denominational work. The publication work has grown to such enormous proportions that it is impracticable to continue it and the Home Mission work under the same management. It will, therefore, be necessary for some action to be taken, looking to a separate management for these departments.

Educational Board

Upon the recommendation of the President the headquarters of the Educational Board was moved from Washington to Nashville. This recommendation was made with the view that the Educational Board would have the cooperative aid of our Publishing Board, and, at the same time, be near the center of the Negro population.

It was clear to the mind of the President that the Education Board could be greatly benefited by being in close touch with our Publishing Board, and it would greatly facilitate its work by using our periodicals as a direct and close medium through which to advertise. Professor Wilson, the Secretary assured us while in attendance at the State Convention of Arkansas that no time would be lost in pushing the interest of his Board. So far as the President of the Convention knows, very little has been done through our Educational Board to promote the interests of this special line of work.

Baptist Young People's Union Board

Not since the organization of the National B.Y.P.U. Board has there been such an awakening or activity among the Baptist young people as has been evident during the past year. State and district organizations have been perfected all over the country, and special pride in them is being manifested by the Baptist young people. It has been a difficult matter, however, to secure sufficient contributions from the B.Y.P.U. work to meet the expenses of the Board. But this condition will not long maintain, for the reason that the people are beginning to understand the benefit of such an organization.

Dr. Isaac has had to divide his time between the work of the B.Y.P.U. Board and the editorial work of the National Baptist Union. This should not be, and the Convention should provide a salary for the editor of the Union and his entire time should be devoted to it. It has been held by some that the National paper is not a necessity and that our State and local papers can amply serve the interest of the denomination. It will only require a moment's reflection to see that such a theory is impracticable and could result in but one thing—that of confusion or misunderstanding in the national work.

National Baptist Benefit Association

The Convention launched the National Baptist Benefit Association at its last session and created a Board to promote the object of such an association. This Board located its headquarters at Helena, Arkansas, and elected Rev. W. A. Holmes as its Corresponding Secretary. The Board has opened an office, and, after having incorporated under the laws of Arkansas, is now doing business. I should call attention to one feature of this work which was not authorized by the Convention. The Board incorporated the provision in its fundamental plan to make all regular Baptists eligible to membership in the Association. I would have you know, however, that I am in harmony with this arrangement and hope it will meet the approval of the Convention.

In conclusion, permit me to say that we are now facing the most critical period and the most delicate problems in the history of our race. We are being discussed by all the people of the world. There is no word in the English language more significantly used than the word "Negro." We are tried by a jury composed of friends and foes, many of whom have already expressed their opinion as to our guilt or innocence and have declared that it will require evidence to remove the opinions already formed. Some of the opinions are, in effect, that we are unfit for citizenship. Our case does not come under ordinary jurisprudence governing the conduct of courts of justice where the accused is considered innocent until proved guilty. But the wheels of justice have been alleged against us. If given an opportunity we will do it. We will prove to the nation that we are the most loyal patriots; that, from the days in which Crispus Attucks fell in the streets of Boston in defense of American independence down to the present time, when called upon we have ever been ready to go to the front in defense of the old flag.

When told that the Civil War was a white man's fight, and that the Negro slaves must remain out of it, we remained at home: not a single insurrection was raised and the home of the master was protected until the superior force of the Union arms crushed the cringing slave and took possession of the devastated plantations, and when the conflict between the North seemed obscured by a cloud of uncertainty as to which way it would turn, and the Negro was told that his freedom and the preservation of the Union depended on the success of the Union arms, 200,000 volunteered on the side of the Union and gave us once more a grand and united country. When peace was declared they settled down and began to plan for what we have here today, as testimony to our progress in education, morality and religion, one of the grandest Christian organizations in the world, with a membership of more than two million people, whose hearts' desire is to live in peace with all mankind and help make America, in deed and in truth, "the land of the free and the home of the brave."

Recommendations

1. That the National Baptist Convention reaffirm its faith in, and approval of, the plan of cooperation as agreed upon between the Home Board of the Southern Baptist Convention and the Home Mission Board of the National Baptist Convention at the Chattanooga Conference in November, 1900.

2. That the amendments to the original plans of cooperation, whereby it is proposed to enlarge the contributions on the part of the Home Board of the Southern Baptist Convention, be submitted to a committee to be reported back to the Convention.

3. That, whereas, the publication of books and other periodicals are distinct from mission work, that the publishing Board of the National Baptist Convention be constituted a separate and distinct Board from the Home Mission Board.

4. That the Home Mission Board of the National Baptist Convention seek in every honorable way to secure the cooperation of all great Baptist organizations who are willing to cooperate with it in

Home Mission work upon such plans as those agreed upon by the Chattanooga Conference.

5. To avoid any friction or misunderstanding between the several Boards as to the future policy or conduct of the National Baptist Union, a committee composed of one member from each Board, and one from the Women's Auxiliary Convention be appointed by the Chairman of each of the respective Boards and the President of the Women's Auxiliary Convention and prepare rules for the conduct and management of the paper, and that the editor to be chosen shall be required to conform to said rules when agreed upon.

Annual Address of Dr. E. C. Morris
President of the National Baptist Convention of America
In Session at Columbus, Ohio, September, 1909

My Brethren:

Once more I have the honor and supreme pleasure of coming before you to report as an officer of your great Convention. For fifteen consecutive years, I have come before you in a like capacity, and at no time have I felt a deeper interest in the work of the Convention or greater pride in the progress of our great denomination, than now.

It is quite fitting that you voted to hold this session of the Convention in this great city and state, which state is the home of the President of our nation. This beautiful capital city, noted for her magnificent public buildings, beautiful parks and magnanimous people, is a delightful place for the representatives of the lowly Nazarene to sojourn for a few days. The word Ohio has a marked fragrance about it to most intelligent Negroes when they recall the unique position it occupied in the anti-slavery movement prior to the Civil War. Ohio, being a border state, became one of the terminals of the "Underground Railroad." Many of the directors of that road lived in other sections of the country, but Ohio, by reason of its situation, was looked upon as the safest ground for the landing of the weary pilgrims who made their escape from slavery. Her laws then as now were protection to the black man as well as the white. As long as a single Negro lives, the heroic deeds of the grand old Abolition Fathers will be held in sacred memory.

The interest which the Negro people felt in Ohioans did not terminate with the abolition of slavery; but they have watched with abiding interest the course of Ohio's great statesmen in time of peace and almost without a single exception, these statesmen have stood squarely upon those grand and righteous principles of equal rights to all, without regard to race, color or condition.

Her great statesmen never faltered when it became necessary to defend the Constitutional rights of the Negro. In that galaxy of wizards in statecraft, who never flinched at duty's call, we beg to mention the names of the late John Sherman, of James A. Garfield, and William McKinley, our martyred President; of William Howard Taft, our President now, and, last but not least, that of our friend and patriot, the Hon. Joseph Benson Foraker: all of whom as Governor,

Senator, or President held the scales of justice so evenly balanced between man and man as to challenge the confidence and esteem of their own countrymen and the admiration of the best people throughout the world. Then again, we are proud of this grand state because of the fact that it has given to our race some of the best men and women to be found anywhere.

But while we rejoice at the fact that a kind Providence has raised up many friends to our race in every part of our great country—which has enabled us to make such wonderful advancement—yet, we cannot conceal the fact that the Negro people are facing some of the most serious problems that ever confronted any people. Problems which are puzzling some of the wisest statesmen of the day. It was not thought by the wisest and most optimistic of forty years ago that those safeguards thrown around the emancipated people by the Fourteenth and Fifteenth Amendments to the Constitution would be attacked after that people had received more than forty years of training in the art of good citizenship. But such is the case. And the people who have waited patiently and long for the color of their skin to give way to the intelligence of the mind and heart, find that there is still much opposition to their having their civil and political rights. But there is hope in the fact that the race agitation is kept alive in most parts by an element that is fast passing off the scene.

There is no class of people in this country more desirous to see a really united country than the Negroes. And, a slight ray of hope broke through the clouds of sectional prejudice at the recent reunion of the Confederate Veterans when the Commander of the veterans, Gen. Clement Evans and General Fred D. Grant clasped hands. We all should hope that it really means that blotting out of sectional lines which must come before that God-given principle of equal rights to all and special privileges to none will have universal sway.

Fortunately for the Negroes, the most bitter contentions at this time are not with them, but, like the Civil War, the contentions are about them; an instance of which is found in the case of the Georgia firemen's strike. I am not an advocate of monopolies or trusts, but I believe that men who are at the head of great corporations and who have invested their money in railroads and other great enterprises should be permitted to operate those enterprises profitably so long as they are within the bounds of the law, without the dictation of any class of people who seek to manage the affairs of others on no better ground that racial prejudice. The right to earn one's daily bread is a God-given right that cannot be taken, and when the effort is made to take that right from the black man, those making it will find themselves facing not only the laws of the land, but the influence of every capitalist, great and small, in our entire country. Hence, we conclude that next to the rights of the laboring man, be he white or black, comes the right of the capitalist to control his investments.

But I wish to repeat here what I have said on former occasions, that the worst and most serious aspect to the race questions in this country is the fact that it has taken the front seats in many of the Christian churches in our country. And in saying this, I do not mean to advocate inter-racial churches for it has pleased all-wise Providence to permit separate churches for the races to exist and prosper. But while this may be in accordance with His will, yet it is inconceivable that Christians of the same faith cannot find a common ground on which they can meet as brethren and, at least in fraternal way express their good wishes the one for the other. Sad to say, instead of coming closer together, the chasm seems to be widening each year.

The gospel of Jesus Christ is either an unselfish gospel or it is no gospel at all. It will either unite the world in one Christian brotherhood, or it will utterly fail of its purpose, and leave its great founder to stand convicted of the most colossal fraud ever perpetrated against the world.

But, thank God, it cannot fail. Heaven and earth may pass away, but His word shall not fail. It may be hindered for a while by those who think more on how to keep alive race hatred than they do on how to get the people of the world saved, still time will change all these conditions. We must admit that caste, color, and race antipathy have done much to retard the progress of the gospel, and will perhaps continue to be a great obstacle in its way. But it will eventually have to give way to the truth of Him who said through His beloved disciple, "If a man say I love God, and hateth his brother, he is a liar; for he that loveth not his brother whom he hath seen, how can he love God whom he hath not seen?"

These sacred rules are yet to become the guide of all the Christian people in this land before we can fully recognize one another as members of one great family, before the unsaved world will believe that "there is neither Jew nor Greek; there is neither bond nor free; there is neither male or female; for we are all one in Christ Jesus."

My friends, the most serious of all the matters which should have the attention of the Baptist churches of America is the work of foreign missions, not only as it affects the constituents of this Convention, but the entire Baptist family. Each passing year brings the countries of the world closer together in commercial relations, and the white Christians are beginning to realize that in dealing with the pagan nations, it is by far more satisfactory where the principles of Christianity have been introduced, and they are, therefore, giving many thousands of dollars annually to their foreign mission work. It is true we are much weaker than they financially, and yet we can and should do more than we have done for the redemption of the heathen.

Our principal foreign missionary efforts have been directed to the redemption of Africa. And, while I do not wish to be understood as advocating a racial gospel, yet I believe that it is well that we have largely confined our efforts to that continent, for the reason, first, that the other great missionary organizations are giving more attention to other countries, following perhaps the line of least resistance; secondly, that the Negro missionary is more readily accepted by the African than those of other races, the African regarding the American Negro as a Joseph who went before to prepare the way for him; and thirdly, that the means at our command have been too limited to reach much further.

Then again, it appears from printed statements and reports of missionaries that Africa is the most neglected, and therefore, the darkest spot on all the earth, and largely because it is the land of our forefathers. I fear the real motive which prompted the early Christians in missionary work has not yet taken hold of our people and that many of those who go out as missionaries are not willing to die, if need be, for the redemption of that land. Of course, the missionaries should be supported; and instead of the $25,000 that Negro Baptists are raising for foreign missions, they should raise $100,000 annually for the work in Africa alone.

If the glorious light of heaven is to shine upon the African and he is to stand transfigured before the other nations of the earth, it will, in my opinion be when the Negro Baptists take him by the hand and ascend to the mount of Christianity and teach him that higher and more glorious civilization which is revealed in the word of God. We cannot do a greater service to the other parts of the world, to say nothing of the incalculable benefit it will be to Africa's sable sons, than to devote the greater part of our means and efforts at this time to the redemption of the Dark Continent.

What could bring greater gratification to the Christian world than to know that an army of 30,000,000 men and 120,000,000 women and children who had roamed the deserts and forests of that unhappy continent for centuries were coming forth dressed in the uniform of Christian soldiers, ready and willing to help turn the barren places of earth into well-springs of joy? Such will be the case when the gospel of Jesus Christ has been given to darkest Africa.

My brethren, I beg that you give the foreign missions cause a deeper place in your affections, to the end that the appeals from the Board will meet with a more ready response.

Woman's Training School

The woman's training school project has assumed definite shape, and the school is to open in October. At first, the enterprise did not receive the hearty endorsement of the brethren for more reasons than one. Some objected on the ground that its object was to teach the women how to work, and others that it would detract from the interest manifested by the women in foreign missions. But each succeeding year has given greater emphasis to the importance of having trained women in the race, if we are to have our share of the skilled labor which will ever remain the basis of real progress in a material war; and instead of diminishing the interest in foreign missions, the school will be a means of promoting the work. The leaders in the Women's Auxiliary Convention are to be congratulated upon the very bright prospect for this feature of their work.

Home Missions

We have not in any sense lessened our interest on the home field, where several millions of our people are yet to be training in Christian life. It is true the Negro has made marvelous advancement in religious matters in the last forty years. He has startled the world in the matter of church and school building, out of his poverty. This fact will ever stand as a monument to the race; but those of you who are most closely allied to the race will admit that there is very much to do even among the professed Christians, before the real, ennobling principles of Christianity have an immovable place in the affections of many of our people.

It is largely the work of our Home Mission Board, through its missionaries, to go among the churches already established and strengthen them in the doctrines of Jesus Christ, by removing the sands of heresy and emotionalism until the rock of unfaltering faith has been reached, to the end that "the gates of hell shall not prevail against it."

In our efforts to strengthen the churches and educate the people to real Christian service, we have had the cooperation of the Home Board of the Southern Baptist Convention, for which cooperation we feel very grateful and cherish the hope that it may be continued.

Next to the human voice in proclaiming the truths of the gospel is the printed page. Our Publishing Board is sending out millions of printed pages each year. It was reported in the *Union Review* that more than 20,000 orders for Sunday School periodicals were filled for the third quarter of this year, which is the best evidence that our efforts to operate a publishing house are meeting with popular favor. It is generally conceded now that the colored Baptists have outstripped all competitors in the matter of a publishing plant. The merits of the publications are attested by the very liberal patronage given to the house and are very gratifying to the officers and members of this Board.

The B.Y.P.U. Movement

The question may be rightly raised as to whether we are doing our duty by the Baptist Young People. Men who live only for the present and whose official connection with the churches is very largely for the present day benefits will not take any very great interest in a movement which can hardly be expected to come in full fruition for several years. But that class of men and leaders who are interested in what the future church shall be, both as to its aggressiveness and stability, will sacrifice both time and money to prepare the young people to occupy the posts after the present leaders have passed off the stage. Unfortunately for this department of our work, the principal officer has been sick a large part of the year, and could not, therefore, do the amount of campaigning necessary to promote the general interest of his Board. But notwithstanding the many hindrances which he has had, he will doubtless be able to make a satisfactory report. We earnestly ask that all Baptist pastors inaugurate the B. Y. P. U. in their churches and give their personal attention to the work until it becomes self-supporting.

The National Baptist Benefit Board

The Benefit Board of the Convention has been able to keep pretty well up with the claims that have come against it. A large number of death claims have been paid in full or in part and some needy ministers have been helped from its treasury. To say that this Board should have a liberal support from every Baptist in the country is putting the matter in the mildest form. It is founded upon one of the noblest virtues that warms the Christian's breast, gratitude. What one is there among us who cannot point back to some word or deed by the old and now worn out ministers, which has been a help to us all through life? And what man is there who having been helped by them will refuse them aid as they go quietly to the grave?

In what is called the Benefit or Insurance Department, no sympathy should be asked, but one fact should not be overlooked, and that is, that thousands of our people are too poor to carry life insurance in the old line companies, and are also too weak to keep alive a company for themselves without the aid of their stronger brethren. Hence, the ablest and wisest ones among us should be the first to carry membership in the National Baptist Benefit Association.

The National Baptist Convention of Jamaica

Petition was made two years ago by the Baptists of Jamaica, B. W. I., for membership in the National Baptist Convention, through Rev. G. E. Stewart, and they were received. I am glad to say that they have since organized a National Baptist Convention of Jamaica Auxiliary to the National Baptist Convention, and that their Convention has been recognized by the government of the British West Indies, their ministers granted the right to perform marriage ceremonies according to the Baptist usage. It is the only organization composed of what they call "the colored people" on the island. The Convention held its 1909 session on the 8th, 9th and 10th days of June and elected Brother Stewart as its President. They are asking for the prayers and assistance of their American brethren in all their efforts to turn their people from the Episcopal bands that bind them to the freedom of the Baptist faith.

District Conventions

The district conventions are not doing, in my judgment, what they were constituted to do. It was presumed that these district organizations would be auxiliary to the National Baptist Convention, and, in a measure, would cooperate with the parent organization in all its work. The President very heartily approved the existence of the Lott Carey Convention and the Convention of the Western States and Territories, as district bodies, and had not the slightest thought that there would ever occur any conflict of authority between the officers of our district bodies and the officers of our National Boards. But it has been reported to us that there has been some misunderstanding between our representatives on the foreign field and those supported by our Lott Carey brethren. This conflict of authority can be avoided, if the rules governing district conventions are followed. We make an exception, however, in the case of the New England Convention, which has at no time attempted to work independently of the National Baptist Convention but rather sought to cooperate in carrying out its objects.

The Federal Council

The Convention at its last session authorized the President to appoint a committee of twenty-five to meet the Federal Council of Churches at Philadelphia on the 2nd day of December, 1908. Owing to the fact that there was no money in hand with which to pay the traveling expenses of the Committee, the President appointed only seventeen persons to compose the Committee, all of whom lived in or near Philadelphia.

As you know, the Committee was not authorized to pledge this Convention to the object of the Federal Council, but simply to learn the plans and report to you, which it will, no doubt, do at this meeting. During the year, 1910, there is to be held in Edinburgh, Scotland, an Ecumenical Congress representing all the evangelical churches of the world. We have been informed that one of the objects is a union of all the churches of the world.

I am sure that you will agree with me that no sect is more interested in that one topic than the Baptists who are now one of the strongest of the evangelical denominations. A union, however, to any well-informed Baptist would mean an open Bible to all, a regenerated church membership and an acknowledgment of Christ as the only head. And unless all others can come to acknowledge this and accept His Word as the only rule of their faith and practice, the Baptists will remain on the field dressed, so to speak, in camel's hair with a leathern girdle about their loins until Shiloh comes a second time. This Convention should by all means be represented at the Edinburgh Congress if for no other purpose, than to enter our most solemn protest against a union that will in any degree compromise the principles laid down in the New Testament Scriptures.

The Baptist World Alliance

Your attention was called one year ago to the fact that the Baptist World Alliance would hold its second meeting in Philadelphia in 1911. A resolution was adopted authorizing each state represented in the Convention to appoint three persons who, with fifteen others to be appointed by the President, should constitute a committee to arrange for the entertainment of our foreign brethren, supplementarily to the arrangements made by the American Committee.

It is quite important that the personnel of that committee be known and announced at this meeting. In my opinion, the 1911 Congress will surpass any gathering of Baptists since the days of Christ on earth, and no pains should be spared on our part to make it so. Indeed, another great Pentecost should break forth from that meeting which should result in the conversion of thousands in a day.

A great many queries have come to the President during the year about matters with which he has nothing directly to do officially. Most of these queries have been about the affairs of the several Boards and could have been answered by the member of that Board from the state in which the one who asked the question lives. We beg to state that each of the six Boards of the National Baptist Convention are chosen by the state delegations while the Convention is in session, and announced by the Secretary. When this is done, neither the President nor any of the officers of the Convention has anything further to do with the affairs of the Boards, except in an advisory way.

I would say, that as soon as the new Boards are constituted, it is the duty of the former Chairman to call a meeting of the new Board and proceed at once to organize it by the election of a Chairman, a Secretary, a Corresponding Secretary and a Treasurer and two others, who together constitute an Executive Committee, with power to act in the absence of the full committee or Board. This explanation ought to put at rest the continual agitation that this or that property belongs to this or that person (unless the states are putting men on these Boards in whom they have no confidence).

The term of every officer expires at this meeting, and the several officers of the several Boards will have no right to return to their respective headquarters to take charge of the business of the respective Boards, unless they are elected to do so; but when they are elected, they become the legal custodians of your property, unless removed by the Board that elects them.

I think every officer of every Board has the same view of his position that I have expressed, and that all come here to abide your will as to whether they shall continue to labor for you in the future or not.

But there is a serious side to the matter of public service. If you will allow me to use a political term I would say, "a public office is a public trust," and such are the official positions in connection with our Convention. The positions belong to the messengers here assembled and will be given to whomsoever they elect. But let me say that in large religious matters, as in all others, every temptation to do evil should be removed from before the men who are elected to serve you. When men are called from their private affairs to look after the affairs of the general public, several things should be taken under consideration. First of all, in leaving one's occupation to accept a position under you, he may be depriving himself of a lifetime position that would at least be a comfortable living for him; hence, every man employed to work for any of the Boards of this Convention, should be paid a sufficient salary to sustain him in case of removal from office until he can procure other employment, and at the same time justify the Convention in demanding his entire time and energies in the work placed in his charge.

When men are put into positions on small salaries, and yet those same men become wealthy while the institutions which they represent remain poor and in some instances unable to carry on their work, it is perfectly reasonable that suspicions will arise to the effect that the officers are giving more attention to their private affairs than they are to the affairs they have been chosen to look after.

Conclusion

In closing my address on this occasion, you will permit me to say that not since the chains of slavery fell from the limbs of our race in this country have the clouds of adversity seemed heavier than now; and, never have the leaders among our people worked harder to throw off the calumny that is being heaped upon them. Notwithstanding these facts the future continues to brighten, and the race continues to climb higher in the scales of Christian civilization. That we may continue in our steady march of progress, it is necessary that the leaders among us shall stand shoulder to shoulder in every effort to advance our racial interest. Let the motto be Race Advancement leaving the following generations to enjoy the luxuries which will come as a result of our achievements. Already much has been lost by the keen, and I may say, unwarranted criticism which have been made by one class of our leaders against the other. The ingenious enemy have stood by and encouraged a division among us upon the great issues in our race development. But let me admonish you, that, if we cannot agree, we should agree to disagree, and yet be united in the work of building the race.

As Christian leaders we should not despair, but when those who are our friends say to us that the door of hope shall not be closed against us, we should thank them for their generous assurance, but we might say to them at the same time, that, when Fort Sumter was fired upon, the God of heaven set before us an open door, and no man can shut it.

Finally let me say in broken rhyme:

In Eighteen-hundred sixty-one,
When God our freedom had begun;
The statesmen all in fierce debate,
Stirred up strife in every state.
The war broke out, and all this land,
Felt the weight of Lincoln's hand;
The Negro people shall be free:
On January first sixty-three.
From that day to the present time,
Cruel efforts, steeped in crime;
Have been devised to overthrow,
The results of the Civil War.
The God of Heaven will not spurn,
A work so righteously begun;
He'll keep the reins in His strong hand,
Till we are loosed from every band.
Until at last we stand complete
As men, not chattels at His feet;
And the nation whose God we serve,
Will grant the rights which we deserve.

Annual Address of Dr. E. C. Morris
President of the National Baptist Convention of America
In Session at Philadelphia, Pennsylvania, September, 1914

> "Brethren, I count not myself to have apprehended: but this one thing I do, forgetting those things which are behind, and reaching forth unto those things, which are before, I press toward the mark for the prize of the high calling of God unto Christ Jesus."

Fellow Comrades, Ladies and Gentlemen:

Forty years ago I enlisted in the army of my Lord and Master, and twenty years ago, was called to the Presidency of this great Convention. It could not have been hoped that all of these years should have been filled with joys, yet I rejoice that I have been counted worthy to suffer for Christ's sake.

Philadelphia's Hospitality

Eleven years ago it was the good fortune of this Convention to meet in this city, a city which has become famous for its even temper and fair treatment of all her people without regard to color or condition. And we were glad when the opportunity presented itself for us to again assemble here. It was here that the first notes of American liberty were sounded one-hundred and thirty-eight years ago, and while at that time, the people of our race were held as chattels and were not included, perhaps, in the minds of those who sent forth those resonant notes; yet the echo which went forth from the "Old Liberty Bell" was but a signal that all the people would be free.

We rejoice that for fully fifty years, the people of our race have been able to join in the happy acclaim, "Columbia, the land of the free and the home of the brave." But not until the country has been baptized in the blood of many thousands of brave patriots, who would rather sacrifice their lives, than see a divided country, and permit a continuance of human slavery.

It was under such inspiring influences as were characteristics of this grand city that Richard Allen, quite a century ago, sprang from his knees and led a small band of Negroes into a blacksmith shop, and there declared for the independence of soul in the worship of God, and organized what is now known the world over as the African Methodist Episcopal Church, and, I may say, that it is such wholesome influences as go out from here that are attracting such large numbers of our people from other sections of our great country.

I wish to congratulate our great Baptist leaders here for the magnificent work accomplished by them in putting the Baptist cause in the forefront in this city. I have been reliably informed, that the Baptists among the people of our race, lead all other denominations, and that they have more communicants than there are members in all other Negro churches in the city. This is of course as it should be.

Our Jubilee Celebration

One year ago at the meeting of our Convention held at Nashville, Tennessee, the attention of the thousands of messengers gathered there from all parts of our country was focused upon the great Jubilee celebration. Perhaps no event in the history of our Convention, or of the race attracted greater attention than that meeting. As the thousands who had gathered there stood upon the lofty pedestal, built up by fifty years of conquest and toil, and looked in review over the achievements of the most indomitable race of people that ever lived on the Western Hemisphere, it seems as if the very heavens smiled upon us, and bade us God-speed.

The journey over which this race has come, has been as a thorny maze, but we have kept up a steady march, at times as if wading through seas of blood, and at other times it would seem that the stars in their courses were fighting against us, but God always has some one ready to speak an encouraging word to those who trust in Him, and say, "Go forward."

Some of the people of the race trusted in political parties to bring deliverance, and some changed from one party to another, but the great masses of people have trusted in God, and while political parties have come and gone, and while others have tried hard to convince the masses that their ascendancy is for the good of the Nation, this invincible race has moved steadily forward and is fairly well prepared to face courageously the second half century of its freedom.

It is quite apparent that the duties and responsibilities of the Negro have increased as the years have advanced, and today find the Negro people face to face with graver problems than have at any time in the past had the attention of the many great leaders of the race.

The race has not gone backward one whit, but has been steadily progressing for fifty years, and too, against the greatest odds that ever confronted any race. These beautiful lines may be applied to these people with double emphasis:

"We are beaten back in many a fray,
But newer strength we borrow;
For where the Vanguard rests today,
The rear will camp tomorrow."

My brethren, can we not truthfully say, "hitherto the Lord has led us," and we believe He will continue to lead us, until we shall have been fully established, *emperium in emperio*.

No Representation in Congress

Notwithstanding the great faith we have in God, and the knowledge we have of His leadership, we must confess that the Negro people have not fully come into their own, and will not until our nation has become fully awakened to the fact that its peaceable perpetuity depends very largely upon the complete enforcement of the Federal Constitution with all of its amendments. Until every black man in any part of the South is as free as any man in Massachusetts.

The patience of endurance of the black man is without a parallel, and this patience under heavy burdens is one of his most valuable assets. But you may rest assured that the present and coming generations of Negroes, whose well-trained minds and keen foresight, which have been taught and developed to expect equal and exact justice under the law, will not be as patient and long forbearing as were their fathers. Hence, it is incumbent upon the leaders of today to rise from their knees where they have been for so many years asking for the amelioration of conditions and carry the petitions before the powers that be, believing as they go that their long-sought prayer will be answered. Ask for a fair and impartial enforcement of the laws as they now stand upon the statute books, though in some sections they are discriminating laws, the race will prosper if the laws are justly and honestly enforced. Just laws and popular governments derive their authority from the consent of the governed, and yet the consent of the black man has not in any degree been sought in many proscriptive laws which disgrace many of the statute books of our country. That these will all be repealed when the effulgent rays of the twentieth century civilization shall fully fall upon them, we verily believe.

As a race we most earnestly protest against being misrepresented in the Congress of our nation, and we would ask for the enforcement of the franchise laws as set forth in the Constitution, for we believe that a people is only half free, when deprived of the ballot.

Woman's Suffrage

The great suffragette movement which is sweeping over the world has its foundation in the fact that, "taxation without representation in unjust," and no class or race is better prepared by experience to enter into hearty sympathy with such a movement than this people.

The dominant race in this American country will not be insensitive to the petition of ten-millions of patriotic citizens who are pleading for fair play, and it matters not what political party may be in power, since our cause is just, we should get a hearing.

My friends, I am in no sense an alarmist, I have faith in God, and the American people, and am glad to tell you that a brighter day awaits the American Negro. As an indication of this, I need only to point you to the organization and work of the great Sociological Congress which is composed of Southern white and black people, and which has openly declared in favor of the equal rights of all men before the law.

A National Problem

Here at the North, where the people of our race constitute only a small percent of the population, your problems are not the same as those which we have who live in the South. As a matter of course you have your problems and they come to you in a way to make the general cause of the race the same. Hence we are in sympathy with you and believe you are in sympathy with us. I am not one of those who are endeavoring to make the world believe that the race problem is one peculiarly the South's and that Northern people should not interest themselves in the conditions. The race question is a national one, and if not checked, will become a world problem.

Race antipathy can no more be confined to a particular section of our country than the exclusion of the Japanese children from the public schools of California could be made a state issue. The Capital of our nation is a hod-bed of race antipathy, and from that great center it spreads in all directions, and will continue until in the providence of God, Negro men shall be permitted to re-enter the Congress and speak for themselves. Why should ten-millions of people be denied representation in the highest law-making body in the nation? Why should matters be so gerrymandered as to close West Point and Annapolis to the educated, aspiring patriotic young Negro men who are anxious to be trained in military science for the good of their country? Is it reasonable to expect the young Negro manhood of the country to be filled with patriotic valor in the face of such discriminations?

As Christian leaders, we are for peace, and we pray for the time to come when the nations shall study war no more, and yet as true Americans, in the face of all discriminations we stand ready to defend the flag of our country against any foreign foe.

Weakness of the Pulpit

In all the years of the past, the ministers of the Gospel have been potent factors in moulding sentiment for right against wrong, but one who has been observant of the trend of things in our country, will be forced to ask, "Has the American pulpit done its full duty toward settling the many perplexing problems which affect the life of our nation?" It is fully admitted that there are many good and great men filling the pulpits in our country, men who have the courage of their conviction and who have not failed to declare the whole council of God. But it must be admitted also that there is a much larger number whose high calling seems too limited or circumscribed by racial or caste conditions. This latter class whose stereotyped notions of race superiority need to have a vision like Peter had, so that the kingdom of grace may be lifted above the worldly notions of men.

It is a serious reflection upon the Christ of God and upon the cause of Christianity, for the chosen exponents of the gospel of peace and goodwill to seal their lips and keep silent upon the many evils which threaten the peace and happiness of the nation.

There is no reason why the minister of the gospel should fear to declare the whole council of God, for His arm has not been shortened, nor has He repealed the oracle which says, "Go ye therefore and teach all nations, baptizing them in the name of the Father, and of the Son, and of the Holy Ghost, teaching them to observe all things whatsoever I have commanded you; and lo, I am with you alway, even unto the end of the world." With such an assurance from the Prince of Glory, the shining lance of Gospel truth should be thrust into the vitals of every evil which infests our land.

The darkest hour in the life of Christ was but three days before His triumphant victory over death and Hell, and His faithful followers in this world should not falter because of the lowering clouds, but should press with vigor on, under the inspiration of that beautiful song which says,

"Ye fearful saints fresh courage take,
The clouds ye so much dread
Are big with mercy; and shall break,
With blessings on your head."

National Cooperation

The relation between the Southern Baptist Convention and the National Baptist Convention is both pleasant and agreeable. In the matter of cooperation the cords have been lengthened, and the great heart of the Southern white Baptists have taken up the task of assisting us to establish and maintain a great Theological Seminary. Already they have proposed to give $50,000 towards this much needed institution, and are agreeably working with us through a committee of nine of the wisest and best men to that end.

In view of the limitations which govern in our cooperation with the Southern Baptist Convention in Home Mission work, and in view of the fact that a large number of the constituents of the National Baptist Convention come from the North and West and beyond the bounds of the Southern Baptist Convention, it seems to me that cooperation with the Northern Baptist Convention should be sought so as to place the Home Mission Board of the National Baptist Convention in the same relation to our brethren in the North and West that it sustains to those in the South. As a race and denomination we yet need both the moral and financial help of our stronger brethren North and South.

Recent Agitation

The National Baptist Convention has been under fire nearly all the year. The criticisms have been keen, the administration has been attacked and very largely the arrows of criticism have been directed personally at the President of the Convention. But the President was unwilling to disturb our great Baptist family by replying to unwarranted and unfounded thrusts from designing, misguided or uninformed persons, hence, he bore in silence all that was aimed at him for the good of the denomination.

The President would much rather suffer wrong than to do wrong, and even though he should be deposed and otherwise humiliated, he is exceedingly anxious that the Convention shall remain intact, and grow in usefulness each year of its life. There are no personal ambitions on the part of the President to be satisfied, and he has long ago felt that the Convention should release him from any official relation whatever to the great work which he has endeavored to lead for the past twenty years.

It is not my purpose to impugn the motives of any man, but you may rest assured that I shall ever stand for free speech and the equality of all members in this great Convention. It has been my steadfast purpose to accord to every member of this Convention the very same consideration and I shall not swerve one hair's-breadth from that purpose.

To those who would seek to tear down the work of a lifetime, and lay my emaciated form at the feet of my traducers, I would say in the words of Shakespeare:

> "Good name in man and woman, dear my lord,
> Is the immediate jewel of their souls:
> Who steals my purse steals trash; tis something—nothing:
> 'Twas mine, 'tis his, and has been slave to thousands
> But he that filches from me my good name
> Robs me of that which not enriches him,
> And makes me poor indeed."

I beg to repeat on this occasion what I said to you one year ago, that I have no desire whatever to be retained at the head of your great organization, and shall rejoice if it is your will to place the mantle of leadership on abler shoulders.

As I close this part of my annual address I beg to say that at no time during the twenty years that I have had the honor to serve you in this capacity, have I had any higher motive than to magnify through this Convention the name of our Lord and Master, and to serve my race and denomination. And now as I come up to the close of this year's work, I have the happy satisfaction in my breast, that I have done everything in my power to please Him who called me into service, and look forward with joyful anticipation when I shall hear falling from the lips of Him who knows the secrets of all hearts, saying, "Well done, thou good and faithful servant."

Specific Work of the Convention

The attention of the denomination is called to the specific work as carried on by the several Boards of the Convention, and the importance of a closer alliance between the Boards and the Convention.

There is no reason whatever for any friction between the Convention and its Boards, for they were created for the sole purpose of doing work for and in the name of the National Baptist Convention.

One year ago, I recommended the appointment of a committee to take under consideration all matters coming up from any of the Boards about which there were differences of opinion. It was clear to my mind that the affairs of the Boards could not be properly considered in a great deliberative body like this, without doing injury to the work.

The proposition seemed to meet with favor, so much so, that the recommendation was amended to include all of the elective officers of the Convention and the Chairman and Secretary of each of the Boards. So far as I have been advised the several Boards with the exception of the Home Mission and Publication Boards are, working in perfect harmony with the Convention's recommendations and the Committee.

There was no other purpose in the mind of the president than to serve through this committee the best interest of the several Boards and the denomination. It is needless that I call attention to the protest so widely circulated against the action of the Committee. As to whether the Committee exceeded the authority given it, may be determined when its report has been submitted.

It is unreasonable to suppose that there will be any war in the National Baptist Convention, unless we assume at the same time that those in charge of the affairs of the Convention are there for selfish or personal gain, such a thought is inconceivable among Christian gentlemen.

No matter what may be said to the contrary, the President of this National Baptist Convention would not, knowingly, do a personal injury to any man.

For nineteen years the work of the National Baptist Convention has been very largely conducted through Boards chosen by the Convention; whatever has been accomplished in these years stands to the credit of these Boards for the service rendered the denomination, beyond that, the Boards have no more claim on the assets of the Convention than the humblest member of it.

Foreign Missions

The oldest of the Boards of the National Baptist Convention is the Foreign Mission Board. This Board has before it the greatest problem of any of the Boards of the Convention. Unlike the others it has stretched out before it in continental lines a heathen world, and coming down upon it is the command of Jesus to preach the Gospel to every creature: and having assumed the responsibility to answer the call of the teeming millions who are pleading for light, it necessarily must have the support of the Christian family on the home field. That much good has been accomplished through our Foreign Mission Board will not be questioned by any who are familiar with the conquest carried on all of these years.

Our people should consider that missionary work does more than lead men to Christ, while soul-saving is the principal object, yet the influence which goes out from a Christian life, is inestimable.

One can see at a glance what effect Christian missions have had upon Japan, and what they are doing for China. The mere touch of Christianity with the people of these two great countries has lifted them up from obscurity and given them a standing among the great nations of the earth.

What Christian missions have done for the yellow races, it will do for the African and other dark people in other parts of the world. If for no other reason, the American Negro should support our Foreign Mission Board out of race pride. The leaders in every district association, district and state convention should see to it, that the cause of missions is given some consideration at every annual meeting.

Educational Board

The next oldest Board in point of service, is the Educational Board, which took the place of the Educational Convention. This Board has a broad field before it, and has for several years been conducting a campaign throughout the country with a view to the establishment of a great Theological Seminary. You will recall that the plans of this Board were somewhat frustrated by a misunderstanding between it and the American Baptist Home Mission Society, but the Educational Board has been kept intact, and is now prepared to report an alliance with the Southern Baptist Convention, whereby the latter organization is to put $50,000 into the building when a site has been procured. At the time this is written, it is understood that the Seminary will be located at Memphis, Tennessee. This school when started will fill a long-felt want among the people of our race, and should have the unstinted support of the denomination.

Home Missions

The cultivation of the Home Field is essential in a Convention like ours. The Home Field should form the base of our Foreign work.

As men are brought to Christ on the Home Field, and become thoroughly imbued with the principles of Christianity, they should at once help to send the gospel to others who have it not. The Home Mission work is carried on by the cooperation of the Southern Baptist Convention and the National Baptist Convention through their respective Boards. It has been said our Home board is helpless in the matter of doing the work on the Home Field, and is dependent upon the Publishing Board for means to operate the work, if this be true, a remedy should be found to cure this defect.

National Baptist Publishing Board

The National Baptist Publishing Board was born out of the agitation which arose in the Convention which met at Dallas, Texas, in 1891, over the refusal of the American Baptist Publication Society to print in the *Teacher*, articles written by Negroes, but did not take formidable shape until the following year at Savannah, Georgia, when a committee composed of one person from each state was appointed to submit plans for the publication of Sunday School literature at the next meeting. The work of this Board met with popular favor from the beginning but did not assume business proportions until after the meeting held at St. Louis in 1896. Since that time its growth has been phenomenal, and now bears the distinction of being the largest publishing plant operated by Negroes in the world.

B.Y.P.U. Board

Among the Boards of the Convention, none are more deserving of special notice than the B.Y.P.U. Board. The work entrusted to this Board has long ago passed the experimental stage, and is now one of the permanent features of our great Convention.

It is clear to every thoughtful man, that if the churches of tomorrow are to be what they should be, the young people of today should be thoroughly instructed in Baptist History and Doctrine. To accomplish this much desired end, it is necessary for the local churches to keep in close touch with the National Board, as general information touching the B.Y.P.U. work must emanate from that source. There is a steady growth of sentiment in favor of the B.Y.P.U. work throughout the whole country.

N.B.B. Board

In calling attention to the work of the National Baptist Benefit Board, I wish to magnify the purpose for which this Board was created, and say that it seems to me more attention is given to life policies than to the raising of a fund for the relief of the aged and worn out ministers of the gospel. I do not raise an objection to the insurance feature carried by this Board but the primary object was, to provide a fund with which to relieve the wants of ministers when they have grown old in the service and become unable to perform ministerial duties. The entire denomination should give its unqualified support to this feature of our work, and every church should cheerfully make a contribution once each year to help the old deserving ministers who have worn out their lives for the cause of Christ and the Baptists.

Union Review

The denomination should have an official organ, one which is absolutely independent of the denomination or any man or men, one which can never be made the vehicle of the personal abuse, but which will at all times stand up for the faith once delivered to the saints, and at the same time keep before the world the claims of the Convention, as represented by its several Boards.

The *Union Review* has been fair and clean in its editorials under the present management, and yet some of the contributions which have from time to time found their way into its columns have been misleading in the extreme, and have caused the outside world to believe that the Baptist family was torn asunder. And too, over two *little fellows* who will in the natural course of events soon have to report to the Judge of all the earth.

The cause of the Baptist is far greater and of much more importance than that of any man or set of men, and the organ of the National Baptist Convention should be left free to magnify these fundamental principles.

In Memoriam

Many of our good and great men have answered to the muster roll since we last met. Their familiar faces will not be seen any more on this side of the river, but will be in the great union on the delightful plains of glory.

Among that number will be one who was officially connected with this Convention, I refer to Professor J. M. Codwell of Houston, Texas, who was one of the efficient secretaries of this Convention. The news of his death reached me on the 4th of August. On the 17th day of June he was present and took active part in the Board meeting which prepared the program for this session of the Convention.

Professor Codwell was one of the most prominent laymen in the denomination, and was active in both State and National work among the Baptists. May his spirit with others of our brethren who have gone before rest on.

I close this my twentieth annual address with an earnest appeal for peace and harmony among my brethren, and beg to say, that I had rather live in the loving memory of those whom I have tried to serve, than to live in a gorgeous mansion with a king.

I most heartily bid you God speed.

Annual Address of Dr. E. C. Morris
President of the National Baptist Convention of America
In Session at Savannah, Georgia, September, 1916

Officers and Members of the National Baptist Convention, Ladies and Gentlemen:

We are happy for the privilege of once more meeting you face to face on this side of the mystic river.

It has been twenty-four years since we had the privilege of holding a meeting of this great Convention in this historic city, which has been made historic by her contribution to religious thought and activities. It was from here that the Wesleys directed the movements of their great organization which has become world-wide. It was from this city and state that the principles of the Baptist first took a firm hold upon the people of our race, and though they were slaves, were allowed to worship God under their own vine and fig tree, and the first African Church is a living monument to that early beginning. Savannah was home of George Lisle, who by frugality and economy saved enough money to buy his liberty from bondage, and after becoming free, became the first foreign missionary to the people beyond the sea. It was here that, that stalwart leader and gospel preacher, who was foremost in the organization of the National Baptist Convention, the Rev. E. K. Love lived and died, and without recounting the valuable historical data of this great city, I would say as Peter said when he emerged from beneath the halo of a heavenly vision, "It is good to be here."

I am sure you will not consider me so vain when I tell you that having passed the sixty-first milestone of a busy life, and having been maligned and abused almost incessantly for the last past twelve months, that I am still happy and as full of hope as I was when the effort to tear the banner from the staff of this grand organization failed one year ago at Chicago, and you, my brethren are to be congratulated upon the brave and successful conquests you have waged against error, and the practical overthrow of oligarchy in Baptist Institutions.

In no year of my life have I been so flooded with letters of sympathy, telling me of prayers which had been made for me, than in the present one. You know that I appreciate them, but if you have not yet learned that God is my refuge, I would modestly say in these words of my Master, "What went ye out in the wilderness to see, a reed shaken with the wind?" The man who would be the least bit vacillating, or undecided at a time like this in your work, is unfit to be trusted by you, and I will add, weep not for me, but weep for yourselves and your children, for when all of us shall have passed to our final reward, the principles for which we now stand, and at which an unholy thrust has been made, will survive the coming ages.

It is marvelous how you have been able to stand against the terrific storms which have raged for twelve months with a velocity which has surpassed anything within my recollection: a storm which has for years been gathering with but one purpose, that, to overthrow the will of the people and bring them at the feet of selfish interests. That you have been deceived will not admit of any questions, for I myself have for more than ten years believed that there was danger of too much radicalism being exhibited towards those whom we sought to regulate; and not until we met at Chicago one year ago was I thoroughly convinced that the utter overthrow and destruction of the National Baptist Convention had been planned.

It has been wise in you to exercise patience with those who banded themselves together to wrest from your hands the trust imposed upon you by the people. Any other course would have delayed for many years clear understanding of the issue involved, but all can now see the motive which prompted the disruption of the Convention. The fallacious statement that the trouble in our ranks was over men has been completely exploded, and all who are unbiased know that the one living issue is "Shall the people rule?" I have never thought that the destiny of our great denomination depended upon any man or set of men, and have considered it a very serious reflection upon the intelligence of the hundreds of great men and leaders which we have; to even intimate that the Baptists were divided over two or more men, and I beg you now to never give any credence to the statement that there is a Morris faction in the National Baptist Convention, for I tell you most emphatically that Morris is with and for the Convention, and I will ever be, whether in or out of office and that he has no greater interest in it than you have.

We are delighted to be able to say that the thoughtful leaders everywhere are with the organization. My official relation with the denomination, which covers a period of twenty-two years enables me to say, that I do not know a single man who may be rightly considered a worthy leader, who has shown a spirit of rebellion against the National Baptist Convention; nor were all of those who at an unguarded moment allied themselves with an insurgent element evil disposed, but they were honestly mistaken as to what the real issue was, but now that they have seen it, are hearty supporters of the people's cause.

The one deceptive slogan used to lead away some from the organization was the taking out of a charter by seven men, and let me say just here that these men acted upon the authority given them by the Commission appointed by the Convention, and will at the proper time submit their report, either to be affirmed or dissolved by the Convention. But think how deceptive was the scheme of nine men, who were themselves a corporation, endeavoring to make the whole world believe that seven men were trying to do what they themselves had been doing for several years, and we may say that their scheme worked like a charm until exposed, and when they realized that they were going to be apprehended, in order to deceive their followers, they told them "you will be the National Baptist Convention unincorporated,": and will be the owners of the Publishing plant. This statement had its effect, and would not have been so soon uprooted had not the Board elected by this Convention entered suit for possession of your property. Having entered suit, the following excerpt from the answer filed by the nine incorporators is significant. *Viz.*: "These Respondents say that it is not true that they claim to be or that they hold themselves out to be the Executive or governing Board, or Committee of the Publishing Board of the National Baptist Convention of the United States, if the allegation of this bill is intended to mean that these respondents claim to be a Board created by or governed by the National Baptist Convention of the United States, or that they claim to be a Committee that derives its authority from any constitution, resolution or action of such Convention, other than that may be hereinafter specifically set forth."

In another paragraph of their answer it is said, "Such offices or positions as these Respondents hold in connection with this corporation were created by this charter and under its provisions and these respondents deny that they were ever elected to office, or that they have derived any authority as officers, directors, or trustees by virtue of any action, or any Convention of the Baptists of this country at any time whatsoever."

The climax of the perfidy was not reached, however, until the deception had turned upon those who had followed the nine incorporators and the man whom they elected as their President submitted what they called "Exhibit C" with a view doubtless to further shield them against the just wrath of an outraged public. The following is the closing paragraph of that Exhibit:

> "You are aware that the National Baptist Publishing Board of the National Baptist Convention is an incorporated Institution, a legal entity created under the laws of the State of Tennessee, and that the National Baptist Convention has no record known to us where the National Baptist Convention owns any property interest or invested any money in said corporation, therefore you will not be expected to enter litigation for possession of the property, or the removal of any of the incorporators, but you will demand in the name of the National Baptist Convention (unincorporated) of the United States of America, free and full advisory supervision as to the doctrine, diction, and policy of all Baptist publications furnished by them to our churches and Sunday Schools under the resolution passed by this Convention." Signed, Rev. E. P. Jones, President; Rev. T. J. King, Secretary.

It may be clearly seen from this last excerpt that the prime object in trying to get up another Convention was, for the sole purpose of having that Convention turn over to these nine men the property which belonged to the people. I am reliably informed that this latter Exhibit was not approved by the meeting held at the Salem Church in Chicago, but that is a matter for them to work out among themselves.

The Convention ordered that the Board elected at Chicago proceed to Nashville, and demand possession of the property there, which the Convention had been nineteen years in building up, and if peaceable possession was not given, to take whatever steps were necessary to restore to the denomination that which rightly belonged to it, and pending the litigation, that the Board proceed to get out a series of Sunday School periodicals with which to supply those Sunday Schools in harmony with the National Baptist Convention. While the task laid upon the new Boards was very great, yet it was wise to give such an order, for the reason, had you continued your patronage to a Board which openly defied the authority of the Convention you would have been furnishing that rebellious Board with both arms and ammunition with which to fight the entire denomination in the interest of what had turned out to be a private corporation of nine men. For eighteen full years the Convention has through the several state delegations been electing a Publishing Board, composed of one member from each state, and all believed that the persons thus elected constituted the Publishing Board of the National Baptist Convention, and perhaps this deception would have gone on for an indefinite period had not matters taken the turn they did at the Chicago meeting. The Convention should see to it that no opportunity be given for a repetition of such a vile course. I would say, however, that there is no doubt in my mind but that the Board elected one year ago will be able to give a good account of itself, and that you will find that no mistake was made in its personnel.

It is not out of place for me to pause long enough to say that finding ourselves without a medium through which to speak to the people, their paper having been taken from them, that we owe a debt of gratitude to the Editor of the *National Beacon Light* and the Editor of the *Christian Banner* who voluntarily made their papers the organ of the Convention and fought its cause as bravely and wisely as if they were defending their personal interests, and while we are thankful to all the Baptist papers which stood so firmly by the convention, special mention should be made of the *Beacon Light* and its able editor, who set aside all personal interest and took up the people's cause.

Entirely too much is expected of the President of your Convention. If he should attempt to answer all the calls of the several Boards and of the State and District meetings and then answer the thousands of letters which come to his office, every moment of his time would be taken and the time of two assistants; but hitherto he has borne these burdens uncomplainingly, and now ask that they be distributed among the hundreds of intelligent leaders in several states, who are sufficiently informed to protect the interest of the denomination in every state of the Union.

The President has been criticized for not answering many of the things said concerning the Convention, and himself personally, but it has been one unchangeable rule of the President to not attempt to chase falsehoods, but leave them to return and haunt their authors. But I would have you to know that I have felt no humiliation whatever because of the unwarranted attacks made upon the administration or upon me personally. You will doubtless agree with me that no man can lose his character until he consents for it to be thrown down. There is no act of the administration which needs defense, for every act has been in accord with orders handed down from the Convention, and yet the rank and file of Baptists have not always known this and having heard and read that things were going wrong, many decided that they would be "neutral" upon the issue before the Convention. But my friends there is no neutral ground between right and wrong, and the deceptive slogan held up to blind the people; and not let them see the one great issue having been exposed and removed, all will now declare themselves either with the National Baptist Convention or with those who sought to divert the people's property to their personal use. With the line thus drawn, there will be no further occasion for war, for if after the people have been shown the scheme of designing men to overthrow their organization, and some of them still persist in following men, no effort should be made to prevent them.

The false representation continues to be made that the Convention pays its President a salary of one-thousand five-hundred dollars a year. The truth is the Convention has never paid its President a salary of any amount since its organization, but the Convention has undertaken to pay the expense account of the President's office, and that of all other officers, where those expenses were incurred in doing the work of the Convention; and I may say that the undertaking has never been fully carried out, but the officers have gone on uncomplainingly discharging the duties imposed upon them by the Convention. It will be interesting to know that the distinguished gentleman who is editor of the paper through which all of these false representations have been made has advocated through that very paper, that the Convention should pay its President a salary of five-thousand dollars a year, but up to now no officer of the Convention has ever intimated that he would like to go into such a trap.

It has been recently said in the papers that the Convention owed its President ten-thousand dollars. Of course, this statement was made to create a prejudice in the minds of the people against the management, and to give further credence to the false statement that the Convention pays its President's salary. That you may be rightly informed, I would say that should the Convention undertake to pick up all that it has attempted to pay on the expense account of the President's office, up to and including the Chicago meeting, it would not exceed four-thousand dollars and no urgent demand has been made for that, even though two-thousand eight-hundred dollars of that amount was spent by him in the promotion of the celebration of the Fiftieth Anniversary of freedom which was celebrated by the Convention in 1913 at Nashville, Tennessee.

The Peace Movement

Our Blessed Master has said "Blessed are the peacemakers for they shall be called the children of God." I most cheerfully and unreservedly apply this to all who have sought to bring about peace with those who have brought war in the ranks of the Baptists, and hope that they may succeed in bringing back to the fold all who have been led away, and I have no word of condemnation for any who may have made such an effort; but I am sure that they have found out how futile such an effort would be when applied to those whose only motive was to lead away such a number of persons from the regular organization, as to make it appear that they had not appropriated the people's property to their personal use.

So far as I have been able to discern there is no division in the National Baptist Convention, and that which has been made to appear as a division is only the unrighteous scheme of those who have sought in many ways to deceive the people. At the Chicago meeting all kinds of devices were resorted to, to overthrow the Convention, but by patient waiting and stubborn resistance to those evil designs, the Convention was permitted to peaceably organize after an enrollment had been made and reported. Finding that the Convention had organized and was moving along in the usual peaceable way, those persons who were bent on the destruction of the organization went into the courts of Cook County, Illinois, and swore out an injunction against the President and seven other officers of the Convention with the hope of getting full possession of it. But the injunction was dissolved and reversed and stands against the "Rump Convention" today. The meeting at Chicago may be called a repetition of the war in Heaven, and I am sure you all know the result of that rebellion.

It has not been generally known that the men at the head of that rebellion, finding themselves hopelessly in the minority so far as the messengers of the Convention were concerned, sent a committee to the Secretary of the Convention and offered him one-thousand dollars for five-hundred badges. Had the Secretary yielded to such a wicked scheme, there is no telling what the result would have been, because the majority of those who would have worn those badges would have been irresponsible persons who were not sent to the Convention by Baptist churches. But we pass from this to that which represents the constructive forces of our denomination.

Making note of the slack way in which the Convention permitted the old Publishing Board to operate the National Baptist Sunday School Congress, and the fact that it, like other features of that Board was being run for personal gain, the Executive Board of the National Baptist Convention at a meeting held at Nashville last February, authorized the Sunday School Board of the National Baptist

Convention and the B.Y.P.U. Board of the National Baptist Convention to proceed at once to organize a Congress of our Baptist young people, which would serve the needs, and the interests of the denomination. The secretaries of these Boards went to work immediately, and after getting the consent of the Baptists of Memphis, Tennessee, to hold the meeting in that city, began to lay before the Baptists of the country the importance of such a meeting and the desirability of all Baptist churches which believed in the rule of the people of our institutions to send representatives to the Congress. To say that the meeting was a success is expressing it in the mildest term. A conservative estimate of the number of progressive young Baptists who answered this call can safely be put at two-thousand. An organization was perfected by the adoption of a Constitution and the election of officers, who are to bear the same relation to the National Baptist Convention as that borne by other auxiliary bodies. The young men chosen to lead these forces are among the ablest and best young men in the race, and deserve and should have the encouragement of the older leaders in every state of the Union. It was also ordered by the general Executive Board of the National Baptist Convention that the Sunday School Board proceed at once to get out a paper as a medium to get the truth before the people and counteract the many false statements being circulated by the *Union Review*. The gentlemen elected by the Convention as the Editor of the Convention's organ was given the editorial management of the newspaper, the *National Baptist Voice*. It is needless that I say one word about the tremendous amount of good accomplished by the *Voice*; but knowing as I do the advantage of such a publication, I most earnestly urge that a substantial plan be adopted for its future. The organ of the Convention should by all means be put in twenty-thousands homes as a matter of education of the plans and purposes of the Convention in its leadership of Baptist affairs throughout the world.

The Southern Baptist Convention

Perhaps the strongest and most influential Christian organization in the South is the Southern Baptist Convention. Sixteen years ago, this great organization, through its Home Mission Board, entered into cooperation with this Convention in missionary work on the Southern field. The cooperation entered into has gradually increased from the time it was formed to the present; but sad to say several years ago, it developed that our part of the agreement was not being faithfully carried out, and that instead of our missionaries doing real missionary work and being directed by our Home Mission Board, they were required to act as the agents of another Board which was not engaged in missionary work. As soon as it became known that this and other infractions of Christian comity were being violated, the President called attention to the matter, and urged that the Home Mission Board and Publishing Board be separated and placed under separate management.

The suggestion for the separation of the Boards was made as far back as 1904 at Austin, Texas, but met with stern opposition, which opposition increased each year—the opponents claiming that the Home Mission Board could not live unless it was under the fostering care of the National Baptist Publishing Board. Two years ago at the meeting held in Philadelphia, a separate management was chosen and the headquarters of the Home Mission Board assumed its original place at Little Rock, Arkansas.

As soon as the new Board was installed and the Home Board of the Southern Baptist Convention had been notified, every agency which the old Publishing Board could employ was set to work with the avowed intention of breaking the fraternal relation between the Southern Baptist Convention and the National Baptist Convention; and had the effort been successful, the result would have been very serious to our denomination and the race in general. To have the leading white men of the South who are allied with the Baptist denomination, in cooperation with the Negro Baptists of the United States in missionary work, and their many churches contributing to the support of our missionaries, awakens an interest among the many thousands of white Christians in the South in the future well-being of the Negroes which could not be reached as well in any other way. I am glad to tell you that all efforts to destroy the brotherly alliance between these two great organizations have failed.

The Law Suit

Much has been said about the law suit entered for possession of the property which has been built up in Nashville with the money given by the thousands of Baptist churches and Sunday Schools of this country, and the officers of the Convention have been severely criticized for not pushing the matter to an early conclusion; but I beg to say that there has not been a meeting of the Convention since the Publishing plant was snatched from the hands of the people one year ago at Chicago, and the Executive Board having no means at its command could not do more than it has done, and is bringing the matter to you who constitute a higher court and that Board stands ready to execute whatever orders may be given.

But may I be permitted to suggest that the matter of forcing the National Baptist Publishing Board to turn over your property to you be carefully and dispassionately considered before any further action be taken. I am reliably informed that the plant is heavily in debt, and mortgaged to the limit, and that as soon as a decision is rendered, which in my opinion could not be otherwise than in your favor, that the principal creditors will at once apply for a Receiver, so as to not alone get the present income of that house, but the money which the loyal Baptist churches and Sunday Schools are sending to the Board created by you for their Sunday School literature. So far most of the burden of paying Attorney's fees has been borne by the Sunday School Publishing Board, which in its present condition is hardly able to bear this responsibility alone, and if the suit is to be continued, the amounts given by that Board should be supplemented by the Convention.

One National Baptist Convention

For several years prior to 1895, we had three National Conventions of the Negro Baptist, but the wisdom of those who were prominent leaders at that day suggested the blending of these three Conventions into one; and that henceforth, every phase of the work among Baptists should be represented by Boards and for twenty years this arrangement was carried out, and I believe will continue, and that those who went off after a tangent, finding that the circle has not been cut, will return and help to make the organization a greater force in the world than it has hitherto been.

There are many reasons why there should be one National Baptist Convention, but I shall mention a few:

1. Because it places the Negro Baptists in a position to be an example to all other Baptists in that they are in no way affected by sectional lines in their organizations. They came on the scene when the Mason and Dixon line had been practically wiped out by the Civil War, and therefore, there was no reason for a Northern Baptist and Southern Baptist Convention among them.

2. Because one great organization with a following of three million people will give them standing with other great National and International Societies which could not be attained if there were more than one.

3. Because it affords an opportunity to prove to the world that the black race is capable of self-government under democratic form.

4. Because the black people of the world are to be touched, and lifted up by the American Negro and it cannot be effectively done through a multiplicity of organizations. It has been marvelous how the leaders of thought among the people of our race have endorsed the idea of one great National Convention of Baptists. Such strong organizations as the New England Convention, the Lott Carey Convention, and the General Convention of Western States and Territories have approved the plan and are loyal supporters of it. I am sure you have been impressed with the magnitude of such an organization, and the mighty task of holding such an army as we have in one great Convention, an army far greater than that which Moses led out of Israel to the border of the promised land, and whose accomplishments far exceed that of the Israelites for the first three-hundred years of their freedom.

One National Convention
Of Baptists for this land;
Oppose every contention
To break this Christian band.

Danger of a New Era

Just at this time when the thoughtful men of the denomination are getting themselves together for effective work in the future, and when the good Lord is carrying us through His winnowing fan, there is danger of us allowing division to creep into our ranks. Already there has been some talk of changing this and that man to make room for another, but my friends, a New Era has at last dawned upon the Negro Baptists of this country and the opportunities which now loom up before us are such as to cause us to set aside all selfish ambition; and all unite for the common good. Do you not see the prophetic words of John Wesley about to be fulfilled? In that God is breaking down the barriers and the world is soon to become the parish of the Negro Baptists? In less time than our race has been free, our Boards will be serving the many millions of black people beyond the seas. "Are you ready? Are you ready? Are ready for the day to come?"

If I am competent to advise, I would suggest that whatever ambition we may have, that we put it in the background, and let the cool judgment of the messengers here assembled decide every question which may come before this great body. The charge that we have been disorderly, and that good men are not permitted to be heard on the floor of the Convention has arisen out of the fact that you have been enthusiastic and jubilant over all the success which has come to the denomination. May I ask that you take the advice of Paul and agree that "If eating meat cause my brother to offend, I will eat no more meat," and especially do I urge, as I have done in former years, that you quietly elect your officers in the way prescribed in a resolution adopted two years ago.

The European War, What Does It Mean?

While our nation thus far has been spared the awful carnage and bloodshed which is cutting down the nations of Europe, yet we cannot separate ourselves from them. They are human beings, and all came from one common stock. I am sure that you, like myself, have tried to pray that the end would soon come and that no more wailing of widows and crying of hungry orphans could be heard in the streets of the old world. But the heavens seem to be brass above our heads, and our prayers fall back on us. What can all this mean? Is it that the Man of Galilee is now upon His white horse and is now lifting up the valleys and pulling down the high places and making smooth the path so that His Gospel may run and have free course?

Think ye not my brethren that this titanic war is a white man's fight, for thousands of black men are now pouring out their blood on the gory battlefield daily.

A movement has already been started among the Christian forces in this country to carry the REAL Gospel of Jesus Christ to these people, and while we cannot do much in a financial way, we can do something; and the least we do for Jesus will be precious in His sight.

Our Condition In This Country

Our situation in this country is not what it should be; nor is it what it will be in the future, for I assure you that true white Americans are getting their eyes open and are rapidly considering the importance of treating their black brethren with fairness and justice. The strong Christian societies, and the great organizations like the Sociological Congress, have already recognized the black man as a brother; and you may rest assured that these mighty forces will ere long control the legislation of the country and will cause the scales of justice to evenly balance between man and man, and why should it not be so?

There are no truer patriots than those found in the Negro race. Their fidelity to a principle, or trust, reaches beyond the days of their freedom and was fully exemplified during the Civil War; for while their masters were at the front fighting to tighten the chains of slavery on their limbs, they lived up to the charge committed to them; and if there was a single instant where they betrayed their masters, it has not yet been reported. That they wanted to be free is not questioned, and yet they put their honor above freedom and waited until the Union armies had come in reach of them before they made any effort to enlist in their own behalf or for a restored Union. But once free, they stood ready to follow the flag even into the jaws of death; but one thing can be said of the Negroes and that is he never put the National ensign above the banner of the cross; for as he follows the flag of his country, he sings aloud:

> "In the cross of Christ I glory,
> Towering over the wrecks of time."

In a way the people of our race have been marked by a large element in the dominant race. Every Negro is held under suspicion by that element, and when any crime has been committed by the lowest and most debased Negro, the whole race is by that element charged with that crime. This ought not to be and is itself a crime against the upright members of the race; but the redeeming feature is that such a sentiment does not represent the best white people, and they know that the best black people have as much respect for the law as any white man can have.

Now my brethren as I come to the close of this address, I can say without any hesitation whatever that I have for twenty-two years endeavored to serve you faithfully as the President of your Convention, with no hope of reward except such as finally comes to the faithful in Jesus Christ. And in all these years, I have nothing but praise for my brethren everywhere. You have followed me from Boston, Mass., to the capital of Texas and no distance has been too great for you to go and answer when the roll was called. If there were those who sought to destroy my good name, I freely forgive them and pray that the good Lord may have mercy on their souls; but I fully realize that I am now living on the shady side of life, in the evening of my days—they are beautiful days to me, and no regret will be felt when the sun sets, and I am called to join my faithful comrades on the other side of Jordan.

It would be inexcusable if I should close this address without pausing for a moment to pay a deserving tribute to those of our brethren who have departed this life since we last met in an annual meeting. The prominence of each and all of them was such as to be deserving of special mention, for they were loyal supporters of the kingdom and faithful followers of the King. But it will be readily conceded that among the faithful members of the National Baptist Convention, none were more conspicuous than was Dr. Booker T. Washington, who periodically came to us with a great message of love and goodwill for all the people. In his death, this Convention sustained an irreparable loss and the country has been deprived of one of her foremost citizens.

But we can truly say of him that his life and works are still with us and will be passed from one generation to another as an example of what can be accomplished by one, even though born in poverty, if that life is dedicated to the uplift of his race. The greatest desire of Dr. Washington in the closing days of his life was that the National Baptist Convention might remain united. Perhaps one of the last acts of his life was to write a letter to the man who sought to tear asunder this great organization asking that he go no further until he could see him personally.

The National Baptist Convention will greatly honor itself if the many hundreds of prominent leaders will throw the full weight of their influence in favor of raising the Two-Million Dollars Memorial Fund to perpetuate the work of the greatest man of his times. I am sure that suitable resolutions will be passed by the Convention in honor of all of our brethren who have died during the year.

I know no better words with which to close my address on this occasion than these lines written by A. L. Crawley to the Baptist World.

> I saw a raging storm cloud rise one day
> Which hid the sun and darkened all my way;
> It came at noon and raged an hour or more,
> And then moved onward toward the Western shore;
> And I moved onward until I reached my home,
> And saw from there a change in Heaven's dome;
> For that same cloud which loomed so dark at one,
> Was bathed in glory at the set of sun.
> So shall the clouds of every child of God,
> Which seemed so dark above the way he trod;
> Be seen transfigured from the home above,
> Bathed in the light of God's eternal love.

And now, finally, let me earnestly appeal to you to grant me rest from official responsibilities in connection with your great Convention, and I here and now promise you, that during the remaining years of my life, I stand ready to use whatever influence I may be able to command to increase the efficiency and usefulness of this the greatest organization among Negroes in the world.

Thanking you most sincerely for the many unmerited honors which you have seen fit to confer upon me, and for the unlimited confidence you have reposed in me, I beg to remain

Most affectionately yours,
E. C. Morris

Recommendations

1. I recommend that the Constitution be so amended that hereafter, the membership of the Convention be composed of representatives from churches, associations, and conventions, provided that those who are now life members may retain their membership and that no other life certificates be issued.

2. That the Constitution be amended to provide for a Corresponding Secretary in addition to the Recording Secretary and the four assistants; and that the Corresponding Secretary be required to maintain an office to which he shall devote his entire time.

3. That a Church Extension Board be created, which Board shall raise funds to help needy churches and to build churches where the people are not able to build for themselves.

Edward Perry Jones

Edward Perry Jones (1872 - 1922), the eldest son of Rev. George P. Jones and Lavinia Jones, was born February 21, 1872, Cayuga, Mississippi. He graduated from the city schools of Vicksburg and Natchez College. He attended Alcorn A & M College during the presidency of U. S. Senator Hiram R. Revels. The Doctor of Divinity degree was conferred upon him by Rust University in 1906.

He served as a member of the S. C. of M. at Philadelphia for six years and represented the Odd Fellows of America at the A. M. C. at Burton-on-Trent. He pastored at Mount Heroden for seventeen years and served as chief secretary of the Baptists of Mississippi from 1895 to 1908. He was chairman of the Republican State Convention in 1912, and represented the state in the National Baptist Convention at Chicago in 1912.

He was elected President of the National Baptist Convention at Chicago in 1915 and served seven years (1915-1922).

He pastored Mount Zion Baptist Church at Evanston, Illinois, during which time he erected a building at a cost of $100,000.

He was considered by his contemporaries as one of the most eloquent orators and ablest divines the race has produced.

Annual Address of Dr. E. P. Jones
President of the National Baptist Convention of America
In Session at Kansas City, Missouri, September, 1916

Brother Vice President and Messengers to this the 36th Annual Session of the National Baptist Convention of the U. S. A. and the Isles of the Sea:

Up from the hills and prairies of my native state twelve months ago I went as I have often done before to the great National Baptist Convention which convened on the 8th day of September, 1915, in the great city of Chicago, a city whose marvelous growth staggers the most optimistic. I had the honor there of being appointed by the President presiding to one of the most honored positions in the gift of the Convention. I refer to the Tellership handed me without solicitation of the then-united Convention. You will distinctly recall that I went about the discharge of those duties not unmindful of the great responsibilities that rested upon my shoulders. I did not seek nor covet the distinction. I presumed that in a great Convention composed of brethren gathered from the four corners of the earth that there could be but one intent and purpose and that was to see that even-handed justice was meted out to all, irrespective of their convictions or position upon the great question which hung like a pall and threatened to rend asunder friendly relations that had existed for years and years. As we proceeded to pursue the duties assigned us, it soon dawned, not only upon me, but upon every fair-minded individual present, that steps unfair, unjust and void of every semblance of Christian motive were to be put in execution to stifle and thwart the will of the majority. Volumes have been written in defense of the actions of the minority on that memorable day. Energy, which, if properly directed, would work miracles, has been spent to controvert the truth and make plausible the attitude of the hopeless and forlorn, but all the scholarly attainments of ancient Greece and the modern eloquence of the Ciceroes cannot alter or change the facts which stand out like signposts to guide the traveler that 504 votes were cast to 310 to not sustain the chair. No man in these United States, whether he be black or white, rich or poor, saint or sinner, can defy such an expressed authority and retain the respect and obedience of the Baptist ministry. Ours is a church of liberty and doctrine. Although our triumphs have been many, although we have grown in fifty years and stand out as a marvel in our accomplishments, there is not gathered here today, I hope, a single individual of the ministry, or the laity, who would consent to make a sacrifice of the principles for which our fathers died in the hoary past. May that day never come in the history of this nation's life when the privilege to think and act as God gives and imparts light shall be denied the humblest citizen. Better defy an army of Teutons of a million men bent on conquest than a hundred determined Baptist preachers whose lives are dedicated in maintaining one Lord, one faith and one baptism. To adjourn a convention of Baptists, a majority to the contrary notwithstanding is a flagrant usurpation of power that in the ultimate will make the trembling and quaking of Belshazzar insignificant and inconsequential to the disrepute and condemnation that must follow such a course. This was the very signal of a heated imagination that rent in twain the mighty brotherhood. Lest you might forget the issue, I again urge that you recall that in the face of the fact that the Convention had gone on record more than once in condemning the procuring of a charter; that illegal and unauthorized efforts did on May 17, 1915, in the city of Washington succeed and make of record the incorporating of the National Baptist Convention of the United States of America. I do not need here to tell you that the provisions encouched within that unbearable and disgusting measure scent unto the heavens and enviously seek to control and manipulate and with malice aforethought assassinate that industry for which we have striven these many years. It is acknowledged that the only purpose for which these unnecessary and strange innovations had their origin were selfish and ambitious and they were absolutely void of the warmth of the Christian spirit, but cold and barefaced in the attempt to reap where they have not sown.

Our Publishing Plant at Nashville is the greatest of its kind owned and operated by black men throughout the breadth of the universe. Mississippi, my own native state, gave birth to our own Dr. R. H. Boyd, whose industrial eye and honest business capacity add lustre to this Convention and our great denomination. He has done for us and our children's children that which no Negro of this century has achieved. It was his opportunity; God gave him the light. He went forth in the fact of discouragement and a thousand other besetments; caught a vision as if by inspiration and founded an institution which today employs your sons and daughters and makes possible their advancement. The Publishing Board is composed of brethren well prepared for their duties and they hold in trust for you and for me and every Negro Baptist in this nation this property about which more calamitous fairy tales have been told then could be recorded by a thousand scribes in a thousand years. It appears to me that this Convention is absolutely competent to understand and define its relation to the publishing plant, and that if any defects existed legislation and not destruction would be the remedy. To the maintenance of the National Publishing Board as now constituted and this the National Baptist Convention of the United States of America, I have dedicated the past twelve months of my life, and as I take a retrospection I am none the less willing to continue in my feeble way the defense of these fundamentals which underlie not only the very future of the church, but would turn back the pages of the Negroes' progress for the next quarter of a century. Others may subscribe and give their hand, voice and vote to upset and disgrace that which we have vouchsafed these last twenty years, but until fiery revelations from God's heavens, like stars at midnight, shall picture the irregularity and unreasonableness of my course, I shall go forward believing that whithersoever I go, He who guideth the destiny of men, will lead me on.

I submit that the records at Nashville in Davidson County in the State of Tennessee, and they are open to the inspection of earth's millions, show that there are seven conveyances of property, real and personal, made over in fee simple to this our National Baptist Publishing Board; the first conveyance is the conveyance of machinery, printing paraphernalia, stock, etc., conveyed by R. H. Boyd and wife to the National Baptist Publishing Board of the National Baptist Convention and their successors in office, filed for record at Nashville, Tennessee, Davidson County on the 20th day of May, 1899, at three-o'clock, five minutes past. The second conveyance is a warranty deed from R. H. Boyd to the National Baptist Publishing Board of the National Baptist Convention and their successors in office, filed for record on the 10th day of December, 1901, at nine-o'clock, twelve minutes past. The third conveyance is a warranty deed from H. L. McNish, trustee to the National Baptist Publishing Board of the National Baptist Convention and their successors in office, filed for record on the 12th day of December, 1903, at two-o'clock, fifteen minutes past. The fourth conveyance is a warranty deed from W. H. Leickhardt and wife to the National Baptist Publishing Board of the National Baptist Convention and their successors in office, filed for the record on the 12th day of December, 1903, at two-o'clock, fifteen minutes past. The fourth conveyance is a warranty deed from W. H. Leickhardt and wife to the National Baptist Publishing Board of the National Baptist Convention and their successors in office filed for record on the 6th day of June, 1905, and is recorded in book 314, page 259. The fifth conveyance is a warranty deed from Georgiana Albury to the National Baptist Publishing Board of the National Baptist Convention and their successors in office filed for record on the 18th day of May, 1905, and recorded in book V.V., on page 220. The sixth conveyance is three lots in the Panama Canal Zone. The deeds are conveyed in the Spanish language and set for lots Nos. 16, 17 and 18 in block 6 in the City of Panama and were conveyed June 15, 1909. The seventh conveyance is from States Campbell and Ira Waters to the National Baptist Publishing Board of the National Baptist Convention and their successors in office. None of them are made to R. H. Boyd or to the wife of R. H. Boyd or to any of the heirs of R. H. Boyd. Our committees find that this property is well insured and has a commercial value of $350,000.00. By what other means are we to conduct our business other than through these Boards? They are here to make their reports and it will be a revelation, pleasing and delightful, to hear of their hard-earned success. The incorporators are managing their pretended Publishing House just as we are managing ours, other than that, they have a lawyer as the Corresponding Secretary while we have a veteran Baptist preacher. Which of the professions do you prefer?

Mightier than our presumptive contemplation have been the changes in the world's history since at Chicago we bade each other God's blessings and moved on to again assume the duties assigned us. Singing on! Marching on! Praying on! From mountains and from valleys we come here to review our efforts and accomplishments of the last twelve months, and to offer for your consideration fundamental measures, the enactment of which will dignify the causes we espouse and challenge the admiration of the thoughtful nonetheless, kindling fire of inspiration, the light and reflection of which shall make visible the eternal truths of God.

These are days that try the souls of men and every hour is pregnant with changes, the possibilities of which dumbfound the most profound and paralyze the thoughtful Nature, boundless in her resources with locked and bolted doors, denying entrance to the mighty men of the past, is trembling as keenly as she observes her mysteries unfolded and harnessed to man's service. Science reluctantly disgorges her apparent indifferences to the word of God and in the main not only substantiates its supernatural originality, but cruelly victimizes adherents to the contrary and signalizes its approval; "That in the beginning God created the Heavens and the Earth and the Earth was without form and void, and darkness was upon the face of the deep. And the spirit of God moved upon the face of the waters. And God said, 'Let there be light,' and there was light, and God saw the light that it was good."

Back yonder in the front line of the mystic onset. Back yonder in the shadow of Omnipotent loneliness! Back yonder in the realm where man's wandering imagination become blind in its limited anticipation! Back yonder in the dawn of time when her fingers first wrote greetings to a new creation, when none were there to gainsay or behold the brilliancy that illuminated the first day, God said, "'Let there be light;' and there was light, and God saw the light that it was good." Our God, therefore is a lover of light. He is our Father. Children partake of parental likes and dislikes; hence count it not strange, my brethren, that we should work while it is day, for the night cometh when no man can work. "Remember," said Dr. Phillips Brooks, "by continually looking upward our minds themselves grow upwards." And as a man, by indulging in habits of scorn and contempt for others, is sure to descend to the level of what he despises, so the opposite habits of admiration and enthusiasm for excellence impart to ourselves a portion of the qualities as admired. Here, as in everything else, humility is the surest path to exaltation.

I have striven with a consciousness of duty to impress the thousands to whom I have spoken that this Convention now rounding out its 36th year of usefulness, stands squarely and unalterably and unequivocally opposed to selfish aggrandizement and a policy of rule or ruin. We who are here have been tried in the first and may with grace from these heights of eminence diagnose a present whether in church or state unparalleled for its restlessness and revolutionary tendencies. Nations are without justifiable cause or reason engaged in ruthless warfare, the proportions of which the Napoleons and Caesars in the noontide of their conquest would have trembled to conceive or imagine. Submersibles like plumed demons of night plough the sea and their commanders dream dreams of tomorrow's flight while superdreadnoughts once the hope and ideals of natives scamper to harbors of safety or find repose in death and ruin, as torpedoes flashed by these under sea dogs pierce and shatter armors, once held indestructible, while the heavens once of peace are aflamed with muffled fury taking flight to earth make Dante's Inferno a blissful desire, and the times do not presage the end of carnage of rapine murder and ruin. Diplomats and statesmen are juggling words in efforts of peace, but the more they write and surmise the greedier appear these dogs of way. Well might the church of God ascend the Hill of Zion and assume her duties and be about her Master's business, and you, my brethren, "I charge thee therefore before God, and the Lord Jesus Christ, who shall judge the quick and the dead at His appearing and His kingdom; preach the word; be instant in season, out of season; reprove, rebuke, exhort with all longsuffering and doctrine. Henceforth, there is laid up for me a crown of righteousness, which the Lord, the Righteous Judge, shall give me at that day: and not to me only, but unto all them that love His appearing." (2 Timothy 4:1-8)

Emphasize the doctrine, stress its outreach, make permanent its glories. Remove not the ancient landmarks. Hold fast to the truth as proclaimed by the Fathers. Let vengeance be of God. Seek divine approval. Covet not thy brother's property. Envy not the angel of hope, but walk under the shadow of her immaculate wings and in the day of adversity be not dismayed nor afraid. There shall not any man be able to stand before thee all the days of thy life; as I was with Moses so I am with thee. I will not fail thee nor forsake thee. Be strong and of good courage, for unto the people shalt thou divide for an inheritance the land which I swear unto their fathers to give them. Do according to all the laws which Moses, my servant, commandeth thee. Turn not from thee to the right hand or to the left that thou mayest prosper withersoever thou goest. This book of the law shall not depart out of thy mouth, but thou shalt meditate therein day and night and then thou shalt have good success.

Prosperity is a mark of God's approval. Success is from above. Colossal and gigantic industries are supervised, constructed and manned generally, if not always, by the prudent, prayerful and just. The indolent and haphazard seek to reap where they have not sown and the envious-hearted poisoneth the waters and addeth hate to malice, but their course shall be calamitous. Remember Joshua's command, "Sun, stand thou still upon Gibeon: and thou, moon, in the valley of Ajalon." So the sun stood still in the midst of the heaven and hastened not to go down about a whole day. One day lost to earth's calendar: the world one day behind since, and so the victory cometh to the prayerful and he that waiteth upon the Lord shall not be ashamed. And now, forgetting the things that are behind, let us press on to the mark of the high calling which is in Christ Jesus.

Illiteracy is on the wane and decrease. Ignorance is a bane to any people and is a twin sister to discontent and lawlessness and it is imperative to the perpetuity of every government that opportunity to advance and cultivate should not be denied its humblest citizen. Let no man upon these American shores mislead himself to conclude that the American Negro is disinterested or unconcerned as to this vital question. His yearnings for the higher and nobler outweigh the dearest environments and with tear-bedimmed cheeks he unwillingly faces the unknown that his children may drink of the fountain of intellect. His comprehension of education is as broad as the spacious heavens and his grasp for attainment can only be measured by God's unknown intention in man's creation, in other words, his ambition swings from pole to pole and then hopefully defies and laughs at every barrier that other than enhance a new sunburst of vision. We are Americans unhyphenated. Our love of country is written in the blood of our forefathers, who fell at Bunker Hill, Fort Wagner, Miliken's Bend, Richmond and San Juan Hill, that this government founded as an asylum for the oppressed should not perish from the earth. We loved her industries, her pursuits and activities, and sing her songs of triumph. Every rippling rill murmuring and singing to the sea carries in its wake the stamp of liberty, liberty to move in its God-given channel and perchance bear upon its bosom that which the fingers of an unknown kinsman may trickle and conjure from the bosom of Mother Earth and thereby establishing and making necessary a merchant marine to be manned and controlled by Americans, and that they shall be white-winged messengers of peace unfolding and permanently establishing that heaven-born and undying sentiment that must yet fill the earth as the waters do the sea—"God our Father, Christ our Redeemer and man our brother." Lynching will then be unknown and our courts unhampered for the inherent right of a trial by a jury of peers should not be denied an American citizen. Let us thank God that the conscience of the entire nation—East, North, South and West—is being awakened to its sense of duty. As prohibition gathers strength and the teachings of character, morality, virtue and honesty the cornerstones of Christianity are erected and reverenced so these hydra-headed enemies of civilization and progress are relegated and utterly routed. The hope of every nation is in its home training and the hope of every home is in Christianity; and it is here that we must sound the alarm and kindle an interest that will make prayer an essential and longing privilege. The resentful, haughty and arrogant individual is a menace to the peace and harmony of any community and bring punishment to the innocent. We emphatically plead that the guilty be punished and the innocent protected. To ask less or demand more would be unmanly, insane and hypocritical.

A training ministry with heart and soul guided by the Spirit of God is the call of the hour. "Go ye therefore into all the world and preach my Gospel unto every creature and, lo, I am with you always" is the commission handed you from above. It has not been changed or amended and is of more honor than any parchment or credential ever handed ambassador or minister plenipotentiary by emperor, president or king. Ours is a mission to save, and much depends upon our ability to cope with the issues of the day, and if we would maintain and foster the coming of the kingdom on Earth our feet must be trained to walk the highways that eminently dignify an exalted station. Our lips taught make the welkin ring with songs of praises while the force of our lives must so shine as to scatter dismay and dispel hopelessness and encourage the life of righteousness. I urge you in the fact of these conditions to inaugurate plans here that will make sure in the near future the erection of a theological seminary. Its necessity is futile to discuss. Philanthropists will help us if we help ourselves, and I recommend that the greatest caution be exercised in the selection of your Educational Board and that that Board in selecting its Secretary look wisely to the demands of the hour. I recommend in this particular that at this session a committee of three be appointed or selected to solicit subscriptions to be paid at the next sitting of the Convention to be known as "Educational Jubilee Fund," and that our energies be directed to the raising of $10,000 for the erection of such an institution. Are there not two-hundred of the genuine, real invincible followers of progress now ready to subscribe to this fund? And as I have said before, this will be a nucleus demonstrating our earnestness and out of that zeal will come friends of whom we do not dream to aid in making possible this absolute necessity. Vague, abstract and theoretical sayings must be buried with the past while our forces resurrect and teach the concrete and the practical. Better ten-thousand times a hundred thoughtful, thoroughgoing, faithful constructors than a million blind, thoughtless, uncontrollable obstructors. The task may seem great, but remember dead fish can float down stream, but life's energy and courage are the elements necessary to stem the tide.

The National Baptist Layman's Movement is a child of promise.

It only awaits your acceptance into your care as an auxiliary working under its own constitution and rules, none of which are repugnant or in conflict to the Constitution of the Convention. I recommend your endorsement of the movement and the appointment of a committee to do such things as will make permanent this helpful and potent force heretofore neglected and unmentioned. Our laymen are competent, resourceful, earnest and willing factors to whom we may look in every emergency of church life and it is proper and befitting that they be thus honored and ordained to go forth and uplift as they climb.

Our Woman's Auxiliary Convention will, ere you close this session, have moved on to conquest, and I bid them Godspeed as they journey on making better the world by their devotion and lives of usefulness. What is home without a mother? What mishaps are overcome by the church through our Godly women? Man without her softening, winsome, tender care would degenerate into barbarism. For God knew when he beheld man that eventful morn that there yet remained unfinished the glorious and beautiful creation, and when in rest and repose Adam slept, God took one of his ribs and made a woman and brought her unto Adam and Adam said, "This is now bone of by bone and flesh of my flesh and she shall be called woman" and happily their hearts were entwined and today we are contented, truly delighted that our good women are here to bless and help us in the vanguard of Christian endeavor.

Dr. J. D. Brooks, Corresponding Secretary of the Home Mission Board, and Dr. R. Kemp, Corresponding Secretary of the Foreign Mission Board, have done the best they could under the circumstances, and I tender them my gratitude not only for the work they have done to make this convention a success, but to aid your executive in hours of trial. Dr. S. R. Prince, Secretary of the B.Y.P.U., has ceased not to declare the whole truth and his success has been assured from the very beginning. Dr. S. T. Floyd, Secretary of the Benefit Board, and Dr. J. S. Anderson, Secretary of the Evangelical Board, are each alive and sensible of the duties before them and should be encouraged to pursue their already well-prepared plans. Dr. Jno. H. Frank, editor of the *Union Review*, is recognized as a high-class, capable, fearless, intrepid writer and his breadth of thought and unanswerable editorials are gems for future references. His replies to those who would besmirch and delve into thoughtless venom and spite have sought the snow-covered mountain top and added lustre to a cause as eternal as the heavens.

Compromises

Invariably these suggestions have come from friends well meaning in their intentions, but unacquainted with our differences. Dr. Boyd, true as the needle to the pole, has referred these suggestions to your executive for consideration. They have been many and presented many phases, but I promised you at Chicago by the help of God to meet you here. I have kept my word. I cannot close this message without tendering my thanks to each of you who have labored in and out of season for the success of this meeting. Dr. Charles H. Clark, the surgeon of the race, upheld my arms and encouraged us at all times. Dr. Henry Allen Boyd, the youthful, tireless business product of a worthy sire, has not slept at his post, but unassuming and yet determined has given every possible aid. The plumed knight and veteran, Dr. J. F. Thomas, has been as active as if in the commencement of his great life, and time would fail me to name each of you to whom my heart goes out for demonstrations of affections and kindness.

Dr. W. R. Toliver, our Field Secretary, closed down his eyelids in slumber and rendered an account before the Great White Throne. Kind, affable, erudite, eloquent and fearless he was an exponent invincible and failed not in the discharge of his duties. Dr. G. W. Railford of South Carolina, auditor and pastor, launched full high out to sea and entered the haven of rest amid the sunshine of noonday. Both died in harness! Both are resting from their labors.

Servant of God well done,
Rest from work's employ;
The battle fought, the victory won,
Enter your Master's joy.

And now, my brethren, language fails me in the attempt to express my gratitude to each of you for your loyal and unchallenged support you have given us. It has been my pleasure to stand upon old England's shores and there represent the proudest and greatest fraternal organization known among black men, and I can never forget the unbounded enthusiasm and the unlimited and hospitable welcome accorded me throughout that great and powerful nation. But all of this fades into insignificance when I recall the splendid ovations tendered me throughout this entire country, since last September. I would not have you presume that I for once attribute these great outpourings of love and affection as representation of my own popularity and ability, but rather the cause for which we stand and for which we will die has found a ready response in the hearts of the true and devoted Baptists throughout the entire union. They know that this Convention stands for an open door for every black boy and girl whose eyes have seen the brightness of the sun, and it matters not to me what course others may pursue, with this hand extended to God, I promise you now, henceforth and forever, that I dedicate anew the modicum of talent I may possess to demand that special privileges are contrary to the rule and law and equity, but to every individual is inherited the right to think, to act and to serve God as he pleases. I thank you.

Annual Address of Dr. E. P. Jones
President of the National Baptist Convention, U.S.A.
In Session at Atlanta, Georgia, September, 1917

Brother Vice President and Messengers to this the 37th Annual Session of the National Baptist Convention of the U.S.A., Africa and the Isles of the Sea:

Toward the sunset in a prosperous, thriving, busy city we met just one year ago. Story nor song can ever tell of the unlimited enthusiasm manifested nor the cordial welcome extended to us. That session is now history. Read if you please the record, note the faultless composition, and join me in extending to our Secretaries thanks for their painstaking efforts. They sought not the abbreviated or endless course of publicity, but wrote as writes the happy and true sanctioned by the righteousness of their cause and, yet, you who were present will ask in vain for the living, inspiring, wonderful fellowship which permeated and took into its mastery the fashioning of that session. I can't tell about it. Gifted sons, though you are singled out and called from the very foundation to describe, unfold, preach and teach, learned and kept by a power that is not your own, finished in the art of expression, training to give shape and form to the mysterious, will you not agree that truth had a hearing and at times the angel of peace walked by our sides and now as we approach the threshold of this the 37th Annual session in the Athens of the South, where college hills loom from every angle and prophets of disaster premeditatedly misinterpret our purpose! God gives us light to travel on. Help us as here we review the past and lend our limited conception in fathoming the necessities of the future to so impress the thousands of this city, Commonwealth and nation that the glory of God may be magnified and the kingdoms of this earth become the Kingdoms of our Christ. Abuse, Scandal, Hate, and Prejudice are the cornerstones of the Temple of Envy and the pretended songs of Triumph are but the dirgeful wails in their own fury seeking contemptuous remorse. "For whatsoever we sow that we shall also reap." There can be no space here for vilification or its kindred elements. Such were not the dreams of the fathers like William J. Simmons, Dupree, Richard Pollard, Joseph Smothers, R. H. Boyd, G. W. Gayles, Geo P. Jones, Adam II, Davis, some of whom have fallen asleep and let us here and now adopt anew and re-ordain that the faith and practices made eternal by His groans upon Calvary and sent home to the hearts of millions through the preaching of His word, shall be forever maintained and that the honor and exalted wisdom, extolled through the past shall shine forth, growing in solemnity as ages shall pass before his ever watchful eye, and slumber in the bosom of divine consciousness. "And all the trees of the fields shall know that I the Lord have brought down the high tree, have exalted the low tree, have dried up the green tree and have made the dry tree to flourish: I, the Lord have spoken and have done it." Ezekiel 17:24.

God's methods are at variance with those of the world. Look at the Antediluvian and Noah, Pharaoh and the Israelites. Goliath and David, Haaman and Mordecai, exemplifying his policies. The great founders of Christ's Kingdom go forth. Fishermen, plain, humble, preaching not a religion of metaphysical subtleties, not elaborate doctrines or profound dogmas of philosophy; not a splendid system of pompous ceremony, but the lowly doctrines of the weak. What are the aims and objects of this our National Baptist Convention standing now at its 37th mile post? Are you gathered here from your various fields of labor as exponents of character building an industrial might and power or mere onlookers? Have you turned this way from the general trend of comforting the distressed and left those near and dear longing for your return simply to selfishly satisfy some temporary passing whim or desire? I answer, no! A thousand times, no! I do not mistake your purposes.

Our representation and authority rest fundamentally in the individual churches. We are here as a volunteer Association of Baptists. There can be none other than New Testament directions and all roads lead to Jerusalem and the banks of Jordan. There can be no secondary condescensions and transgressions to satisfy ambitions and personal desires for the Golden Rule fore-shadows and dispels even such contemplations. Here we study and nurture humility. Here we spurn cloture that deprives freedom of speech and by all the rules associate justice and liberty as ideals first born in the government of this our grand old Zion.

Because Thomas Jefferson occasionally visited the Baptist churches of old Virginia and studied the democracy and rule vouchsafed, he was enabled to write immortally, and upon the world's horizon picture new hope that shall yet make tottering thrones and unfounded discriminations heritages of the forgotten unchristian past. This Convention, its followers here, and its constituents, to the ends of the Earth contenteth not until, "Nation to nation is just and man to man is true." Dead fish can float downstream. Drift follows the current. Criticism is the tact of miscreants. "Unto the pure all things are pure, but unto them that are defiled and unbelieving is nothing pure but even their mind and conscience is defiled." Titus 1:15. Let us study to "show thyself approved unto God a workman that needeth not be ashamed rightly dividing the word of truth." 2 Timothy 2:15. Our duties are complex and require in their execution much patience and longsuffering. Upon the shoulders of the anointed rests the fabric of nation and tongue and out of your silence will come reddened valleys and rivers of blood, for death and hell ask no defiance, save as "Peace be still," is heard cautioning the maddened whitecaps like lambs to rest at his feet.

The power of centralization is dependent upon the general or individual realization. Cities are great in proportion to their utilized surroundings. Rivers are dependent upon their tributaries and never ceasing hidden springs; and our Convention must look likewise to its Boards, Associations, Conventions, and other Auxiliaries, for its life. And these feeders grow and augment so their source of supply must be multiplied that the broadened opportunities of our great Convention be not circumscribed. I think I can say truthfully, that under the circumstances, each Board has done well. Our secretaries in the main have gone forth heeding the call of duty and as a result you will note an increase of fully one hundred per cent over last year. The reports will disclose an awakening to the interest concerned in heretofore undeveloped territory. I tender each of them my unstinted commendation in their gallant stand and sacrifices demanded. Loyalty to this Convention has marked their every step and perfect harmony exists in every department. I appear to you out of the very depths of my heart to make the incoming year one of conquest and from every department. It is vital to the whole that the weakest link be accorded more than the customary; and out of your wise dispensation fear need not be entertained. The Publishing Board has had its very vitals held to ridicule and is it not a reflection upon the denomination as well as the brotherhood to see published glaring falsehoods in which hypenated treachery is made the weapons of Time-Servers. Those who stop to inquire into these misgivings recognized at once that because of the success of the Publishing Board it is made the sole issue. The folly of their argument is answered by the creation of a similar Board possessing similar powers and duties. The old mossback, time-worn artful deception, "That the property has been stolen from the Baptists of the nation," no longer serves to mislead, for it is now patent to every thoughtful interested layman that the records at Nashville show unmistakably that from cellar to dome the Publishing House is the property of the National Baptist Publishing Board, and that Dr. Boyd, Dr. Clark and all the officers are regularly elected and that a majority of this Board may, as other Boards, make such changes as they deem necessary. All was peace. All was warranted and guaranteed until the Board in the exercise of its power failed to re-elect a certain officer. Then and there it is amusing to note that all the records of the past become veritable fallacies, foreign to truth and men of character, force and manhood sink into ingrates. There are some who could wish that the Board had continued its policy of useless expenditure, but none can deny that its acts were of legal delegation and usurpation. It ill becomes the building of a prison cell, when incarcerated for crime, to decry the bars which hold him fast. Of his own making and construction it rather deserves his encomiums. Strange philosophy that seeks, after a quarter of a century of uplift, to pull down and stigmatize. The wherefore is individualism versus the interests of the many. I had rather have walked in silence and with folded arms sought solitude, or defied a thousand erratic destructionist than to have handed down to history a page of such glaring inconsistencies, four and furious in their poisoned extremities.

Laymen's League

Child of twelve months since recognition of the necessity and service is now universal. That there must be a better understanding of the doctrines, polity and practices of the church none will gainsay and particularly is it essential that our Laymen in their united capacity be given an opportunity to work out the glorious destiny within their grasp. Many leagues have been organized. Rules and regulations may be had from the National Organizer, Professor C. T. Hume at Nashville. When you recall that William Harrison of Oklahoma leads and is supported by Benjamin W. Currie, Ben J. Davis, L. L. Toney, W. H. Williams, and others influential and determined, it is not to be thought that other than a splendid report will be rendered at this meeting. If you as pastors will join with this movement it is not a distant day when this child of yesterday will contribute and in every way assist the parent body.

The *Union Review*

Weekly for eighteen years this paper has served this Convention. Its course has been unchangeable, and no periodical in this United States bears upon its pages matter more wholesome. It's a messenger of goodwill and fellowship, and many of its contemporaries would do well to come into its presence and there abide until properly charged with the current of truth. Read it, subscribe, hand it to your neighbor; through it express your views and become a contributor in disseminating that information necessary for progress and advancement.

The National Theological Seminary and Training School

On May 21st, while attending the State Convention of Illinois at Carbondale, I urged and insisted upon Dr. Boyd that upon his arrival at home that he at once take every possible step to make the operating of the Theological Seminary and Training School possible. It is useless to appeal to the people, for during the last twenty years every conceivable promise has been made and in the face of their liberal donation only airy castles have been constructed and it would not only be humiliating, but our own conscience would revolt under such circumstances. Prayer brought the results, for in a few days a telegram brought the possibilities of the coveted desire. It is useless here to enter into every phase of the subject, suffice it to say that for $25,000.00 the site and buildings have been secured and at this session you can be depended upon to redeem your pledges and lend heart to a denomination perfectly willing to do, but out of heart because of infidelity. A conservative estimate of its valuation is $100,000. We have gone forward relying upon your endorsement and support. Dr. Boyd at first hesitated, but I convinced him that in the sunset of his wonderful life he could do nothing grander or more beneficial to the denomination to which he had devoted his time and talent than to unite with the Educational Board and make possible this Light House from an eminence that overlooks the city. Every detail will be gone into when the Educational Board makes its report and when you are absolutely satisfied, let us join hands and redeem the promises so lightly considered. Throughout the length and breadth of the land this effort has been applauded. Enthusiasm prevails and friends are daily rallying to its support. If we would be worthy of existence as a convention, this is opportunity. It's yours now to do or choose a policy that has met no uncertain condemnation by the people. One is constructive, the other is destructive. One is a benediction, the other is a curse.

Unveiling the Toliver Monument

As ordered by you at Kansas City in October last, I unveiled the beautiful monument erected by you to the memory of the late Dr. W. R. Toliver. It was an impressive occasion and hundreds were present from all parts of Texas. Dr. L. L. Campbell, the sage and genius of Texas, stood by my side and made possible the fulfillment of your decree. It was befitting that William Robert Toliver, himself an orphan, should sleep and find rest at the St. John Orphanage. This gray marble shaft stands yonder in the "Lone Star State" as a mute tribute of grateful hearts for one who knew not how to falter, but fell in harness.

And now I thank each of you for the loyalty and devotion you have at all times extended to me. I have done the best I could. I have not been able to accept the many invitations extended. Out of my heart I have spoken as God has given me light. I have had in mind the betterment of mankind, the elevation of Kingdom on Earth and the promotion of this convention.

The Exodus of Our People

The exodus of our people deserves more than passing notice. I have insisted before and now that this earth was made by God for His children; that the earth is the Lord's and the fullness thereof and what's my Father's is mine by inheritance. We are now fifty years from slavery. That which satisfied then will not satisfy now. Progression must be the course of the race in every pursuit. Lawlessness must give place to legal authority. Opportunities to educate our children can no longer be denied. Accommodations fit for manly men and refined women must be provided upon every common carrier. We simply demand that for which our forefathers died. In the mighty conflict now engaging the millions of the earth, we are willing and ready to die that the Flag of Liberty shall be unfurled. A world's democracy can mean only a land of justice and liberty.

Let that day be not distant when the words of the immortal Booth shall no longer be theoretical but practical. Said he, "This Republic shall live the incarnation of freedom, the embodiment of the power and majesty of the people. Baptized anew, it shall stand the Colossus of the nations—its feet upon the continents, its sceptre over the seas, its forehead among the stars."

In that day the Fatherhood of God and the brotherhood of man shall be the religion of every tongue. "One Lord, one Faith, and one Baptism," shall be a universal text—every pulpit a burning fortress of righteousness and the children of God shining stars, radiant in splendor, marching on in their conquest.

Recommendations

1. That there shall be elected at this session, a Board on Church Extension or Aid with corresponding secretary and chairman as are other Boards and full recognition shall be given said Board by this Convention.

2. That the first Sunday in March annually shall be designated as Union-Review Day, and that all pastors and superintendents be requested to make this day one of the greatest possible, advantage to the management in every way particular and especially by the way of securing subscribers.

3. That a committee of three be elected by this body to present our necessities to the Southern Baptist Convention, and inform them of our Theological Seminary and its readiness for operation.

4. That each church, association, or convention, desiring to furnish a room in the school be given an opportunity and that the name of said donor be placed in some conspicuous place of said room.

Annual Address of Dr. E. P. Jones
President of the National Baptist Convention of America
In Session at Columbus, Ohio, September 8, 1920.

Brother Vice President, Messengers, and Friends:

An unbroken silence as solemn as death marks the twelve brief months since last we met and rendered an accounting of our stewardship. Those were hours elementary in our study of service to God and man, and here in this city, the very center of thought and activity for a section remarkable for its love of liberty and justice, our every act should evidence "a burning of the midnight oil" and an attainment fraught with no uncertain intentions.

Ere we pass into the concrete of these happy and privileged moments, let us stop and meditate upon the goodness of our God. Stop and wonder that in our simple nothingness, he has yet made us heralds of his loving kindness and champions of his infinite purposes. Well says David in the 108th Psalm:

> O God, my heart is fixed.
> I will sing and give praise,
> Even with my glory.
> Awake psaltery and harp;
> I myself will awake early.
> I will praise Thee O Lord among the people,
> And I will sing praises unto Thee among the nations.
> For thy mercy is great above the heavens,
> And thy truth reacheth unto the clouds.

Music is now and has ever been the soul's inspiration and home, and angels find unabridged ecstasy in the hymns of praise occasionally shaking the mountains, and then again, murmuring as the zephyrs in rhythmic harmony. A people singing on, working on, and praying on is not distant from the eminence wherein abideth those rights as sacred as virtue and for which life has been offered since, "When the stars in the courses fought against Sisera" (Judges 5:20) to yesterday, when Soviet Russia collapsed and fell before organized society.

These are days when every heart yearns for freedom, when the caged nightingale longs for the beach and from its fetters marks the changing clouds as they dip now to curtain "old oceans gray or unfold from Pisgah's top to greet the sun at morn." A breath of freedom says addition is worth a lifetime of slavery. Man to man must be brother, not master; advisor not dictator; friend, not foe; kind, not haughty; true, not false.

Strange indeed how in the very ranks of the ministry will be found the "dwarf and freak," the upstart and the sage. You will pardon my analysis. The dwarf is that assuming misfit in the pulpit who, because of some fortunate surroundings, endeavors to impress his importance at the expense of his less fortunate brothers, and may I here add, that class has no standing in an orthodox church or convention. We be brethren. A freak is that stupid pretender whose location in some big city has so lost his senses and so far forgotten the rules of Christian ethics as to imagine to himself some authority foreign to the whole. Thank God there are but few, and here and now I desire to emphasize that we be brethren, and that the standard of measurement is service, not vaunted selfishness. Forget your vanities. Lay aside your follies and preach the Word. Preach it as God has given you the light. Countenance no alternative but preach the Word.

"For there are three that bear record in heaven, the Father, the Word, and the Holy Ghost, and these three one. And there are three that bear witness in the earth, the Spirit and the water, and the blood, and these three agree in one"—I John 5:7,8.

Yours is an imperishable mission. A consecration of God and not of men. Of heaven and not of earth.

Ye servants of the Lord,
Each in his office wait;
With joy obey his heavenly word,
And watch before his gate.
Let all your lamps be bright,
And trim the golden flame;
Gird up your loins, as in his sight,
For awful is his name.

Watch! 'tis your Lord's command:
And while we speak he's near;
Mark every signal of his hand,
And ready all appear.
O happy servant he,
In such a posture found!
He shall his Lord with rapture see,
And be with honor crowned.

Today five years ago, in Chicago, a liberation from attempted thraldom came as truly to the Baptists of this nature as that which followed the immortal proclamation of the preserver of a nation. In both engagements the conflict was intense and brothers fought against brothers, each possibly assuming their cause to be just, but even now from every viewpoint, the slave owner was as much justified in his contention as the Committee of Seven who sought by intrigue and strategy to create an oligarchy inconceivable in its treacherous contentions and more to be despised than the magnified injustices of an administration that sought only its own aggrandizement. That infamous charter sought unrestrained power. Its hand would grasp a denomination's printing plant. Yea! all its earthly substance and entrench its personal prejudices, nor would it here be content, but like a dragon fed upon its own blood, raving and distracted, undermines the faith handed to us by the fathers, made sacred by the blood of the martyrs, baptized and ordained in the Jordan; it was foiled and forever doomed while "One Lord, One Faith, and One Baptism" shall be preached to all the world.

Lawsuits

It is incomprehensible how, in the face of records as well as court proceedings and publications, thousands are misled. It matters not if the cost of the court in all instances is assessed and levied upon our incorporated brethren, they take heart and find some interpretation akin to their preachments to stir anew fealty and hope. If they had been half as easy to satisfy in the onset as now, love would have been enthroned and truth walked for unwounded. Let us stop here and hope that never again in the history of our denomination will strife and unmanly criticism as well as unchristian utterances be found in our ranks. All cannot lead. Some must follow, and let it be known now that the servant, whether in the chair of the National Baptist Convention as President, in the pulpit as pastor, or in a thousand other pursuits, deserves considerations as well as sympathy. The editor of the *Union Review*, and I say it free from all unfriendliness, might have used its columns to assist our work, but alas! not a word in commendation. We wonder if it has ever occurred to him that the struggle in Chicago made it possible for him to continue to write editorials.

Constructive Ideas

New methods have marked the course of this Convention since our incumbency. I have striven to have the humblest as well as the most exalted feel the same sense of duty and honor. The college-bred and graduate as well as preacher of experience. Both are God's messengers. The one is as the other, a servant. No more, no less.

Your Theological Seminary is not in operation. You owe less than $15,000. Its valuation is $300,000. It was bought and will be paid for under this administration. Is that constructive? Is that the work of reactionaries? It is at least worthy of mention and particularly when you remember that for more than a quarter of a century it has had its theoretical existence.

Preparation should always follow a call to the ministry, and in this school we are bending our every effort to arrange a course commensurate in all details for the demands. You have come here to see that the last dollar unpaid is raised, and let us hope that your general campaign committee will find itself so engaged as to be only concerned with the vital affairs of that committee. These are the days of opportunity, and if we would make sure the spiritual and intellectual future of our denomination, our efforts at this session must be centralized, emphasized, and broadened.

The Interchurch World Movement

For once, the versatile editor of the *Union Review* sought to advise us as to our course and suggested that I go to New York and Atlantic City to conferences. I immediately wrote him in which I advised that he could attend, but I would adopt no such policy. This Convention had not spoken. It was not in my province to speak in advance and bind you in the absence of any specific instruction. The Northern Baptists at Denver had looked askance at the movement, and approved it with strict reservations. The Southern Baptists had unanimously disapproved of the entire proposition, and from every viewpoint, it had come so clothed in raiments of royalty as well as measures unbaptistic that even until this day, although it has gone the way of all the earth, our thoughts find no sorrow in its dissolution. The moment it sought to regulate the location of a Baptist church and make it subject to other than New Testament directions, it became woefully disappointing and wholly out of harmony with those teachings dearer than life and for which the saints faced death. This was not, however, its greatest sin. Every line pointed toward episcopacy. Every sentence was drenched in the stream of conquest; for when Baptists interchurch, they unchurch their own churches and make fickle the dogmas and doctrine for which the Son of God on Calvary drank to the dregs the cup of death. Ours may be the course of unpopularity, but it's the only real way. It may not please men, but it pleases God. Better ten-thousand times to walk alone triumphing on a good conscience penniless, yet rich on promises, than go meteoric-like with kings and be deceived. The one means hope verified; the other, loss of confidence as well as consistency.

The Publishing Board

It has been less than a miracle that this Board has been able to stem the current, and only God's assistance and wise management combined have made it possible. High cost of material, labor problems, and a thousand other inconsistent scheming and wicked attempts have operated to its detriment. Without a wise mariner its wreck would have long since told the story of prejudice and antagonism. Let us hope and pray for its success and at this session pay up our subscription to the *Union Review*. It cannot survive without our help. Dr. Boyd and the Board deserve sympathy, not criticism; and at this meeting, we must come to the rescue of this Board whose expenditures, because of the lawsuits, have been enormous. The depressed and inflated conditions gnawed mightily, and at times these officials have despaired, but out of it all has come an experience rich in the lessons of admonition, and now a better day is just ahead. For while preparing this address telegraphic communication tells me that the business of this Board has reached more than ten-thousand dollars above its greatest high-water at any time before our misguided brethren led off a few of their following. I know you will rejoice when the Board reads its Twenty-fourth Annual Report. God preserve to us such characters as Dr. Chas. H. Clark, Dr. R. H. Boyd, and the young and gifted Rev. Henry Allen Boyd, whose farsightedness in these days of fog and confusion stands well this institution.

Foreign Mission Board

Your Foreign Mission Board is steadfast and unswerving in its ceaseless efforts to redeem Africa from throes of darkness. For Dr. John H. Frank, the Chairman, and the Corresponding Secretary, Dr. R. Kemp, I have only words of commendations and goodwill. Their souls are wedded to the righteous phase of our national work, and we who stand aloof and criticize them and this Board may find a lesson in the old adage that a child may find spots on the sun, but it took a God to make it. Rebuke and fault-finding sleep on the tip of the tongue, while honest, heart support is the golden reed, radiant from afar, splendid to encourage and assist. Help them. Pray for them. Dr. Kemp is indisposed. His work for this Convention has been untiring. No man upon the floor has done more for its advancement and maintenance, and you will do well to honor him. He has been unable to travel. The Chairman, Dr. Frank, would greatly help the cause if at times he would visit us and tell us of its work. The editorship of the *Union Review* and the chairmanship of this important Board embody much work and with the splendid array of talent to be found in this Convention; it is a reflection that the burdens as well as honors should, no doubt to Dr. Frank's desire, be placed upon others. It might have been proper a few years ago, but not now in these days of opportunity. No man should hold, at the same time, two of the most important positions. If you will, in your prayers, seek guidance, the work of this Board must prosper. Hasten the coming of His Kingdom to Africa and may every heart who knows not Jesus here and everywhere have unto them the light given.

Home Mission Board

Here is the work misunderstood and half-heartedly supported. I have wondered a thousand times why. Charity begins at home and spreads abroad. Home Mission efforts are primitive and essential. Dr. J. P. Robinson, the Chairman, desires to see this work succeed. You could not find in all these United States a character more greatly beloved or more highly honored than he by those who know him.

I hope you will rally to their aid as never before. I cannot close my reference to the work without commending the labors of the Field Secretary, Rev. S. J. Dixon. Brimful of energy, as true as the needle to the pole in his labors, it is not to be wondered that the result has been a three-fold increase in good accomplished. Pray for him.

B.Y.P.U. Board

Drs. W. L. Drane and S. R. Prince need, at my hands, no introduction. Both have stood unswervingly for your work. Both are capable and competent and their reports will go far in directing you as to their necessities and you should carefully hear them and take steps to remedy their crying needs. The B.Y.P.U. is an auxiliary of vast importance, and we must hope for a better day with such splendid men in the vanguard. This Board will in the coming years in the hundred-fold repay every activity in its behalf. To the Chairman, Dr. D. W. Drane, and the Secretary, Rev. S. R. Prince, this Convention must always be grateful for their untiring zeal and devotion.

Evangelical Board

Fortune smiled upon this Board at its last meeting when Rev. A. A. Banks came into the actual service. His efforts have been wonderfully successful and God has pushed forward the work. He has had the assistance of his Chairman, Rev. D. P. Jones, as well as the cooperation of the entire Board. True to himself and to the work this young and energetic Gospel herald deserves unstinted praise.

Other Boards

Time would fail me to enumerate and set before you the various enlargements as well as work of all your Boards. The Church Extension, the Temperance and the Benefit Boards are forces in their spheres that need financial assistance to bring them forward and let us hope for that realization.

National Baptist Aged Ministers' Home

With our Publishing House busy and distributing ten-millions of religious tracts annually, and your Theological Seminary and Training School in operation, thus affording an opportunity for the present and future generations, I do not hesitate here and now to appeal to you from my inner soul "to stop, look, and listen."

Passing recently out of St. Louis on to Chicago, these words gained my attention and for more than a block I saw a heap of scrap iron gathered from every section of the country. The railroad management had sent out its employees, and as a result safely guarded and housed this useful material. Has it occurred to you that no such consideration is given the aged Baptist minister, but rather, like brick bats, they are thrown away and forgotten? May I call your attention to the fact that last winter in the poor house at Chicago, a minister whose life had been spent honorable and who had done valiant service was, just a few days before his death, because of the activities of our Alliance, saved from burial in the potter's field. He had been loved in his days of usefulness, but forgotten in his hours of weakness, and you are responsible for this sad neglect and blight upon the history of a denomination true to its leadership and always anxious to perform their duty. This movement will mark the most advanced step in the life and work of the Negro Baptists in these United States. I do not now pretend or suggest any interference with the work of the Benefit Board. That department seeks to provide for the widows and orphans when the mainstay of the home is gone, and for its work I have only the highest commendation and words of praise. But, it is easy to distinguish the difference between the two institutions, and if I shall accomplish, with your assistance, the erection of this home, my heart shall have attained that joy unspeakable and satisfactory. Out in Illinois a strong and influential body of Christian women have for many days struggled to accomplish this desire. I refer now to Mrs. Sallie B. Thomas, Mrs. Eva C. Hooper, Mrs. M. E. Mitchell, Mrs. I. Dean, Mrs. D. J. Marion, Mrs. Hattie E. Childs and others. They have toiled and worked incessantly. They have on hand quite a thousand dollars and would no doubt join hands with you in pushing forward this constructive and most wonderful, as well as self-preserving institution. I have talked and told how necessary it is that this home be build from yonder in Chicago, where the dashing waters of Lake Michigan break in their fury around the shores of a great city, to the sweet and pleasant groves of Florida, and then again in my own native state and throughout the entire Southland where the stars shine brightly, and everywhere one hearty accord has followed this proposition. Already there are those who are boasting that this Convention will follow in the pathway of others in giving countenance and support to this movement. I have come to plead and pray with you and to tell you that there never was before such an opportunity for real and genuine work as is afforded in this special and worthy institution. There are those here today who stand ready to make a contribution to this particular cause. It is not because they think that in the early future they may find refuge within its consecrated walls, but it is because of that Golden Rule to "Do unto others as you would have them do unto you." Not unmindful of the fact that self-preservation is the first law of nature, you, like evangels of hope and philanthropists of mercy, have spoken in behalf of every cause of charity as well of educational value. You have gone forth and triumphantly stood by the projects that looked toward civic pride, and when red-handed war has dropped its pall and mantle over this country, not one of you have failed to respond and do your full duty. I congratulate you for having chosen well to respond to these calls, and what indeed would be the conditions prevailing here and everywhere if you had not gone forth to teach and to preach and to tell of the matchless love of the wonderful Christ? It may not be yours and it may be mine when honored age shall place its golden locks upon ours to need the care and shelter of the home for which I now plead, and as to whether we shall profit is not the question. There are those who have given their lives for the cause. They have gone forth as pioneers and erected tabernacles for the service of God, and today, because of old age, and because those who knew them have gone across the Great Divide, they are neglected and forgotten. Let us today resolve and dedicate our very life for this cause that demands assistance. This great Twenty-five Million Dollar Drive that is to be fully launched at this session and continued for the next ten years will receive impetus and assistance as well as stamina and love when you shall at this session write firmly upon your intentions the erection of a National Baptist Home for Aged Ministers. There could be no higher or nobler step taken, and three million Baptists will respond eagerly to your call and demonstrate their love and affection.

Once again, referring to the instance in the city of Chicago and such instances have occurred time and time again over these United States, death had marked our lamented brother and soon his remains were to be interred in the potter's field but hastily we gathered $200 and had him removed to the Home for the Aged, where he was properly administered to and in a few days thereafter when death came, he found relief, relief in the arms of the blessed Christ. Relief because he knew that his brothers had not forgotten him and came to him in the moments of his calamity.

There is an action natural to every idea, and there is also a natural normal increase in its activity as it is maintained in consciousness. This action is the will. The normal increase and natural development of this activity is the normal progression of will, and herein lies its greatest effectiveness. Shakespeare must have referred to this same principle when he said: "There is a tide in the affairs of men which, taken at the flood, leads to fortune," for truly one's ability to carry out any idea in the most successful manner consists in his ability to keep an even balance with the normal development of the underlying idea or ideas. Another writer has said: "The most irresistible thing in the universe is an idea whose time has come." Any idea after it has developed to a certain point will inevitably find its own expression, just as a seed planted will grow and bear fruit. This is but the working out of the law that as a man thinks so is he. And well might we conclude here that in all this mighty concourse of mighty men representing a mighty people, there is not one who is not of the opinion and thoroughly convinced that this is the one idea that finds in this hour and this moment its consciousness. The question and the only question is whether you will to do it. I believe you will conclude now to make a certainty out of that to which our very natures should be wedded. In order that there may be no suggestions or references or hindrances or postponements, I present to you and they herewith follow the names of brethren who have been true to this Convention and who have expressed a desire to work in the interest of this Home. If you will elect them and they do not hold any other official position in this Convention, I will assure you that at your next session you will be satisfied with what we have done:

Texas: Revs. J. C. Curtiss, W. H. Holland, S. A. Pleasant, C. L. Humbler, J. H. Wynn, J. C. Calhoun, S. E. Diggs, L. R. Johnson, T. S. Wright, P. A. Prince, W. C. Barnes, W. Lofton, H. N. Bowden, J. S. Sutton

Louisiana: Revs. A. Hubbs, A. Carter, G. W. Davis, M. W. Grimble, P. B. Lewis, J. S. Love, W. Woods, Bro. Wells, W. L. Burrough, Bro. Fisher

Missouri: Revs. J. W. Hurse, J. W. Holley, A. A. Banks

South Carolina: Revs. H. H. Hill, J. C. White, T. M. Boykin, J. A. Watson, J. W. Weatherspoon, F. Seal

North Carolina: Revs. C. M. Cartwright, J. T. Williams, M. McDaniels, C. W. Webb, Z. B. Wynn, J. A. Melborne, J. J. Hines, J. H. Robinson, J. W. Wood, J. W. Ransay

Florida: Revs. H. M. Dilliard, A. Arnett, D. H. Kine, W. M. Marshall, P. C. Harrell, E. A. Granlin, V. A. Roberts, J. H. Brown, I. C. Nimmons, W. J. Ballou

Virginia: Revs. N. D. Leinsford, McLelland, L. J. Alexander

Mississippi: Revs. T. H. Walker, R. H. Reid, H. B. Boyd, G. L. Kelly, R. C. Burton, W. H. Johnson, A. W. Looney, H. B. Black, S. L. Fox, E. Herrington

Georgia: Revs. K. C. Masdox, G. C. Chapman, E. D. Dallis, N. J. Jackson, R. B. Webb, L. J. Wilder, E. J. Rozzel, H. C. Blackshear, E. Hall, L. Clowers

Alabama: Rev. A. J. Jones

Pennsylvania: Revs. G. Richardson and E. M. King

Kentucky: Revs. E. H. Pinck, A. F. Fox, V. S. Smith, E. T. Offutt, T. H. Bradis, R. B. Butler, J. C. Cross, H. Kutter, W. Brown, T. Timberlake

Ohio: B. D. Scott, T. J. Smith, F. P. Green, P. H. Hill, L. W. Gray, A. G. Freeman, B. R. Reid, Bro. Curry

Oklahoma: Revs. R. D. Wess, I. W. Stephenson, C. Johnson, J. W. Knowles, W. L. Harris, J. B. McFarland, R. Y. Corbin, Y. R. Jordan, S. P. Harrison

Tennessee: Revs. J. Brown, J. L. Harding, Sr., H. A. Alfred, H. M. Burns, H. A. Boyd, G. B. Taylor

Illinois: Revs. W. H. Carter, J. D. Davis, J. M. Haggard, J. E. Priestly, H. W. Knight, J. R. L. Gibson, E. P. Jones, L. Drane, M. L. Porter, H. E. McWilliam, G. W. Prince, B. Johnson, J. H. Hallman, W. H. Woods, G. W. Alexander, C. C. Phillips, W. L. Washington, J. A.

Royal, B. H. Hunter, L. C. Clark, W. H. Snowden
To be associated with such other trustees as the N.B.C.A. shall elect.

The approval of this address can mean and will mean that these brethren are the elected trustees for this, your National Home, and that they will be given such authority as is necessary to put the same in operation. There may be those here who will desire changes in this recommendation; but may I suggest since you now have nothing whatever in this particular and since I have conferred with each of these brethren and since they have signified an earnest willingness to go forward in the discharge of this particular duty, and since they are supporters of this great Convention and connected in no capacity officially, I insist that if you thus recognize them you not only extend the influence of this Convention but you bind by a closer tie these particular brethren whose hearts are enmeshed in this demand and necessity. God help you to see and to go forward in the discharge of this wonder and deserved privilege.

$25,000,000 campaign

The greatest conflict since the world commenced ended two years ago. It was a struggle most titanic in strength as well as destruction. When the two great forces faced each other in deadly conflict, and when the struggle was over, men saw as never before that big things and big accomplishments were to be achieved through big ideas. Your Convention at Norfolk gave to your committee full authority and power to go forth in bringing to you for all phases of your work for the next ten years this large and splendid sum. The Executive Committee of the General Campaign Committee, Drs. L. L. Campbell, Edw. P. Jones, C. J. W. Boyd, J. P. Robinson, S. R. Prince, F. H. Cook, R. H. Boyd, J. W. Hurse, C. P. Madison, E. R. Carter, and W. W. Hill, have gone forth, and at this session presents to you a systematic course of procedure which, if followed, will accomplish a general survey and make easy an estimate from which may come the accomplishment so much desired. When we remember that in this general summary will be found provisions for Foreign Mission, Home Mission, Education, Church Extension, the Widows and Orphans, in fact every department of religious activity, it must at once be apparent that the call has in it all of the substance and essence that would bind those whose vision rises above the valley and swings to the mountain top. Let each member of this Convention not only at this Convention pay to your committee every dollar that has been raised for this cause, but after the survey has been made and an equalization placed, go forth to make fast the dreams which, if brought true, will raise a higher and greater standard for the cause of Christianity. Every denomination upon the globe is striving now to enlighten, to enlist and to enlarge, and we cannot afford to do other than to take the vanguard and on every hilltop and in every valley carry the Gospel of One Lord, One Faith, and One Baptism, and that while we live on earth we must construct for the oncoming generations who will take measure of our capacity in proportion as we have lifted as we climb. Every moment of this Convention had its glorious advent forty years ago. Those who then saw the opportunity decided that when all of the States of the Union as well as the territories should meet in this annual session, and then and there renew their obligations, the results could only be enhancing, inspiring, as well as advancing to the kingdom of God. Many of them are now asleep. They live only in the affections and admiration of you who gather here to honor their memory.

We have come to this great city not for sightseeing or recreation, but for work. We have come to tell the story, the story that has been the thrilling, consistent, and wonderful inspiration since Cain slew Abel. The story of Calvary's Cross. The story of the Living God. The story that had its origin in Genesis 3:15 when God said: "and I will put enmity between thee and the woman and between thy seed and her seed; it shall bruise their head, and thou shall bruise his heel." Injustice from that day until this has dared enter conflict with righteousness and righteousness and truth have ever held their heads high and marched with determination to continue the struggle until every vestige of injustice and unrighteousness shall have been driven from the earth. This old world must be renovated and for a thousand years his children shall rule. It was at Chicago that the Baptists of this nation marched forward in solid phalanx to forever set their seal of disapproval upon every act which sought to leave the teachings of God's Word. The question there was whether truth should be fettered, right imprisoned, and the doctrines of a church slain in the hands of its friends. You wrote your determination once for all that until the judgment morn the legacies and practices of the fathers should remain unchanged and that you would report to God and not to man for your actions. I can never forget your support. I can never forget your confidence. It filled my heart then with joy and every fibre of my soul today is filled with that same inspiration. The wonderful work that you have accomplished since we met in Chicago is indeed admirable not only in deed but in contemplation. Your

Railroad Commission seeks to see that Jim Crow laws are abolished and that travel upon every highway of America is given with similar equality to every American citizen, and then that vice and spirit of injustice in which the law is taken in the hands of the mob and American citizens lynched without judge or jury is forever swept from the American continent. Freedom is the common lot and heritage of every man and no man is free who does not enjoy as his neighbors the full freedom of equality and justice. I here make no special reference to what some would call social equality; in every man's hand rests or should rest his social relationship.

Society has its own regulations and rules, and the law in no particular should seek to control or to bind these particular privileges, and I seek only that equality before the law which warrants and guarantees as the constitution proclaims the rights of an American citizen.

And now, my brethren, I have done the best I could in these five years of service. They have been years and days of concern and deep study. I have, from the pulpit and the hustings, on the hills and in the valleys, in the cities and in the country, before the learned and the unlearned, before brothers and before enemies, attempted to carry the message of a risen Lord and of a church dearer to me than life. My mistakes in this period have been many and the many ordeals through which I have gone have been trying, but I have endeavored to see a brighter day. Lawsuits and a thousand other impediments have hampered our activities and at times it has appeared as if our last session had been held. A great many times, out of my own pockets, I have had to advance money to keep the old Convention going. I have called upon Dr. Boyd and I want to say today that his heart has at all times moved in unison with those intentions that would fundamentally construct and lift up this Convention. I wish that I might today call the names of those who in the front of bayonets fought that this great heritage might remain steadfast and immovable. I can never recount to you the struggles through which we have undergone. God alone has preserved and made possible this wonderful achievement and I thank God that we are here today to take fresh courage and to move forward as never before under the martialing power not of any man but under the power of the Holy Ghost. I want you to forget me and to forget all with which I have been associated with you in trying to do these five years. Stop and listen to the voice of the Apostle Paul as he speaks in 1st Corinthians 13:1: "Though I speak with the tongues of men and angels and have not charity, I am become as a sounding brass and a tinkling cymbal; and though I have the gift of prophecy and understand all mysteries and all knowledge, and though I have all faith so that I could remove mountains and have not charity, I am nothing. And though I bestow all my goods to feed the poor and though I give my body to be burned and have not charity it profiteth me nothing." And so today if there are those who bring charges and who impute imperfections to our deeds and to our administration, I desire to have you read the ninth verse of the same chapter: "For we know in part, and we prophesy in part, but when that which is perfect is come, then that which is in part shall be done away. When I was a child I spake as a child, I understood as a child, I thought as a child, but when I became a man I put away childish things."

Inexperienced in many things because we had not gone this way heretofore, it was natural that mistakes would be made, but I have done the best I could. I make to you today this report and offer no apologies for one single act that I have done during this administration. I do not serve men or bow to them. I only serve my God. The office of President of this Convention is one of honor and distinction, but when it comes to the time that my own conscience is not to be my guide and God my judge, and that a few who imagine unto themselves some peculiar authority shall govern and control, I shall no longer attempt to lead, but as long as God lives and you, by your suffrage, shall see fit to place in my hands your leadership and shall advise me to go forward in the discharge of that duty, I shall see no favorite few nor shall I seek to place upon your shoulders burdens without your consent, and then, too, I would have you understand as I conclude these remarks that I know I have a building not made with hands, eternal in the heavens with God.

Since last we met, first, that sweet and loving soul, Rev. C. F. Whitenburg, of Spartanburg, S. C. placing his hand in the hands of the Redeemer, stole away from his congregation and he is absent in body today; and then Rev. T. J. James, one of your Vice Presidents, unflinchingly marched down to the Jordan and moved across the dark river, catching a glimpse of the other side of the merciful Saviour, he too, is absent in body; and then you will remember that little giant and wonderful evangelist, the Rev. J. W. Paul, of Charlotte, N.C., who wrapped the drapery of his couch about him and silently took his seat in the Land of Pure Delight; and just the other day in Chicago, having made all preparations for this meeting, Dr. John F. Thomas, the most remarkable man and a gospel preacher of depth and power, bade an adieu to his family, to his friends and his congregation and found rest in the bosom of an ever-ruling Providence. And like true, noble-hearted brethren, let us here resolve and remember those sweet and beautiful words —

Guide me, O Thou Great Jehovah,
Pilgrim through this barren land;
I am weak, but Thou are mighty,
Keep me with Thy powerful hand.
Bread of Heaven, feed me till I want no more.
Bread of Heaven, feed me till I want no more.

When I tread the verge of Jordan,
Bid my anxious fears subside;
Bear me through the swelling current,
Land me safe on Canaan's side.
Songs of praises, I will ever give to Thee.
Songs of praises, I will ever give to Thee.

Recommendations

1. Be it the express sense of this Convention that the National Baptist Home for Aged Ministers, as heretofore recommended in the message of the President, and the plans suggested are approved, and that said trustees are authorized and empowered to do any and all things necessary in the premises, and that it is the earnest wish as well as desire of this Convention that all possible haste be put forth to bring about this Home, and that the Trustee Board, as aforementioned, is given the countenance and support of this Convention.

2. I recommend that each messenger present at this Convention and enrolling will present to the Executive Committee of the Campaign Committee statistics necessary for the information of the committee, in order that the Committee on Equalization may, in the progress of our present financial drive, intelligently give information to the various churches, associations, and other bodies connection with this Convention in order that the duty incumbent upon all Baptists may be borne equally.

3. That the President be authorized to appoint a Commission of Five, whose duty it shall be, as they deem wise, to commemorate the work and deeds of its late Treasurer, Dr. J. F. Thomas.

4. That the second Sunday in October will be known as Union Review Day, and that the Director General of the $25,000,000 Campaign Committee be authorized to do everything possible to increase the circulation of the *Union Review* to one hundred thousand.

Annual Address of Dr. E. P. Jones
President of the National Baptist Convention of America
In Session at New Orleans, Louisiana, September, 1921

Brother Vice-Presidents, Friends and Messengers to this the Forty-first Annual Session of the National Baptist Convention:

The sacredness of this hour and occasion cannot be overestimated. "If there be therefore any consolation in Christ, if any comfort of love, if any fellowship of the Spirit, if any bowels and mercies, fulfill ye my joy that ye be like minded, having the same love, being of one accord, of one mind. Let nothing be done through strife or vain glory; but in lowliness of mind let each esteem the other better than themselves." Phil. 2:1, 3.

"Watch ye stand fast in the faith, quit you like men; be strong." II Cor. 16:13. Ever displaying hopefulness and at all times considering the extreme difficulties in the pathway of the church, the wonderful and greatest of all the Apostles presents to us a clear and unmistakable plea for unity and humbleness of mind. Behind him were years of fortitude and consistent endeavor and in the might of his accomplishments had come an experience, right in its superior alliances. Dreaded, hated and maligned, and scored by the superficial society of his youth, his discernment is fortified and crystalized into gifted expositions, which horrify the impenitent and lift high the believer. As a father expects and yearns that his son may cover the good and digest the intellectually pure and walk the ways that concern the hopeful, in these words we have that calm and majestic sweetness combined with an everlasting assertiveness which sweeps away the cobwebs of the fine spun fanciful and brightens those elements which add to the soul's delight and keeps the "kinship of God," ever alive in man. Our separation these twelve months now in the past has seen and marked events worldwide in the world of invention, kingdom building of our God. Education is the world's greatest need, and especially Christian education; of it and for it man fails in his attempt of description, as well as necessity. We must educate or we must perish, are words as true today as yesterday; but that education which concerns itself chiefly with its own importance dovetails into selfishness and digs its own grave. It isn't to be wondered at that the Apostle as in the onset of this address sought for fellowship, accord, and one mind. We meet to continue, to uphold and to forever perpetuate those undying and wonderful principles that actuated our fathers when to lend heart to heart and to study his word meant happiness and joy. It was not the intention of the founders to do other than to foster brotherhood, inspire fellowship, kindle friendship, augment study and so expose the doctrines as to make unchangeable the faith stubbornly contested by the Apostles. Arrogance had not assumed the proportions of today, but throughout ran a genial disposition, whose hands were open, whose songs of cheer made the Convention a school of methods; where every messenger sat to learn and to worship. These were days in the gone by for which we must pre-eminently hope, they must come, they will come; for when we remember that after all we are brethren, bound by sympathies and ties of devotions as well as afflictions, it must appear that we cannot under any circumstances afford to do other than uplift and comfort each other in all efforts pertaining to the advancement of God's kingdom. Remember that the real preacher and pastor generally must overcome two-thirds of the opposition of both the officers and the congregation if he would do constructive work. It does not appear to me that our brethren in the Convention would realize that we are in no position to bring about divisions or to enter into scurrilous charges. It seems to me but yesterday when in Chicago, we united and stood for an uncompromising doctrine as well as for a convention that stands for uplift and science, art, and religion. Time forbids that I should here and now take up these particular subjects in detail. The field in which we are called to work is so complex and varied, a thousand minds looking in a thousand different directions must be harnessed by the Gospel of the Christ and focused upon Calvary's Cross. Around that tree of life, all of the world's stupendous events must fall as the unsupported rain drop, or the angel of darkness, when doomed by God's displeasure, to the inferno, not before nor since, more truly painted than by Dante. The music of the spheres, the grandest orchestra of earth, the sublime and sincere quartet that gather around the thrones and principalities as well as the crimson-bought millions, whose tramps shall be the marvel of eternity; all alike must sing and wonder and take consolation and comfort out of the immutable love of Christ.

Forty-one years ago Baptists first met in a National capacity. The gruesome tide of slavery had scarcely fallen from its crest when our forebears stepped to the front and saw in such a gathering as this an opportunity to sow seed which would ripen into a harvest potential for the advancement of faith and practices as well as the doctrine, dearer than life, and as hallowed as love. It was here that the learned and unlearned should forget their differences of attainment and blend in heart and soul for a fellowship genuine and pure. If there be those who to themselves assume for themselves an air of superiority because of their advantages educationally, they will find themselves out of place in the old school which assembled forty-one years ago. If to me there shall come criticisms and dislikes because I do not differentiate between the profound in scholarship and the humble, or less scholarly, I would here and now emphasize that wisdom is the principal thing, but with all thy getting get understanding. The preacher who understands and is led by the Spirit of God is the true exponent of the word and has wrought marvels in the unity. It would be out of place here to picture the scenes of that memorable conflict. Suffice it to say that it was rugged as well as dangerous; it tried the souls of men and after the smoke of battle had cleared away for five years, and even until today, the embers of animosity may be seen full aglow. Ours is not to fan the flame or keep alive these prejudices, but rather by our work to show and demonstrate to the world the capacity of our great church to do great things. We have reached the turning point in the life and history of our denomination. The lawsuits and propaganda initiated and fostered have all fallen for want of facts and this year has found the right of our existence as a convention undisputed for the first time in its history. We have had to contend for life. We have had to sound the alarm, and work in season and out of season to make possible this meeting at this hour in this the greatest city of the Southland. And never before have we met in a city where Baptists are depending upon you to leave an impression that will assist them in making sure the very foundation of the church. It is here that contentions run rife; that the leaders of our denomination must face every conceivable force of disintegration and destruction. I come today in this message to plead that fellowship and love, brotherhood and Christian ideals would sit enthroned in the hearts of you, my brethren, whose struggles to maintain the ideals of the church brought to you undying glory and luster of which the succeeding generations must read and take pride. The world looks to you, and you only as the real constructive force of Baptists in this nation. Not a bird's nest other than that you have feathered exists as yet where civilization abounds.

Forty-one years have gone and presuming that one thousand dollars were raised annually, then forty-one thousands have been raised as told from a thousand pulpits to erect a National Theological Seminary, and yet I stand here to tell you that the only Theological

Seminary and Training School owned by Negro Baptists in all the wide world as a National institution is your school, which from its eminence kisses down in shadows its modern architecture from the banks of yonder placid Cumberland. There are those today who doubt its existence. I invite you to walk with me and see its outstanding prominence. Look at its towering dome. Contemplate its mighty future and listen to the footfall of the students who matriculated this year from Iowa, Illinois, Mississippi, Texas, and Florida. Stop! and hear the words of instruction as they fall from the lips of teachers whose hearts were entwined in the hearts of the student body, and whose hopes fashioned the walk-ways that shall make patent the dreams of the now sainted dead whose memories are heritages more valuable than the cedars of Lebanon, and far more precious than the undiscovered mines in yonder land of Africa. What are we going to do here is the question uppermost in my mind? Will we enter into useless bickerings and division or go forward to discharge our duties as Christian leaders? Will we make true the charges that Negroes are as helpless babes that must be held in the arms of other races and nursed in the useless, or will we challenge these unsupported theories and demonstrate our own capacity to lead and to unite our forces? The eyes of the world are upon you here today in New Orleans. It is either do or undo. Make the church or undo the church. Give reasons for this convention by doing that which the hour demands, or agree to disband and hand over to those whose only stock is unfulfilled promises, laden with childlike hope, that some master hand will find the time to guide your destiny and wipe out your ignorance and shame. This is the day when the world is awake. When the sleeping slumber of yesterday has been everlastingly wiped out and all look forward with hope in the future. When we stand and watch the events of today, the great combinations of capital, and the uniformity with which nations are blending their efforts to stabilize, we are reminded that the church of God has in its wake made possible civilization. It has been the citadel from which every highway of reverence, valor and discipline lead, and along its course inspiration for every song of praise, every poem that has attracted the world's attention. Its disciples have at times been driven to seek seclusion and protection in the wilderness, but their words of encouragement as well as hope remain even until now to dispel every murmur of discord and brighten the way of peace.

The grandeur of God ought to rebuke our reliance upon creatures. All creatures are His. He made them, He governs them. He will govern. Not a sparrow falls, or an angel sings or a devil blasphemes, without Him. All else shall fail us. They will soon fail. They are even now failing. Friends sink around us! Hopes perish! We carry the seeds of death in our mortal bodies! And this wide world and these sweet heavens themselves, shall pretty soon vanish away at the sound of the final trumpet! Our God in grandeur and our world on fire.

Oh, give us hope and treasure in God. Give me some solid foundation to build upon. Give me my house founded upon the Rock of Ages! Give me this, and soon when I stand a disembodied spirit on the ashes of a burnt world and see the heavens rolled together as a scroll, I shall be able to say I have lost nothing. And then taking my way up to that Mount Zion which cannot be moved, I shall be able to exclaim I have gained everything. Because God, speaking in the grandeur of grace which belongs to Him, has issued the promise to the poor and contrite spirit—"the mountains shall depart from thee, neither shall the covenant of my peace be moved." Would to God that we persuade every immortal soul here to give up the treacherous world, and rest itself on the bosom of this vast and gracious God—immeasurably great and immeasurably good. Our mission as Baptist preachers and harbingers is as much to save souls at this meeting as when we are gathered in the greatest revivals in our respective fields.

Foreign Mission Board

"Quit you like men" is applicable to the work of this, one of the most important boards of our Convention. "Go ye into all the world and preach the gospel unto every creature" inspires the hearts of Baptists the world over. In our ranks, let it be hoped, that the indifference to the cause of Foreign Missions has long since ceased to exist. The Master's coming is foretold and understood by all the apostles, but its delay must be hastened on by the church, and not until the rock-ribbed hills of Africa and the frozen beaches of Alaska shall hear his words shall the end be. Our mission is to evangelize and instill the love of Christ and as we tell the story of the Cross to those in foreign lands, we glorify the sufferings and emulate His life. "For God so loved the world that He gave His only begotten Son, that whosoever believeth in Him shall not perish, but have everlasting life." Your board must have your cooperations as well as your prayers and assistance. And in their report you will see the advanced progress made during the past year.

Home Mission Board

Charity begins at home and spreads abroad aptly warrants this board to go forward in its work. The Secretary, Rev. Dixon; Dr. J. P. Robinson, the Chairman; and Dr. J. S. Ladelle. The Secretary has done much to demonstrate the capacity of this Board for effective work and they will tell you of their needs to which I urge you to give special heed for the Home Mission field of your own convention is alarmingly in need of proper information and let us hope for a brighter day and that the denomination will realize how important and necessary it is that we give our insistent attention to this department of our work. They cannot do effectively the work of the field unless responses are made to their appeals. The untold opportunities in Panama, as well as those about us, call in loudest terms for our assistance. A revolution must be had along the line of this particular endeavor if we would keep pace with this phase of our work.

Temperance and Church Extension

These two distinct Boards evidence the advanced ideas of today. The demon drink with all of its attendant evils, finds none at this day to pay it homage. Intemperance in all of its forms is ruinous and regretful and it is wholesome to contemplate that in the near future, our fair land will be free from this demon.

There are broken hearts and tears mingled with blood that argue the crime of intemperance. This Board has before it a great and wide field. And if it does nothing more than to distribute a million tracts denouncing this particular class of intemperance it will have done sufficient to warrant its existence. I earnestly appeal to you to stand by the Secretary, Dr. F. H. Cook, and pray that he will put over a program with the other members of the Board that will bring credit to the denomination.

Church Extension must be developed. Your Board seeks to make possible this work. Thousands of Baptists have gone north, east and west, and have joined other denominations; and in nine cases out of ten, give as their reason the inadequate accommodation of our great churches. Wonderful as has been the growth of our denomination, we have not as yet reached that point where we can countenance the loss of membership for want of church houses. With a Corresponding Secretary and a Board overflowing with the desire to extend the church, this department would find ready support.

Publishing Board

Colossal in its transactions and far-reaching in its influence, it rises mountain high, as the greatest accomplishment of any denomination under similar circumstances and conditions in the world. Its enemies have been many. Within and without its foes have carried on a constant warfare. The cost of material, as well as labor, and a hundred other adverse circumstances have arisen to stop and hinder the work of this Board. Our venerable Dr. R. H. Boyd sits in the lookout and in his observation and wide range, observes the storms, lessens their force, and thus the great old ship moves forward. The bond issue was a result of many considerations, all of the great institutions called to their assistance this feature of finance. And let us hope that when the report of this Board is made that such an understanding will be reached that all messengers present will readily respond and purchase bonds, thereby relieving a condition forced upon this Board by the unscrupulous and gainsaying. That it is the property of the Baptists of the nation, is no longer to be disputed, and the message carried to the World's Sunday School Congress by the Assistant Secretary, Dr. Henry Allen Boyd, told even in Japan, of the board and extensive work accomplished at its quarters. The *Union Review* has served this Convention long and well, and if we have not agreed with the editorials at all times, it must be said that the management has stood four-square and above board for a clean publicity void of the meaningless but anxious for the constructive. For the veteran and pioneer, founder let us stop, and in these moments ask Him who doeth all things well to spare to our denomination and people his wonderful and masterly mind.

Evangelical Board

Tireless, energetic and filled with a relentless spirit, Rev. A. A. Banks, and Rev. S. W. Toles, the Secretary and Chairman respectively, of this Board have gone forth to their work. Splendid offices have been fitted up in Kansas City and as not before the dawn of a new day in prospective under this Board. It needs your help; stand by them.

B.Y.P.U. Board

The work of retaining the young people and interesting them in the Master's cause has always been one that deserves serious reflection. The B.Y.P.U. offers an opportunity for their enlistment and enlightenment. It is the unyielding hope for their concern. Our B.Y.P.U. Board does not deserve censure. It may not have done all for which we have wished, and in that particular all of us have failed, but there are evidences of a better day. The Chairman, Rev. L. Drane, and the Secretary, Dr. S. R. Prince, will tell you of their success, and I earnestly entreat you to awaken to the obligation of this particular work.

Benefit Board

The mind was indeed right in comprehension that made possible the work of this Board. It seeks to relieve the distressed widows and orphans. It is a pity and yet it is true that we do not cherish the memory of our departed brothers to the extent of assisting their widows. Hear their report and join the great procession marching onward and forward and extending assistance to the needy. The Chairman, Rev. J. D. Leonard, and the Secretary, Dr. Floyd, are anxiously awaiting the hour when they can tell you of their needs as well as their demands.

National Baptist Ministers' Home Board

The only Board under your supervision without any liabilities but with an asset, is this the youngest Board of your Convention. On page 24 of the Journal of the Convention which met at Columbus, Ohio, it will be seen that you authorized, instituted and elected a Board of Trustees and in compliance with that order, Rev. J. S. Earle, of South Carolina, Dr. I. W. Crawford of Mississippi, Dr. F. H. Cook of Columbus, Ohio, and Dr. George W. Alexander of Mississippi were put in the lead of this Board and they have done splendid service. Fanatics succeed in many instances because of their intense zeal. This Board hopes at this session to have your order to purchase interest-bearing bonds until a sufficient amount have been raised to erect this home. If you could but trail the footsteps of the many old and aged ministers of our denomination who are without help and penniless and in many instances in houses of charity, you would arise in your might and free the denomination of this galling neglect and make possible the composure and rest of these veterans in their slumbering hours. They deserve more than scraps of iron, they are human. Their trade was soul-saving and making the world better, and if out of that particular effort they had hope at least for a pillow of straw upon which to rest in their closing days and disappointment comes because of inefficient pay, may I not appeal to you at this convention to set forward the hand on the clock of hope when they shall have this crumb of comfort.

Educational Board

A standard unequalled and untouched by any of its predecessors is the work of this Board. Dust thou art and dust thou shalt ever be is the heritage handed the present Board by those who have gone before it. Not a penny nor a blotter was handed them at Chicago. Empty-handed they faced the world. They met at every turn of the road the condemnation of having to reap a harvest without a sign of evidence of their sowing. The task was hard, the road was rugged and dangerous, dangers lurked in the pathway, but none of these things moved the invincible leaders of your Board. The opportunity came, it was seized and today every dollar owed upon that splendid property worth $250,000 has been paid, with the exception of $12,000. Nor would I have you forget that for two years its doors have been open and last week in the city of Chicago, two of its brightest students stood upon the floor of our association and told of its wonderful influence and expressed their hope that in the days nearby it would be fitted up and prepared to accommodate the many who had to be turned from its doors for want of facilities.

The Corresponding Secretary, Dr. C. J. W. Boyd, Dr. G. L. Prince, the Chairman of the Board of Education; Dr. G. B. Taylor, the Chairman of the Board of Trustees, and Dr. J. L. Harding, Secretary and Treasurer of the Board of Trustees, have done their part and deserve at your hands encomiums of honorable mention. Like gifted sons of the morning, they have stood and contended in your absence that this one and formidable asset should stand sacred and honored to your efforts as were the Greeks in their worship of Apollo. Twelve-thousand dollars must be raised at this convention and that institution saved or the world must know that the great Baptist family has not entirely forsaken the rut of hopelessness. What will you do to relieve the situation? Quit you like men, be strong, watch ye, stand fast in the faith, emulate the great men who have gone before. Forget the pygmies who openeth not their eyes like the mole, until the day of death, and run with patience the race that is set before you. If here today we shall contract honestly with ourselves and with posterity, God will give unto us a goodly heritage.

The flight of years through which we pass leave their telltale of the happy memories of those whose presence is no longer with us.

Columbus had its page of mourning and here in New Orleans, we shall dedicate another to the memory of those splendid men whose eyelids have been closed in slumber. Illinois bows in submission and with silence, recalls that twelve months since with us stood Rev. G. H. McDaniels, educator, financier and preacher. He was true and tried to every trust and won the admiration of all who knew him by his frankness and uprightness. South Carolina has felt the burden hand for their splendid chieftain and leader, the late Dr. J. J. Durham who passed into a happy beyond and gathered unto himself the beauty of a life well spent and to those who stood nearby well said, "I have fought a good fight and kept the faith." Texas mourns the loss of the late Rev. W. M. Jones, concerned with all that looked of interest to this convention and ready when called upon to shoulder the responsibility. Each of us will drop a tear for his absence, but will reverence his memory, and while the solemn zephyrs in yonder plains shall sing their mournful requiems, our hearts will be nearer the righteous because of his splendid example. W. H. Higgins and Seymour M. Miller, all of my native state, are asleep. Let them rest, and to their memory in our hearts let us carve a monument of love, and as the shadows fall therefrom the break in our sincere affection, let us redouble our conviction to stimulate and cheer the broken-hearted and teach the lessons of the Christ who tempers the wind to the shorn lamb:

Weeping soul no longer mourn;
Jesus all thy griefs hath borne.
View Him bleeding on the tree,
Pouring out His life for thee.
There by every sin He bore.
Weeping soul, lament no more.

The Sunday School Congress

At Little Rock in June, an army of ambitious, studious visionists drank from the wholesome fountains of intellect and are today alive and keen for work. A better investment for uplift and enlightenment is not ours to point out. Every moment was used and every illustration was welded into one great mass of ideals heavy with sentiments wonderful for refinement as well as classic in outlook.

Evanston invites the next Congress to come and partake of its hospitalities, and if the management opens its eyes to the real conditions and opportunities held out by these followers it may even now be said that all doors ajar and yonder on the shores of Lake Michigan you will find a welcome royal and absolute.

Racial Suicide

The sad and alarming conditions disclosed by the recent census must concern you and all who are interested in mankind. The records show a population of 11,000,000, and under all the rules of natural increase at least 13,000,000 should have been the calculation. What is the cause of this serious neglect? The serious policy of despised motherhood? This assuming attitude of racial suicide? The answer is not far nor hard to disclose. The country life and life of the fireside, rich in opportunities and upon which rests the very foundation of good government are being forsaken and the haphazard conditions of the city life chosen instead. And it is not now to be argued, but all are agreed that nature in her ideal bestowals lavishly dispenses there a thousand comforts denied in the crowded ways of the city. The call must be and better conditions prevail in the rural districts. Law and order must prevail. Lynch law must be abolished and better schools established. Let us hope that these elementary conditions are not far in the distant future. Peonage, a dark page in the history of semi-barbarism, must not find tolerance in these hours of noonday democracy, when the roar of cannon and smell of poisonous gases still vex the peaceful. Unless they died in vain, unless the crimsoned soil of France mocks and jeers at the lives given for freedom's cause, America, the chosen home of the oppressed must awaken to her true status and hold high to the nations of the earth that liberty guaranteed by the constitution for which the fathers died and make glorious a thousand battlefields. And let it here be said that in all the mighty conflicts and achievements the American Negro has been foremost and consistent and stands today ready as of yore to aid his white brother, but at the same time demands an opportunity to educate his children, live happily with his loved ones and serve God according to the dictates of his conscience. To ask more would be in vain; to ask less would be unmanly.

The accommodations upon some of the railroads of this country offered to some of its patrons cannot be too forcibly condemned. It would in a number of instances be remedied if the proper steps were taken for improvement. A law that imposes the same rate of pay upon one class of citizens without the same accommodations is unjust, unreasonable and ere long must be relegated. Truth and justice are eternal and will stand when falsehood and error are blighted pastimes. The upheavals, contentions and unrest throughout our own beloved country as well as the world will find settlement only when the rule of righteousness shall prevail. "Do unto others as you would have them do unto you," is the standard and rule of action whatever life is secured. Prosperity cannot come and will not come to any people where lawlessness prevails and murder is constant. It is not surprising that every American citizen is contemplating the recent organizing of the "Ku Klux Klan." It may be that the fire and smell of lawlessness with which the Klan of '75 and '76 was weighted does not now touch the garments of the organization of similar name, but dread suspicion and condemnation must follow wherever this organization is found because of the relationship which it takes upon itself by assuming this particular incorporation. Rest and contentment cannot come and will not come until the law as written in the Constitution of the United Sates, as well as the constitutions of the various states is upheld and enforced in every particular. The law should know no color or condition and its violation should find punishment to all. Let us hope that the accusation and charge that the rich may escape its penalty while the poor suffer shall be discountenanced forever. There should prevail an interest between all mankind that binds the one to the other. That makes one grand brotherhood so that the women of the world could find protection at the hands of all. Security must be given, not only to life and womanhood and character, but a trial by jury ought not be denied the humblest. The Anglo-Saxon, upon whose shoulder civilization has rested for more than twenty-one centuries owes it to his forebears as well as posterity, to stand between injustices and wrong and suffer no infliction to the contrary. Let us hope and pray that such outbreaks that occurred in Chicago and Tulsa, Oklahoma, and in other communities, will find their adjudication not in the frenzied and heated passion of the job but in the cool, calm, collected judgment of those in whose hands have been imposed the execution of the law. I know it is argued that the policy powers invested in the various states preclude any enactment to prohibit these violations. But if the Congress of the United States will pass a law giving to the heirs who survive the victim of mob violence a right of action against that particular county or parish and removing the officer of the law whose duty it is to protect from office, mob violence will cease. Let us help to build up a sentiment wherever we live that will argue potentially for law and order. But we must not fail to impress upon our own country as well as the nations of the world, our severest condemnation of misgovernment and our heartiest admiration for law enforcement.

I recommend and urge that this convention at this session organize and elect an International Welfare and Civic Commission, and that said commission will be empowered in the name of the Baptists of these United States to present to the President, the Honorable Warren G. Harding, such a petition as will have him understand our position upon all matters relating to the rights of citizens and that said commission will also be empowered to take up with the English government such modifications of the law in its possessions of Africa as well as the work of the missionary, and that said commissioners elected will also constitute the delegation to the World's Congress of Baptists to be held in London. And I recommend the commissioners:

Alabama, Revs. C. B. Williams, J. H. Easton, L. Hawthorne; *Georgia*, Revs. E. R. Carter, Ernest Hall; *Louisiana*, Revs. W. W. Hill, J. M. Carter, W. M. Grimble, A. Hubbs, C. S. Collins, E. W. White, Geo. W. Davis; *Texas*, Revs. L. L. Campbell, J. H. Winn, S. R. Prince, Ed. H. Branch, M. E. Robinson, O. Edwards, I. H. Kelly, J. C. Lott; *Virginia*, Revs. C. P. Madison, R. H. Bowling, T. J. King; *New England States*, Revs. W. B. Reid, R. Paul Russell, A. Wyatt; *Ohio*, Revs. F. H. Cook, J. F. Hughes, W. H. Williams, W. C. Hall; *Kentucky*, Revs. J. E. Wood, F. C. Lucas, R. B. Mitchell, Jno. H. Frank, F. C. Locust, R. B. Scott; *Indiana*, J. D. Leonard, I. M. Hendon, Chas. Lewis, J. D. Johnson, W. M. Ferrell; *Tennessee*, Henry Allen Boyd, G. B. Taylor, C. J. W. Boyd, H. Alfred; *Illinois*, W. P. Washington, C. C. Phillips, J. B. Beckham, W. H. Woods, J. A. Royal, R. B. Darden, H. W. Knight; *South Carolina*, J. S. Earle, E. W. Bowen, A. W. Hill, A. W. Puller; *North Carolina*, T. C. Phillips, C. M. Cartwright, W. M. Daniel; *Oklahoma*, S. B. Harrison, J. H. Smiley, D. C. Cooksie; *Missouri*, J. W. Hurse, G. L. Prince, N. T. Lane; *Mississippi*, G. W. Gayles, R. H. Hilliard, W. M. Mallory; *Florida*, K. R. Britt, J. E. Ford, A. L. Anderson, H. S. Nichols; *Pennsylvania*, Rev. W. A. Jones, Williams, Johnson, T. H. C. Messer; *Wisconsin*, Revs. S. L. Russell, W. J. Singletary; *Michigan*, Rev. Francis M. Story; *Colorado*, Rev. David E. Overs; *Arizona*, H. C. Williams.

These brothers will make a commission competent and will attend its sessions. There are others equally as able about whom I have said nothing.

I thank you now for the support you have given us these years filled with errors and mistakes as well as misgivings, but I have sought divine guidance and at no time have I had but the kindliest treatment of the entire brotherhood. I hope I have done all that would uplift and nothing that would pull down. I have preached and lectured and made wherever I have gone "One Lord, One Faith, and One Baptism" the chiefest of my theme. I have wished that I might visit every pastor on this floor. And the hillsides, far in the rurals as well as the city have been no exceptions. I have argued and told of the great good that comes to the pastorate as well as the people of continued service and emphatically denounced the itinerant method which at times I have noticed. The church of Christ must be advanced. It cannot be done through haste and the greatest churches as well as the greatest congregation are those with a settled pastor. Let us in unmeasured terms condemn the parasite who makes it his business to endeavor to seek honors where he has not labored and ease where he has not builded it. It is but a reproduction of the efforts of that class of Christians who find it impossible to go into the tall timbers of the wilderness to seek the lost, but rather come into the already organized house of God and create the dissatisfaction and bring a severance of church relationship to the childlike and simple.

What the church wants and what we must stand for is construction in the pulpit, construction in the association and construction in state conventions and construction here, and may I here and now urge that this Convention close its ears to those who seek office and go about endeavoring to tear down and to wring untruth from the garments of those who in comparison with their own is as the fiber of silk to the hastily spun cobweb. Let love raise her hands above each of our heads, let our lips speak only the truth as regards each other. Break down disagreements. Let none of us think ourselves better than the other, but with that earnestness of heart and contrition of spirit let us go forth in the might of prayer contending for the faith and upholding the truths of God's word, remembering that "Upon this Rock I will build My Church and the gates of hell shall not prevail against it." And may I in conclusion call your attention to the eighteenth and nineteenth verses of the Epistle of Paul, chapter one and of Philippians: "What then? notwithstanding, every way, whether in pretense, or in truth, Christ is preached; and I therein do rejoice, yea, and will rejoice. For I know that this shall turn to my salvation through your prayer, and the supply of the Spirit of Jesus Christ." Sweeping over the difficulties of the past Paul acknowledges and offsets every argument of those who underestimate the power of prayer. Prayer has been the weapon with which I have striven to fight since I saw the wonderful hope in Christ, illumined and magnified by His love and sustained through His death. In the bright morning promised to His redeemed church we shall stand amid the sanctified throng yonder beyond the realm of man's imagination and shall sing the song of triumph. I ask of you as I conclude this address only your word of sympathy, I have done nothing worthy of praise, my best efforts have been failures but I hand to you as the results of these six years' labors an escutcheon as clear and as clean as earth can afford. Every lawsuit has been won and when you have raised her $12,000, the property in Nashville worth $250,000 will be clear of debt and if I shall be trusted as your standard bearer, I promise as one of the planks of which we shall stand, that not again shall a mortgage be placed against it. It is easy to criticize and to find fault but remember no man can see and know the requisites of a position until he has filled it. Thanking you again and again. As it is written, "For my sake we are killed all the day long, we are accounted as sheep for the slaughter, Nay, in all these things we are more than conquerors through Him that loves us, for I am persuaded that neither death, nor life, nor angels, nor principalities, nor powers, nor things present, nor things to come, nor heights, nor depths, nor any other creature shall be able to separate us from the love of God which is in Christ Jesus our Lord." Romans 8:36-39. Honor and shame from no condition rise, act well your part there all honor lies.

Recommendations

1. That every pastor affiliated with this Convention will be requested to lift a special collection on Watch Meeting night for Foreign Mission, and that the amount collected and allowed shall be remitted on the first day of January, 1922, to the Corresponding Secretary of the Foreign Mission Board.

2. That this Convention authorize the Corresponding Secretary of B.Y.P.U. Board in cooperations with the B.Y.P.U. Board to present such plans to the Convention for its approval as will remove all doubt with regard to publishing of B.Y.P.U. literature.

3. That every pastor attending this Convention, will be requested and urged to pay their subscription for the *Union Review* and that the management at once arrange means by which said subscriptions may be collected.

4. That the Constitution of this Convention shall be so amended as to prohibit dual office-holding and that the Constitution, when so amended, shall be construed as barring any and all members of this Convention from holding more than one position to which is attached any remuneration, directly under the supervision of the Convention or any of its Boards. The object being to see that the honors and burdens are equally borne.

5. That the second Sunday in April is hereby fixed as Educational Day and that each pastor shall request of each member of his congregation a donation of twenty-five cents for education, which amount will be sent to the Corresponding Secretary of the Educational Board.

6. That no agent or missionary shall be deemed as holding a valid commission from any Board affiliating with the National Baptist Convention unless said commission is signed by the Chairman of said Board and attested to by the Corresponding Secretary.

Annual Address of Dr. E. P. Jones
President of the National Baptist Convention of America
In Session at Nashville, Tennessee, September, 1922

Brother Vice President, Officers of the Various Boards and Messengers:

The grace of our Lord and Saviour Jesus Christ and the communion of the Holy Spirit rest and abide upon you now and forever more, Amen. Seven brief years have come and gone filled with historic memories since first you, who gather here, in your own hands and under your immediate supervision, declared that a New Testament Church would suffer its own ruin and disaster when it even winked at intimations and teachings, not taught by the Christ. The power of God, the power of the courts and the law, the power vested in the people throughout the United States have upheld and strengthened our arms from that day until this. And so, under the shadows which fall in silence from the hills of the Capitol, we meet to take account of our activities and reach conclusions free from prejudice as to whether success or failure have attended our efforts.

At New Orleans, you decided to meet in Denver and it is proper that I should here have you understand why the change was made to Nashville. I need not be elaborate in this discussion, for at the January session of your Executive Board, a communication authoritative was read agreeing that this session should meet here. The only invitation before the Board was that presented by the Baptists of Nashville, as well as the citizens, and no other course remained open and hence this, the forty-second Annual Session of the Convention assembles where for more than twenty-five years has centered the material life and ideals of the denomination. In response to more than a thousand letters, sent out from our office, making inquiry as to where we should meet, the replies were so unanimous that a blind man could have seen how anxious, interested and concerned the Baptists, from the Everglades of Florida, the Prairies of Texas, the Mountains of Virginia and the Magnolia-dotted hills of Mississippi, yea, everywhere in America take hopeful interest in the hum of the thousand wheels which make up the machinery of the greatest Publishing Plant owned and operated by Negro Baptists in the world. I could make no mistake if I should say that it is the greatest institution of its kind owned by Baptists, irrespective of color or race. For when we remember the opportunities of our brethren north, south, east and west and compare their financial rating and remember that in the wake of their footsteps have fallen a civilization hoary with centuries supported by countless opportunities and upheld and sustained by ever possible advantage. I repeat and challenge contradiction that there can be no greater evidence presented throughout Christendom of unity and devotion. But without thy mind would I do nothing; that thy benefit should not be as it were of necessity, but willingly. (Philippians 1-14) It has been done because of necessity. No man could tell of the tears and sorrows in accomplishing that "willingness" as the venerable, earnest and conscientious Dr. R. H. Boyd, upon whose brow has fallen needless criticism, charges and countercharges, unwarranted by facts; but in the main ignorantly alleged and for reasons personally sinister, advanced and maintained. If every charge made against the management of the Publishing Plant was true, the good it has accomplished in ten-thousand ways is sufficient to demand the goodwill and support of every man whose heart is open to conviction and whose desire is to give opportunity to a people stepping yesterday from thralldom and standing today in the sunlight of the mightiest civilization that has ever dawned in the annals of time. Let us here remember that it has ever been thus: The greatest benefactors have in their own day and time found the arrows of hate and malice, envy and prejudice fattening on their heart's blood. It is so with those of you here today, it will be true of those who shall succeed you for the carnal mind is at enmity with righteousness. Caesar fell wounded at the hands of Brutus. Lincoln, the greatest American for all times to come, drank of the dregs of hate and fell a martyr to the cause of liberty. But so clean had he washed his hands from the seductive influences of passion and hate that his immortal documents grow whiter in purpose with the years. Whittier, Summer, Conklin and Douglas though a hundred years in advance of the hours in which they lived and each of them paid the toll of condemnation and saw that which we see today, but they faltered not and it is equally true of the patriarchs and prophets. Abraham, the father of the faithful, Enoch, who walked with God. Noah, the antedeluvian preacher, Moses, the world's greatest law-giver, Daniel, the interpreter of dreams, David, the man after God's own heart, Solomon, the wisest of each, John the Baptist, the forerunner of Christ, Peter, the impetuous, Paul, the philosopher, psychologist and greatest writer and preacher since first the flight of years, all suffered. But they found unmeasured joy and an unfailing assurance in the words of the blessed Sermon on the Mount. "Blessed are they that are persecuted for righteousness sake; for theirs is the kingdom of Heaven. Blessed are ye, when men shall revile you, and persecute you and shall say all manner of evil against you falsely, for my sake. Rejoice, and be exceedingly glad: for great is your reward in Heaven: for so persecuted they the prophets which were before you." (Matthew 5:10-12)

Self-Examination

It becomes us now to look into our own misgivings and to answer the many who inquire as to why our Convention should exist. If we cannot now and here in argument, present and give tangible reasons for this Convention, then I agree with our assailants that we should disband, return to our homes, and from every pulpit, admit our failure or make such amendments to our procedure as will bring the desire to our hearts. This Convention struck at Chicago for freedom and as one of the fundamental accomplishments; I speak for that loyal and true ministry of this Convention, there has never existed in a Convention a greater freedom than that which we enjoy in our deliberations. We are brethren. We have like sympathies and experiences and our every effort has been dedicated to the cause that in its deliberations all are equal and that it matters not whether we come from the city where the towering spires hinder the light of day in its rising or the humble districts in the valley may all enjoy, discuss and decide upon questions affecting the life of our denomination. Secondly, we challenged the fraudulent securing of a charter which struck at the vitals of a liberty-loving denomination and stood four-square for the New Testament and its teachings as the guide and only charter necessary for Baptists. We stand there today and from its ancient landmarks and dogmas, we unyieldingly hesitated our approval. Thirdly, we stood for the principle that God helps those who help themselves. The evidence of the rightfulness of that proposition is demonstrated in all the success of the children of God for at no time has God blessed any individual until that individual has done that which is a part of his inherent possibility. Whosoever will, let him come and drink of the water of life, but there must be a willingness executed, affirmed and put into action and we are unmoved today as we were then from this position. Fourthly, we condemned unalterably the raising of money for one purpose and using it for another. For more than twenty-five years, money had been raised for a Theological Seminary and Training School, but the school was a myth and hearts had become faint because of this painful neglect and although we have done nothing in comparison to our obligation, yet you will agree with me and the people of these United States, will also agree that if on tomorrow the Earth should open and some mighty earthquake should sink into oblivion as has been done in the past, your Seminary standing yonder on the banks of the Cumberland, there could not be found in all the world, a single institution of its kind purchased and owned by a National Baptist Convention. This may be failure, but if such, you class it, then you are lost to find another of which to tell. It will be yours, while here to visit its walls, and walk over its campus and as there you stand in the presence of its beautiful architecture and overlook this city, the Athens of the south, you will observe that nature has favored this hilltop and that the finger of God pointed the way that there might stand an everlasting lighthouse where the generations of tomorrow might come to enlist and be enlightened to do service for the King. If this be failure make the most of it. Last month, here at the Board session, it appeared as if this advantage was to be lost, but I shall never forget how your Board entreated God that we might come here today and point you to your own and I am of the opinion that when you leave Nashville, you will be able to tell those who are waiting your return that the program of Education and religious training written and emphasized and made a reality from Chicago to Nashville has not failed. The record is clear, the record is true and a strange coincident will bear relation here that those who have stood in the front and have given to make possible this Institution are found today harnessed marked contending for its on-going, and the criticisms so bitterly heaped have come from those within our own ranks, and if the record is demanded, it will disclose their sullen attitude to its advancement and their failure to contribute to its success. It is true in the church life and each of you have observed it that in the heights of success the reactionaries find fault and would in their vanity destroy. But thanks be to God the trumpeters have gone forth as did Gideon and have won for Israel to the dismay of the Midianites a victory wonderful in its consequence. You have been the savior and the mighty leaders who have made possible these achievements and your decision, if I do not mistake you, will be to go forward for there are heights yet unattained, battles to be fought and victories to be won. And the Lord spake unto Joshua, saying: "Be strong and of a good courage; for unto this people shalt thou divide for an inheritance the land, which I swore unto their fathers to give them. Only be thou strong and very courageous, that thou mayest observe to do according to all the law, which Moses, my servant, commanded thee; turn not from it to the right hand or to the left, that thou mayest prosper whithersoever thou goest. This book of the Law shall not depart out of thy mouth; but thou shalt meditate therein day and night; that thou mayest observe to do according to all that is written therein; for then thou shalt make thy way prosperous, and then thou shalt have good success." (Joshua 1:6-8) God then reiterates and strengthens the command for thus saith He in the ninth verse: "Have I not commanded thee? Be strong and of good courage; be not afraid, neither be thou dismayed; for the Lord thy God is with thee whithersoever thou goest." These promises to Israel on the banks of the Jordan may well give encouragement and hope to the Christians throughout the Earth. Courage and strength as well as faith are indescribable, infallible, necessaries to the ministers and Christians. The inheritance and possibilities are no less valuable. Consciousness of duty is immortal, but without execution and man's help, the flesh pots of Egypt are still inviting. There must be a keeping of the books of the Laws, they must not depart from our mouths and upon them we are cautioned to meditate day and night and prosperity, like a shining orb unbroken shall emblazon the path not only of the people but the preacher. Fright and dismay shall under the tender touch of our Father's omnipotence vanish into frills and forbiles less attentive than is the grain of sand to the mighty Mogul Engine dashing down the mountainside under the skill of the experienced engineer who knows the time of the arrival of his train and stops only when time permits. We are the engineers and for seven years in the sight of Jericho, we have been coming, but today we stood on time and although humble in our conquest there are those who will hail with delight and an outburst of hallelujah the courage and unchanging valor that has made for our God a name in Israel.

Education

We must educate or we must perish is as true today as yesterday. Every school house is a lighthouse and every successful mariner who would steer clear of the countercurrents and make sure his haven reckons with these obstructions. Look about us and around us and let us pay tribute unmeasured to those now asleep, who opened these doors of hope in the years gone by when slavery fastened its maddened hand and left a trail of superstition and vice in its wake, and kindly invite the assistance and aid of all mankind for no race has attained the zenith where it does not seek and desire the pure and yet unreached heights wherein is kissed down that wisdom unblemished and unsullied often God's own heart. Let us hope that the mighty army of Baptists north and south will yet realize that because we recognize their own obligations to their own that we claim by every right, not only of brotherhood but all that pertains to Christianity, manhood and civilization concurs in that rule untarnished by centuries. "Do unto others as you would have them to unto you." We cannot, however, wait. We have not waited, we go forward today asking assistance but remembering that if from the dust the butterfly would rise, its own efforts are essential and that the winds upon which it sustains itself in its flight gives no assistance except that which comes through its own efforts and that it can never sip from the flower the sweetness thereof until it rises and finds the unfolded blossoms. We have recognized that education is a failure unless it is of a Christian nature, therefore, in this day, we open the doors but declare no man or woman prepared or fit to teach the young or old unless in their own acquirements may be found a recognition of the Bible and of Christ Divine; you are here in arm's reach of the records of Davidson County and the State of Tennessee and if the tongue of the slanderous would have you surmise that perchance the property of your Seminary is so deeded as to question its ownership, go and see for yourself and then you will find that every grain of sand, every brick, every blade of grass and the beautiful trees which stand as nature's adornment are owned by the Baptists of the United States and that the trustees elected by each state in the Union as well as those elected by this Convention at-large hold in trust this property and its ownership can never be questioned; and while I unhesitatingly point to the Publishing Plant as the property of the Baptists of America, I cannot forget that the very individuals who had in charge the making of the deeds were so unprogressive as to resemble the scuttlefish, which through its own mischief and somersaults so befog its course as to become blind in its travels. Our travelogue is clear. The port is before us, we have only to be of good courage and go forward.

Foreign Missions

In the organization of the National Baptist Convention, it was distinctly a school of methods and acquisitions. The annual gathering was a source from which could come lofty information and the presenting of patterns from which the student and the sage might form worthy and beautiful ideas. They had no drams such as now find embodiment in our Constitution. It is true that they saw the whitened fields of Africa and the Islands of the Seas and told of the wretchedness and idolatry that stalked high-handedly in the dense forest as well as the shores, but today we are concerned more than they, for our vision is clear and while we are determined to have the Gospel of our Christ preached from every hilltop, throughout Heathendom, we recognize that in order to keep pace with the industrial moment of this day and generation, we must establish sawmills, brick yards, and raise that line of agriculture which will make independent or kith and kin yonder in the land of the world's first civilization. Out of Africa have come the arts and sciences and we languish far behind them in many of our present and remarkable discoveries. Can we afford to neglect to send them the message that is dearest and all to mankind? The Kingdom of God must be given them. It is in our hands and if we prove recreant the responsibility will fall heavily at our door. Let that day never come when this Convention will be charged with negligence in the care of its foreign or home mission fields and let us today rededicate all that we possibly are to the salvation of the fields that are white unto harvest: The giving of the Gospel of Jesus Christ to another is the highest mission ordained to man. No minister plenipotentiary or ambassador finds in the gift of his redemption a commission such as we, "The spirit of the Lord God is upon me; because the Lord has anointed me to preach good tidings unto the meek, he hath sent me to bind up the broken-hearted to proclaim liberty to the captives and the opening of the prison to them that are bound." Foreign Missions under our Board must be supported and shall occupy the first place in our hearts. This session should make it possible for our beloved Dr. E. D. Hubbard and family to escape those privations under which they are now laboring. Every dollar for foreign missions should be sent through Dr. John H. Frank, our Chairman, and Dr. E. W. Bowen and any distrust shown them is a reflection upon this Convention.

Northern Educational Society

I cannot and will not agree to the organization of any Convention or Society which seeks to divide the forces of the National Baptist Convention. Our program is sufficiently adequate and we challenge the denial that we have not done as we have promised. There was organized throughout the north what is known as an Educational Society co-extensive with the Northern Baptist Convention and they seek to establish a University for the education of our people. To commence with it is not needed for there are institutions of every kind whose doors are open and make welcome those who would seek training in every way and especially first and second-line Christian workers. Why then should an organization seek to put in operation a school of this kind when all around them and about them are just such institutions? It does appear that they would remember that throughout the Southland the same advantages may not be had and they would decide to put forth their energy in building here and not where preparation and arrangements are complete. I unhesitatingly disapproved of the movement and used my limited influence to prevent the saddling of a $250,000 indebtedness upon our people when they might use the same money to assist in fields more urgent. I cannot endorse such a movement nor will I agree to support any Convention which makes itself co-extensive with certain territories. The world belongs to the church and when the limits of our usefulness is confined to any section we are narrow and imitative of a prejudice against which we are struggling; the world is the field of the church and the saving of all mankind its object and it is now too late to circumscribe its labors.

Alien Immersionists

The great church of the Redeemer must be freed and liberated from every semblance of heresy. The landmark handed down by Christ must be followed word-for-word and letter. There must be no inclination because of friendship to lose sight of the doctrines and practices ordained and made sacred by the New Testament. A regenerated church born of the spirit and baptized must be the demand of God's church if it is to take its rightful position in the affairs of men. There must be no compromise. One Lord, One Faith and One Baptism are the three inseparable, unconquerable, unchangeable cardinals upon which we must rise or fall. A Baptist church that will accept into its membership any individual that it knows has not been baptized by a regular ordained Baptist preacher into a regular Baptist church, unchurches itself and should be denied fellowship with churches that are orthodox. It must stand for a baptism ordained of God and by God and that baptism must be regular. May I also call your attention to Union revivals and if my position is unpopular, I fearlessly accept the odium that may come because of my stand. I cannot see how a Baptist Church can unite with any other church in the conducting of a Union revival for as a result there must be a side-stepping of those rules and ethics for which the New Testament is the foundation. It had been better that one true and tried soul should be born anew and have properly instilled the teachings of the Bible than that a thousand through other means should be led into an attitude which finds no endorsement in the Word of God. I do not mean here to lend any assistance to disruption or to influence division and hate. But the rights of the church and its duty as well as the right of the preacher and his duty must be held sacred. Friendship is one thing and the gospel is another.

Sinners in Service

Let me here pause to condemn the course of any Sunday School or pastor who permits an unconverted man or woman to teach the young. It is impossible for an individual who has not acknowledged Christ and who has not publicly accepted him as their Savior to teach them who are in their same plight. No unbeliever can teach a believer, nor can we condone an organist being of service in the church and leading the song service unless they have been converted. It may be true that at times an organist perfectly qualified or a teacher properly qualified may not be convenient, but the day has not come and let us hope that it never will, when the converted sons of God and His daughters cannot find means to praise Him and to tell of His triumphs. Greater, stronger and more influential will be the church of God when she has the world to understand that the cattle upon a thousand hills are His and that recognition of His Son is the first element of usefulness.

Our Sainted Dead

Stepping out of the ship which he so wonderfully manned, our lamented Dr. C. J. W. Boyd at New Orleans went forward on the great ocean of eternity where the soul finds anchor and the seas are not disturbed. His last words were encouraging. It is ours here and now to study his record and emulate those noble virtues he possessed and enlarged. Dr. Kemp, the Secretary of Foreign Mission closed his eyes upon Africa and her whitened fields and went to sleep with his fathers, princely in ambition, courteous to a fault, tender in his sympathies, he followed, hurriedly on and then Dr. James E. Haywood styled the "Weeping Willow" in slumber closed his eyelids and awakened to take up the duties incumbent upon the elders in the land of light. I saw what was mortal of him as it slept beneath a wilderness of flowers brought by loving hands to his memory and I saw then what I now say, it had been ten-thousand times better if while he lived those who loved him most would have touched his inner heart with kindness and scattered in his way those flowers and made less burdensome the task for him. He fought and won. Each of these leaders left families. It is a reflection upon our great denomination that no adequate means are as yet in operation to relieve them of the distress through which they must pass. Let them sleep on and take their rest. We, too, shall soon join them where the wicked cease from troubling and the weary are at rest. Let us like men rise and support our Benefit Board in its efforts to assist these widows. I recommend that every minister attending this Convention will join the Benefit department and pledge five dollars to be paid on the first day of our next Convention to this fund and that the amount raised be equally divided among the widows of the brethren who died in the service of this Convention. Time would fail me to tell of the many whose absence is marked, but in dedicating to their memory our love and attention to their widows and orphans we step forward in the pathway of progression. I hope at this Convention that on Saturday at 5 p.m. we will journey to yonder resting place and unveil a humble monument to the memory of the late Dr. C. J. W. Boyd, who was truly a martyr to the cause of duty.

Restlessness

The world, our own country and our immediate community have acquired a restlessness never in the history of the universe observed. Anarchy and ruin are apparent, monarchs and governments are tottering, war is imminent, peace is nowhere. It is a day of trial, it is observable in every walk of life, the home life has drifted from its moorings of obedience and we stand aghast, wondering what will be the news of tomorrow, lynchings and burnings at the stakes of human beings without judge or jury is a daily occurrence and the Law seems paralyzed and yet it can be accounted for because the hearts of men have not been turned to God. This is distinctly a day of the church and the story of these outrages will never cease to tantalize the minds of the Christians until every pulpit shall become the mouthpiece of our God and the church shall rise in the might of its influence and demand an adherence to the Law and authority. The Dyer Lunch Bill should be passed. It is not a racial matter, it is a question as to whether America, the land of freedom, shall become a bedlam of lawlessness and disorder or crime: Shall be condoned and its citizens protected. President Harding has well called the attention of Congress to these outrages, but the church is the master in the premises. That citizen who goes forward to preserve the flag of this country when it is endangered deserves its protection wherever it unfurls. Let us hope that the day will never come when our people anywhere or at any time will resort to these measures. He who preaches war, strife and hate must perish. It is the Gospel of peace which the world needs and soberness of thought that must lead aright. A right life, rightly lived should win right treatment everywhere and the hand that punishes the innocent for whatever crime is the hand of a felon. "Do unto others as you would have them do unto you" is again the one rule of action.

Our Country

The United States of America is our country. We are citizens by all the laws of consideration. We came by invitation. We have come to stay. Our duty to that flag is the duty to life. Its folds must ever have our respect and our regard and the pages of history do not portray a single incident wherein we have failed in the discharge of our duty. If you scan the pages from the days of the revolutionary wars down to the last mighty conflict when the liberties of the world were in balance, you will find written high upon the scroll our own sons, who went from every quarter of the globe to see that an insatiate ambition did not survive. They fought from Boston to Valley Forge. They stood in the front from Fort Sumpter to Vicksburg. And then they went side-by-side in the glories that came to the Americans at Verdun and Chateau Thierry. They fought that men might be free and that liberty should be the unchallenged right of free men and well did they fight and under nobler flag no man has ever stood. The Stars and Stripes represent the loftiest ideals in the achievement of government and let us never suffer its ridicule or abuse for liberty and justice to all men are the fundamentals upon which it rises. With malice towards none and charity to all, let us ever be found in the rank and file of that patriotic citizenry whose eyes are quickened with the thought that the hand which gives aid and succor to the needy is the hand of right. That God has ordained that together we should live in peace and hasten the coming of His Kingdom when the story of Calvary shall be the story of His creation.

Industry

The races of the Earth are today as never before seeking to engage their young and prepare them for fields of usefulness as that may arise. It is the hour of competency. These are the days of the survival of the fittest. And he who lags and seeks not to improve for the future will be ground into powder. It is true of the church, it is true of the home and it is true of the individual. We must do all that others are doing. Our banks, our drug stores, our grocery stores and various fields of pursuit must not be neglected. Take the Jew of today and while he represents a small percentum of the population, he is yet the financial backbone of the world and the race that can produce a Julius Rosenwald whose hand of liberality and philanthropy touches every schoolroom in America deserves the highest commendation. It is not to be wrought through prejudice nor is it to come about through presumption, but there must be a quiet, dignified, Christian-like observance of our duty. And it is time we were "going-to-it." The world admires the doer. It hates the quitter. I am delighted to tell you that everywhere, north, south, east and west, the new man is finding new fields of labor as new opportunities present themselves, and is grasping them with the idea of giving greater opportunities to his children.

Exodus

Thousands of our people have gone to new fields of endeavor and are facing conditions new in every particular. It is not mine to advise as to the wisdom of their course. Every man has a right to make his home where he chooses. If he desires the hut of the rudest Hottentot or the land of Senigambia that is his privilege. I do not now discuss or differentiate with regard to his choice. I have come to point out the conditions in a large number of cases which affect our denomination. It will show why your church Extension Board should have your support. The population of some cities has been increased five-hundred percentum while the increase of church buildings has not been adequate and as a result, many of the churches of the large cities are overcrowded and there are many true to the denomination who have not joined churches in their adopted home. I hope that you will impress upon those who leave their home to take membership immediately in the cities of their selection. No member of God's church can faithfully discharge his or her duty unless they are united to the church. If these truths are impressed and sent home, the work in the great northwest and elsewhere will be lessened.

Literature

Upon this subject, time has failed me to write. As a man thinketh, so he is; that which one reads, governs much his growth from every aspect. The hope of every race is in its literature. The songs of our fathers and mothers must not be permitted to go unsung. It is difficult to understand how the American Negro in a number of instances will appropriate to himself with delight that which is out of harmony with his past and present and disdain that which is glorious in his past and elevating in his future. Let us keep alive the history our forefathers have made. Let us sing of their triumphs as well as heartaches and let us remember above all else that in preaching the gospel of Jesus Christ those to whom we preach are not giraffes standing twelve feet in height, but at times the lowest in comprehension and therefore must have the gospel given them in a manner easily understood and illustrative in its comprehension.

And now, my brethren, I must conclude. There remains much unsaid about which I should tell. Evangelism is the keynote of the day, the church as never before is seeking the unconquered fields where ignorance and idolatry hold sway. Unto us have been given those wonderful doctrines and gospel by which the world shall be redeemed and we must enter upon the discharge of our duty with a new vision and a determined effort. There must not be any equivocating or the shaping of policies to please men. The God of Abraham, Isaac and Jacob still lives. His ways are past finding out. "Canst thou by searching find out God? Canst thou find out the Almighty unto perfection? It is as high as Heaven what canst thou do? Deeper than Hell, what canst thou know? The measure thereof is longer than the Earth, and broader than the sea." (Job 11:7-9) And so Job under the stress of affliction and woe had absolute confidence in his Maker. He went forth singing his praises and contemplating the hours and years when his soul would be at ease. You, I am sure, had like experiences and have at times condescended to inquire as to the ways of God but they are beyond our limited comprehension. His provisions for our salvation is as yet the question uppermost in our minds and why He should have chosen weak men to go forth in the discharge of such duties when Angels might have been chosen, the student will long ponder and study. And not only has He taken the man, but those selected have been men who possessed some inconsistency or fault. From the days of Abraham down to the present, the mightiest of the gospel defenders have found their pathways at times obstructed by the enemies of progress. But under every ordeal and circumstance they have unflinchingly stemmed the tide and made the name of the blessed Christ the name of Salvation. His name must be lifted up. It is the Name above names. It is a Name that brings adoration and makes souls realize that it was born to live not in Earth but above the Earth. It is the Name that stands on the shores of Galilee and then quietly walks upon the sea and speaks with authority and the maddened sea becomes as quiet as the tempest and as lovely as a bed of roses. It is He whose Divinity marks the fall of the sparrow, takes charge of the church in its infancy and follows her through the wilderness of despair until she reaches the goal of hope and lifts the banner up of a conquering King that men may worship everywhere. He so dispenses His love that the Earth may find in Him a common Father. And where the children of men are dispersed and divided, and the rattling guns of that are pouring their shot into the army of His believers, His voice is heard above the conflict saying, "Peace be still. It is I." Go down into the land of Moab and see the prophetic mastering in that land and turning the heart of Ruth in order that the Bible may be fulfilled. Here Naomi when two of her sons have fallen asleep and are resting in the bosom of the land of Moab when she decides that she will leave this land where she has come and had been for years and return to the land of Bethlehem, Judea and observe Ruth as she follows her mother-in-law and says to her, "Entreat me not to leave or to return from following after thee: For whither thou goest, I will go, and where thou lodgest, I will lodge, thy people shall be my people and thy God my God. Where thou diest, will I die, and there will I be buried, the Lord do so to me and more also, if ought but death part thee and me." (Ruth 1:16-17) Ruth with her splendid qualities and unmatched ideals has enriched woman and made her name the jewel that adorns man's crown and if all the women that should live in the hereafter would become degenerates the fact that Ruth lived and fearlessly walked forth in following would yet break in luster over woman's pathway such as to enlighten and make her capable in redemption. It appears to me that you who have come up to Nashville have come to the same conclusion that found such an exposition in the utterance of Ruth. "Entreat me not to leave thee or from following after thee." And then as Naomi starts down through the wilderness, I see Orpha when she kisses her farewell and returns to the land of Moab and her name is forgotten and seldom mentioned. Those who falter and turn back or swerve from duty are generally weak from vision. I thank God for the men whom I have met and whom I know on this convention floor who are decisive in their conviction. You have made possible this Convention. You are going up to the land that God has provided for His people. It does not matter if the hissing of serpents are heard along the way, your ultimate is the land of Bethlehem of Judea. Naomi reaches home and by her side is found Ruth and they spend the hours of anxiety together. And soon this daughter-in-law, this woman of faith, this woman of conviction, and this mighty intrepid soul after whom the world may take pattern goes forth to glean and soon she becomes the wife of Boaz and unto them is born Obed and in the line comes Jesse and then follows David and thus she makes akin the world and out of this same lineage is born the King whose Name shall be called Wonderful Counselor, the mighty God, and whose throne shall be eternal in the Heavens. And as we go marching sometimes observing obstructions and impediments, let us not forget that the battle is not to the swift neither to the strong but to him that endureth to the end. The battle is on, the results are sure. On our heads have been placed the helmets of salvation and like the Leader who bleeds and blesses we should go forth, suffering, remembering that under the Cross may be found the crown. The mistakes that we have made during these seven years have been many. They have been errors of the head and not the heart and today as I close this address, if on this floor can be found a single minister to whom I have gone who will charge that I have preached other than Jesus and Him crucified and endeavored to increase their opportunities to make good, I am ready now to hand back to you this emblem of authority which you without solicitation handed me seven years ago. You handed it to me when the storm was raging, when the onslaught of many seemed as if death lurked in the pathway. I accepted it because I believed you were right. Because I believed that God had ordained that every man should serve God to the dictates of his own conscience. Because I believed that you would follow as you have followed when right was the guiding star. And I come now to thank you for these honors which I did not deserve. To thank you for the unstinted support which you have given me from sea to sea and if I have contributed my modicum in the outreach and uplift of the church of God, I shall be satisfied. I hand back to you this gavel and upon it has fallen nothing that would besmirch or betray the trust which you imposed. Your Convention at that time was torn into dissention; today we meet under the auspices far different from seven years ago. A wonderful institution, insured for forty-five thousand dollars, marks the pathway along which we have endeavored to travel. I have preached and told the story of your advancement until thousands are today awaiting the results of this meeting. I count it a happy privilege to be a humble servant following with you in the vanguard of that mighty army who believes in the triumph of the Nazarene. Many of those whose hearts were welded into the compact when we stood for liberation have gone down and have taken their places mortally in their windowless palace. One by one we too will cross the Great Divide and shall make our resting place in the bosom of our Maker. Let us here today forget all differences. Decide that we are brothers, decide that as Christians, we cannot allow ambition to destroy another. Decide that in our heart of hearts envy shall be struck down with the bludgeon of love and that we will erect not only yonder's mighty temple of education but that we will build an everlasting monument, a monument of love in the hearts of men of this Convention. Let us hold no ill-will to those who may differ with us upon matters of polity. But let us at the same time declare that the principles for which we fought at Chicago are as dear today as they were in 1915. That a Baptist church is its own sovereign power that nobody can legislate for its government and that all the attempts of men in the past have failed to subject and bring her to shame. Remember that the mighty Christ taught us that in Him was all power, that He was the Giver of Life, and we should follow Him and that in our day and generation, we should work while it is day for the night cometh when no man can work. Three-millions of unterrified Baptists are watching results at this meeting and it is up to us to demonstrate that capacity, and brain and ability are not exceptions in the ranks of the Baptist preachers. Let us get together, let us drive home the facts of our program. Our program is constructive. Our program is fixed. Our program is being executed, and as we plow through opposition, let us remember: It is easy to criticize and find fault, but few are those who can do better. Forgetting the things that are behind, let us press on to the mark of a high calling in Christ Jesus. Sing and pray and work and the victory must come.

John Edmund Wood

John Edmund Wood (1867-1929) was born near Glasgow in Barren County, Kentucky, May 21, 1867. He accepted Christ at the age of twelve and was called to the Gospel ministry at the age of seventeen. He attended the public schools of Barren County and Glasgow. He was an honor graduate of Kentucky State Normal Institute. He received the Doctor of Divinity degree from the National Correspondence College, Vincennes, Indiana in 1903, and from State University, Louisville, Kentucky in 1908. He was a faithful minister of the Gospel for forty-five years and taught school during the time he pastored at Munfordville, Woodsonville, Bardstown, and Elizabethtown. He held teacher institutes throughout the state and conducted private and summer schools. He was President of the Kentucky Negro Educational Associates.

He was united in marriage to Miss Ella B. Redd of Munfordville, February 19, 1891. Of this union, five children were born: Iola Orontes Soders, John Franklyn, Frances Ophelia, Semmoir Ellsworth, and Marguerite Virginia. He was called to the pastorate of the First Baptist Church, Danville, Kentucky in June, 1898. He served for a number of years as President of the South District Sunday School Convention, State Grand Chief, and National Grand Chief of the Independent Order of Good Samaritans. He was moderator of the General Association of Kentucky Baptists for nine years, and for more than twenty-six years, he edited and published, *The Torch Light*, a weekly newspaper.

For thirty-five years, he served as Secretary of the South District Baptist Association; thirty-one years as pastor of First Baptist Church of Danville; twenty years as a trustee of State University of Louisville, Kentucky; six years as President of the National Baptist Convention of America. He was a member of the City Council of Danville for many years.

He died December 15, 1929 at 1:40 P.M. at the age of sixty-two years, six months, twenty-four days.

Annual Address of Dr. J. E. Wood
President of the National Baptist Convention of America
In session at Kansas City, Missouri, September 9, 1925

Dear Brethren in Christ:

We assemble here today from all parts of this great country, a land which bears the name, Christian; to meditate upon things pertaining to the kingdom of Christ. To sit down with the sons of God is a distinction angels might well covet. Not a seat among Wall Street bankers, or in the American Bar Association, or in the Senate of the United States, or in the English Parliament, is to be compared with a place where the disciples of Christ gather to wait before Him, and receive orders from Him.

It is highly fitting at this time of unrest and agitation, that the followers of Him who calmed the seas and hushed the tempest should gather to receive marching orders, that they may go forth to do His will. Millions wait in breathless suspense to hear what message we bear from the Lord; and our action in this assembly will leave our constituents in the valley of despair, or will lift them up into the realms of light and hope and good cheer. May we say to them, the morning dawns with joy and resplendent glory.

I am conscious of the fact that I am not addressing a class of adventurers, money plungers, or followers of the *ignis fatuus* lights of pleasure; but sane and sober men and women of God who wait before the throne to hear their Lord's command, that they may obey. When Jesus Christ commissioned His church to carry the glad tidings to every creature, He laid upon her a task more important and farther reaching in its import than King John's Magna Charta, Jefferson's Declaration of Independence, or Lincoln's Emancipation Proclamation. No edict from any world potentate approaches in importance and dignity the command of our Lord to His followers. And, our coming together here should be for the sole purpose of evolving plans for the effectual prosecution of our mission. It is a pleasure to address such an assemblage. I am inspired by the thought that I am speaking to men with but one purpose — to secure the rule of Christ, and who seek no honor but to make Him King.

This Convention was born of the spirit of love and loyalty to our Lord and His cause, which inspired the work of its founders; and it is kept alive by the same fires which burn in the bosoms of the sons of those noble sires. And the work of organizing the Negro Baptist forces of this country into a national organization, begun nearly a half century ago, for the purpose of spreading gospel truth, and establishing the kingdom in every land, shall not fail till truth shall die, and love perishes and loyalty becomes a delusion and a snare. With trumpet sound, the call to service comes to Baptist leadership everywhere among our people. When every conceivable appeal is made to the emotions, the conscience, and the judgement of our people, the Christian statesmanship, and intelligence and heroism are taxed to guide the Christian ship safely through the turbulent waters of heresies and infidelity and false teachings.

Ulysses, returning to his home from the Trojan war must pass the shores where the sirens with their sweet song and the exposure of their beautiful forms sought to allure the mariners to their death. This is the song they sing:

> "O stay! O pride of Greece, Ulysses, stay!
> O Cease thy course and listen to our lay!
> Blest is the man ordained our voice to hear;
> The Song instructs the soul and charms the ear.
> Approach! Thy soul shall into raptures rise!
> Approach and learn new wisdom from the skies!"

Ulysses, knowing how false was the song and how weak the human heart, chained himself to the ship mast, and filled the ears of his sailors with wax. Only by this was he able to escape the sirens' seductive wooings. And he describes the struggle thus:

> "So sweet the charmers warble o'er the main,
> My soul takes wing to meet the heavenly strain;
> I give the sign and struggle to be free;
> Swift row my mates and shoot along the sea.
> New chains they add, and rapid urge the way,
> 'Till dying off, the distant sounds decay."

The sirens' song is heard in the land today. They seek to lure you from the beaten paths of duty and the highway of service and honor. With beautiful phrases and smooth speech, they picture fantastic fields and most precious treasures. I warn you, bind yourself with the golden cords of love and devotion, to the mast of the ship of obligation and opportunity; and let the hope of achievement and conquest in the battle for truth and righteousness stop your ears against their entrancing song and false pleadings. This Convention is established by Negro Baptists for the purpose of maintaining and operating Baptist enterprises to the glory of God and the good of mankind. To this task, let us dedicate all our powers — our talent, our influence and our means.

Our Program

We have not come here to mark time. We must give account to God, to our constituents and to an intelligent thinking world for every moment, every emotion, every word spoken and every act performed while in this city. The eyes of twelve-million Negroes, yea, of all the world are upon us. If we come here, make a few big speeches, sign up a lot of pledges never intended to be kept, sound a trumpet's blast of boasting and self-praise and then go home to repose in imaginary honor and delusive victory, this gathering will prove a miserable failure. Nothing short of a constructive program which will put every phase of our denomination's work squarely before the world, will satisfy the demands made upon present day religious organizations. Persons who think in our denomination and out of it, want to know our purpose and the methods we have adopted to attain that purpose. If we have a recipe for Earth's ill, we must give it out, and if it proves efficacious, the world will accept it. Someone said, "If a man makes a sewing machine or a mouse trap or builds a university that is better than any other person has made, though he live in the desert, the world will make a beaten path to his house." Whom we may attract to this Convention, and the support we may receive for our enterprises, will depend upon the character of the work we shall perform.

Our program must include a campaign of information. If we are to obtain favor with men the world must know the history and achievements of Baptists; and what this Convention as a Baptist organization purposes. In the past, Baptist contribution to the world's civilization and advancement have been large and munificent. In missions, in education, and in good government and social uplift, Baptists occupy front rank. William Carey was the father of Modern Missions, and Judson, Rich, Beebee Wallis and Dr. Andrew Fuller, all Baptists, were comrades and companions of Carey in laying the foundation for that movement, the mere mention of which stirs the heart of all Christendom. Baptists stand in this country second to none in the promotion of Christian education. The first money ever received for an endowment for Harvard College was from a Baptist, and the Hollis family — Baptists — were among its most liberal donors. Its first two presidents — Henry Dunster and Charles Chausen

— were Baptists, and President Quincy said of them, for learning and talent they were surpassed by no one of their successors. Their great colleges — Brown, Vassar, Newton, Crosier, and many others — stand as monuments to Baptist educational sentiments. And, while these institutions have been established and maintained by white Baptists, Negro Baptists, when measured by their wealth, their opportunities and their numbers are not far behind their white brethren in matters of educational activities. Virginia Seminary, Simmons University, Selma University, Guadalupe College and others are living expressions of Baptist interests in education. Among educators and race leaders, Baptists take first rank. Brawley, M. W. Gilbert, Purce, Simmons, Booker T. Washington, and others no less illustrious than they form a brilliant array that shall illumine the pages of Baptist history through all coming time.

The foregoing record of noble achievements forms the background for our future activities. Are we willing, are we capable of erecting a temple of high aspiration, of duty well done, of worthy victories, upon the foundation already laid?

As we stand in this holy presence can we hear the voice of Him who rules the sea and governs the winds and weighs the mountains, and rules in the governments as He cries out: "Speak to the people that they go forward."

> "No waters can swallow the ship where lies
> The Master of ocean and earth and skies;
> They all shall sweetly obey His will:
> Peace be still, peace be still."

Cooperation Among Baptists

When Jesus Christ prayed that believers might be one, His desire was that they should be one in faith, one in love, and one in purpose. All of His true and loyal followers desire such unity. We court it; we pray for it; we believe it shall come. And we stand ready to go the full length of Bible teachings, and Bible living to hasten the day. In seeking such unity, however, we are willing to recognize Jesus Christ only as Lord and to recognize all His followers as common brethren. We join hands with any Baptist or any group of Baptists in exalting the reigning Christ and are willing to cooperate with all Baptist organizations in making present day society just what Jesus Christ would have it be. We call upon Incorporated Baptists, Lott Carey Convention Baptists, Northern Baptists, Southern Convention Baptists, and in the great hosts of Baptists, white and black, affiliated with no national organizations; we call upon them all to cooperate with us, and we are willing to cooperate with them in the spreading of the gospel to the ends of the earth. But we purpose to operate on terms of absolute equality and fraternity; and we spurn and consider as an affront any attempt or suggestions to have us surrender our independence and God-given Baptist liberty, before we shall be considered as New Testament Baptists, standing before God and men as followers of Him who said, "One is your Master, even Jesus, and all ye are brethren." The attitude of some of our brethren to unite all Baptists reminds me of one of Dr. Booker T. Washington's stories. He said there was a family in which the husband and wife were continually quarreling and fighting. The pastor was called in to quiet their differences, and he counseled them to live in peace and each seek the other's happiness. Said he, "You must remember that you are one." "That is the point," the husband broke in, "and I cannot make my wife see that I am that one." Some of the people who talk loud about union, want to be the union.

Some of our white brethren who have undertaken to assist Negro Baptists to do missionary and educational work seem to confine their help to Negro Baptists belonging to a certain Convention. We do not question the good intention and sincerity of these brethren; but it is our candid opinion that these white Baptists will do little to extend the kingdom among Negroes, till they are willing to include all Negro Baptists in their program.

We regard as significant the following clipping from the *Baptist Advance*:

> "What sort of a mess would we have in the South if most of the Negroes were Catholics?
>
> As a matter of fact, most of the Negroes who are religious at all are Baptists, and that one thing has been worth more to the South than we can estimate. Suppose most of them had been Catholics instead of Baptist. And who can say that it will always be true that most of them are Baptists? Who can say the time will never come when most of them will be Catholics? Who can say that such a time may not come soon? If it should come, would it not make race relation much worse and much harder to handle? The fact that we may not consider such questions will not dispose of the questions or reduce their importance. The fact that we refuse to consider them may increase their importance and make them harder to solve. Certainly the present situation demands that Baptists, of all people, give attention to the religious interest of the Negroes. We can keep them if we will;

> we may lose them if we neglect them. And if Christ has any interest in them, certainly Baptists ought to be interested in them."

While Negro Baptists in the South, we believe, will continue to increase in numbers, and will be strengthened in the faith and in the practice of New Testament principles. Their confidence in and cooperation with white Baptists in the future must rest upon more than mere sentimentality. Whether our white brethren shall prove a help or a hindrance to the progress of Negro Baptists depends upon their intelligence, the Christ spirit and the sincerity with which they approach the solution of this problem.

It is the hope of all thinking Baptists that there shall be formed such cooperation as will build up a Christian citizenship which will insure stable and munificent government and evangelical church membership. The missionary activities among Negro Baptists that will bear good fruit must be work which will enlighten, inspire confidence and strengthen in the faith all Baptists, and the conditions upon which aid is given must be loyalty to Baptist teaching and practice, and not necessarily allegiance to any particular convention or association, for a convention is not a denomination. One outstanding principle for which we contend is "liberty in all matters of conscience; loyalty in all matters of New Testament truth."

Our Compact With the Lott Carey Brethren

At the last session of this Convention, a plan of cooperation was entered into with the Lott Carey Convention by which the two organizations would be able to do kingdom work more economically and effectively. Under this plan we agree to do foreign mission work through the Board of the Lott Carey Convention, said convention agreeing to so amend its constitution as to admit members of this Convention to hold membership in that board. The said Lott Carey Convention agreed and pledged itself, as far as its authority holds, to support, and urge the churches affiliating with that Convention to support the other objects of our Convention, viz.: our Home Mission Work, our Educational Work and our Publishing House. This plan of cooperation, though in its embryonic state, is already bearing fruit; and we have the most sanguine hope that at no distant day Negro Baptists will have the greatest Foreign Missionary program of any Negro denomination in the world. And we confidently expect that through this cooperation we may double our Home Mission Work, and greatly increase our publication enterprise. We believe this compact was entered in good faith by the parties concerned, and, if there are any weaknesses or defects in it, all stand ready to make such amendments as shall secure justice and equality to all concerned. Let it be known this day that all parties to this compact seek only the glory of Christ Jesus and no man is seeking human greatness or worldly honor.

In view of this plan of cooperation by which Foreign Mission activities among Baptists will be greatly increased, we recommend that our Foreign Mission Board will give its attention largely to the dissemination of information and to creating sentiment among all Baptists. Being well known among our churches, this Board will be able to render the new Foreign Mission Board invaluable service in the collection of funds for the enlarged work. We recommend that our Home Mission Board request of the Lott Carey Convention a roster of the churches affiliated with that Convention and seek to enlist those churches in our Home Work. And above all, let the most unbounded love and good fellowship prevail among these affiliating brethren.

Our Seminary

If Baptists would keep apace the onward march of Christian civilization, they must establish and support schools and colleges for the training of Christian leadership. Recognizing this well established truth, the leaders in this Convention, headed by the matchless churchman, the far-seeing pathfinder and God's man of vision, Richard Henry Boyd, purchased the Boscobel property in Nashville, Tennessee, as a foundation upon which Negro Baptists might build an educational institution for the training of men and women for service. It seems to me that securing this property at the small cost for which it was contracted was a gift from God; but while it is a gift from God, it is also a test of our ability to seize an opportunity when presented, and our sacrifice and loyalty under trying ordeals. It also appears to me that the mere mentioning of the demands of this obligation upon the Negro Baptists would be enough to inspire real Baptist men and women to rise up in this Convention today and lay on the tables money sufficient to satisfy the notes held against the property of our school. Twenty-thousand dollars is not an unreasonable sum to request of the progressive, enlisted, and militant Baptist army here assembled. The church people, the leaders in education, the public-spirited men and women, watch to see if we have vision and public spirit and self-sacrifice and heroism enough to do the big thing. The electric wires tingle to bear the message around the world; the newspapers wait to publish it to the ends of the earth, that Negro Baptists assembled in Kansas City have kept faith with the people who trusted them and redeemed their pledge to a great cause by laying down in cash the largest contribution to Christian education ever made by any gathering of Negro Christians. May we say today:

> "And if I should make some resolve,
> And duty did not call;
> I love my God with zeal so great
> That I should give Him all."

That no great undertaking can be carried to a successful conclusion without extensive publicity is a fact too well attested to be questioned. The plan of Christ to push the banner of salvation to the ends of the earth was through intensive advertising. Every great business concern, all the political parties, hope to win the populace to their cause by publishing what they have to offer. The promoter of the baseball, the moving picture, and the beauty culturist, all advertise their business. Shall the children of this world be wiser than the children of light? Religious organizations everywhere are recognizing the power in the printed page. White Baptists, North and South, have inaugurated campaigns to put their church papers into every family. Other denominations are as equally aggressive in this matter. Shall we lag behind? I call upon every Baptist preacher in this Convention to pay for and read the National Baptist *Union Review* and to urge his constituents subscribe for it. It would be a handsome thing for the manager of this worthy paper to receive two-thousand dollars in new subscriptions during the sitting of this Convention. I make this plea not to help the *Review* primarily, but to help the Convention. Every person who reads the *Review* and pays for it gets more out of it than he puts into it. And, then, this paper has been the courageous champion of the Convention's causes from the beginning. There has never been a night so dark but that she stood like a great light house, on the rock-bound coast of the troubled seas, guiding the old Baptist ship with all her precious treasures into the safe haven of security and peace. Let us stand by her; let us bless her with our praise and prayers; let us defend her with our money; let us extend her influence by putting the National Baptist *Union Review* into every Negro Baptist home in America.

Recommendations

The future greatness and permanent usefulness of this Convention depend upon the thorough cultivation of the field. To have a Convention composed of delegates from the large cities and densely populated districts only will never accomplish the thing for which a national organization is established, viz.: uniformity of action and the permanent welfare of the whole denomination. The influence of this Convention should be felt in every church, and the humblest community in the remotest district should be awakened and blest by our activities.

1. Therefore, we recommend that the territory covered by the denomination be divided into three regional districts with a regional secretary in each district who will devote his entire time to the cultivation of the denomination spirit; giving out information and organizing our forces for effective service.

2. We also recommend that a representative of this Convention be appointed in every State whose duties it will be to keep the objects of the Convention before the people of that State, especially the work of missions and Christian education. Where it can be done to the satisfaction of all concerned, we suggest that the Convention cooperate with the State organization in the appointment of such a representative and the two organizations go fifty-fifty on his salary; where this cannot be done satisfactorily, we suggest that this Convention appoint the person and become responsible for his salary.

3. We recommend that these representatives be under the control and direction of the Home Mission Board and that they shall make monthly reports to the Corresponding Secretary of this Board.

4. We recommend that the Statistician be called upon to prepare and present to the Convention, for public distribution, a report touching all Negro Baptist statistics, and especially statistics pertaining to this Convention. That the necessary funds be appropriated to finance this work.

Conclusion

And, now, brethren, we have not attempted to deal in generalities, or to follow in the path of the theorist; but have striven to present some practical suggestions which we hope may inspire us to high and holy things, and guide our minds in grasping the situation which confronts us and dealing with the problems of the day in such an honest and courageous manner as to insure victory. May God seize hold upon each soul here with such a grip as will not let us go till we have put His cause upon a permanent basis that will secure its future. We must deal with our denominational problems, as God's plans and purposes; and not as mere exigencies and man-made policies for the emergency. God's purposes are eternal; He may be ten-thousand years producing a diamond from a cart load of coal soot; but He will neither be hurried in His process, nor frightened from His task; and when it is finished, it will be perfect. And, so, men who would construct a program under God must make their program after God's conception and attributes. My brethren, we can never construct a big Baptist program till that program by God's grace has been formed within us. Let God's kingdom be planted in you and let it grow out as the flowers blossom from the tiny seed planted in the garden walk. When by the grace of God your soul becomes infected with the germ of missions, and world evangelization and Christian training, it will not be a task for you to give your time, and your prayers, and your talent and your money to these causes.

We must have vision. "Lift up your eyes and look on the field." A lady went to her occulist and complained that she could not see at a distance; things were blurred. The doctor asked her what she did. She said she spent her time crocheting. Well, said the doctor, you have confined your eyes to your work till you are growing near-sighted. Every day spend some time in looking at objects in the distance; the far-away mountains and the landscapes and the clouds. She followed these directions and soon her eyes were restored to normal conditions. Many persons have centered their attention on themselves, their pet theories, their selfish advancement, till they cannot see the larger cause. There are persons who are absorbed in a good cause, but the objects of their devotion are not the best; hence the good hinders the best. You are at your best when you are serving all the objects of the Convention in a harmonious and uniform way.

As leaders we must use wisdom, and judgment and precision. We must not permit our feelings to carry us away from the straight and narrow road of duty. A leader must even do the unpopular thing, which will sometimes bring down upon his head the wrath of the populace; but he must be true to his conscience, to the people whom he leads, and to his God from whom he has his commission. Lincoln's war policy not only made him unpopular in the South, but many of the Northern politicians and statesmen condemned him. However, many who cursed him in 1861, adore him in 1925.

My brother, can you not see God's holy church, the Lamb's wife, the bride, as she stands with bleeding hands and feet, and amazed countenance, and weeping eyes and trembling limbs, while a mocking world taunts, and harasses and defies her commission to rescue mankind from hell's enthraldom? Does not the scene move every born-again man and woman here assembled to enlist and carry the blessed gospel to all nations?

A little girl was shown a picture of Jesus Christ standing in Pilate's hall, with His hands tied behind Him, and the cruel soldiers were whipping Him with knotted whips as the blood spurted out from His quivering flesh. As this little girl looked her eyes filled with tears and she exclaimed: "Oh mama, why doesn't some one untie His hands?" When I contemplate the big task before the Master, and the assaults made upon Him by the infidel, the atheist, the agnostic, and the modernist; and how the disloyalty and indifference and worldliness of His professed followers tie His hands, in sadness my soul cries out: "Why don't you untie His hands?"

Ella Wheeler Wilcox has said:

> "Give and thou shalt receive. Give thought of cheer,
> Of courage and success to friend and stranger,
> And from a thousand sources, far and near,
> Strength will be sent thee, in thy hour of danger."
>
> "Give words of comfort, of defense and hope,
> To mortals crushed by sorrow and by error,
> And though thy feet through shadowy paths may grope,
> Thou shalt not walk in loneliness and terror."
>
> "Give of thy gold, though small thy portion be,
> Gold rusts and shrivels in the hand that keeps it;
> It grows in one that opens wide and free
> Who sows his harvest is the one who reaps it."
>
> "Give of thy love, nor wait to know the worth
> Of what thou lovest; and ask no returning,
> And wheresoe'er thy pathway leads on earth,
> There thou shalt find the lamp of love-light burning."

Our Sainted Dead

Since our last session in Chicago, death has invaded our ranks and removed from earth's serious conflict to heaven's peaceful shores some of the most faithful and aggressive workers in the Convention. Among them may be mentioned Dr. Edward P. Jones, for seven years the honored President, a man of rare gifts, of stalwart integrity, of high Christian character and undaunted courage. He fell on sleep, Monday, December 1, 1924, and went to rest with other warriors who waited his coming in the city of unclouded day. Dr. S. E. Piercy, another strong defender of the faith and an ardent supporter of this Convention, went home, Monday, July 27. These intrepid warriors laid down their armor, put off their sword and shield and went sweeping through the gates to join R. H. Boyd, John F. Thomas, J. W. Haywood, and that mighty galaxy of illustrious names whose worthy deeds and high achievements we shall ever hold in fondest memory.

And now, my brethren, I solicit your love and devotion and loyalty to the cause dear to the heart of millions of Baptists on earth and in heaven, who watch our deliberations and pray that we fail not. Shall not the thought of the responsibility resting upon us inspire us to noblest endeavors. Relying upon divine guidance and with confidence in the Baptist brotherhood, let us go forward to dare to do and to die that the banner of truth and righteousness shall never trail in the dust.

> "All may be heroes:
>
> 'The man who rules his spirit,' saith the voice
> Which cannot err, 'is greater than the man
> Who takes a city.' Hence it surely follows,
> If each would govern wisely, and thus show
> Truth, courage, knowledge, power, benevolence,
> And all the princely soul in private virtues;
> Then each would be a prince, a hero greater;
> He will be man in likeness of his Maker!"

Annual Address of Dr. J. E. Wood
President of the National Baptist Convention of America
In Session at Indianapolis, Indiana, September 8, 1926

My Brethren in Christ:

> "A beautiful statue stood in the market place of an Italian city. It represented a Grecian maiden of graceful form, beautiful face, and noble expression. One day, an unkempt, sloven girl came face to face with the statue. She gazed at it in wonder and admiration. It stirred long-dormant instincts within her. 'I can be like that, she said to herself. 'Something in me tells me so.' She went home, washed her face, and combed her tangled locks. The next day she went to the market place and gazed long at the statue, and then went home and washed and mended her tattered garments. Thereafter, day by day she changed. She straightened her shoulders, her form became graceful, her face became radiant and refined, till by and by she transformed into the likeness of the statue."

So many of us coming to this convention see Jesus only during our stay in this city—behold His loving face, His generous spirit, His supremely holy character, till we shall go from here filled with light, love, and life, that men may see: "They have been with Jesus."

Before us lie duty, opportunity and blessings. Shall we be keen enough of comprehension to discern our duty, wise enough to sense our opportunity, and humble enough before His throne to receive the blessings? That one among us who will understand that he who recognizes this occasion to serve the denomination, humanity, and his God, is the greatest among us; will answer the oft-repeated question: What good is a National Baptist Convention? He will pour out his selfish ambition, empty himself of all spirit, of vain glory, and lay his ability, his influence, and his money on the altar to be used of God. He will be found wanting never where duty calls; he will never stand idle when great tasks are to be done.

The ties of love, which bind the hearts of men and women in this Convention into a glorious unity and fellowship, demonstrate the teachings of that beautiful Psalm which says: "Behold, how good and how pleasant it is for brethren to dwell together in unity." Those loyal and self-sacrificing servants of Jesus Christ, who have sponsored the cause of this Convention, who have followed its fortunes in sunshine and shadow, who have sought not their own glory and personal advancement, but have labored to advance the glory of His Cross, stand out today as great heroes in Christian endeavor and brilliant achievements. Some of them have fallen fighting in the ranks, but their lives and labors form a blazing milky way from Earth's toils to Heaven's joys. They labored in their sectors on this great and eternal temple on which we are building and their memory should awaken in our bosoms the spirit to dare, to do and to die, that the banner of the Cross shall wave in every land and among all nations.

The world has a right to expect of us great things today; big things spiritually, big things Godly, big things financially. We shame and outrage the persons who have trusted us and have chosen us to represent them in matters pertaining to the Kingdom if we fail to do a work in this Convention commensurate with our resources, our abilities and our numbers. Shall we fail the cause which we represent? Shall we fail the thousands of Baptists throughout this country looking this way today? Shall we disappoint supporters and admirers? Had I the erudition of a Paul, the language of a Beecher, the oratory of a Webster and the fiery eloquence of a Patrick Henry, I would plead the cause of man's redemption and the call to Christian service before you, till all who sit before me this day would stand upon their feet and swear eternal allegiance to the Kingdom of Christ and bring their possessions—their abilities, their talents, their influence, and their all—and lay them on the altar to be used of Him in reclaiming and sanctifying a lost world.

At the beginning of the year, a group of young ministers sat down for a conference to consider the worthwhile things to claim their attention for 1926. Growing out of that conference, these ministers agreed upon four objectives for which they would ask their congregations to work during the year. These objectives are: Unity of Purpose, Universal Peace, the Proper Adjustment of Inter-Racial Relations, and Personal Evangelism. These objectives, possibly rearranged in their importance, will challenge the thought and sympathy of all thoughtful disciples of Jesus Christ. In order of importance, we might consider: Unity of Purpose, Personal Evangelism, Proper Adjustment of Inter-Racial Relations, and Universal Peace. To our way of thinking, Unity of Purpose is highly important as the essential in all Christian activities and it is secured only by the surrender of our will into the will of Jesus Christ. It can be said of us that we are of one mind, only when we have the mind of Christ.

If we are here today to do His Will, if there be in our hearts a desire that the things shall be accomplished which He wants accomplished. If we are willing to do anything, to be anything, to suffer anything for His glory, each and every one of us possessing this spirit, then we are a unit of purpose. Personal Evangelism is second in importance. Not only the future of the church, but the future of the world's civilization depends upon personal evangelism. Christianity got her big start in the first century through the activities of saved men who made the saving of others a personal duty. My only hope of the world's redemption socially, commercially, politically, is through the teachers of Jesus Christ. As valuable as may be the work of secular education, as useful as may be the service which the community workers and the social reformer render society, if the Gospel of Jesus Christ is left out, these efforts will be ineffectual in rendering any lasting good to the human race. The Gospel of Christ alone is God's saving power and if mankind is to be saved—the African, the Indian, the Chinaman, the Caucasian—it must be saved through this Gospel. The recognition of this eternal truth lays upon every disciple of Jesus Christ the stupendous task of subsidizing every resource to spread the Gospel among all peoples.

May whatever we attempt here have for its ultimate aim the making of Jesus known to all the world.

Much is being said and done nowadays about adjusting inter-racial relations. Pulpit and press, church and state, are giving much attention to this important subject, but I see no solution to this problem outside of the Gospel. To attempt to adjust relations between man-to-man, race-to-race, class-to-class, upon any other basis than the teaching of Jesus Christ, is the sheerest folly. Until the disciples of Jesus Christ accept all saved men and women on equal terms in the scale of brotherhood, the preachments of the adjustment of inter-racial relations is a delusion. A minister told us recently of an experience in his life. He had been raised in the North and called to pastor an influential church in the South. He knew a cultured, consecrated Negro preacher and had heard him address large audiences of white and black, even the Southern Baptist Convention. So he said to him, if in his travel, he ever passed his way, he would be glad to have him preach to his congregation. Some months afterward, he was advised that this Negro minister would be passing through his city, and so he said to his officers that he would be glad to make an appointment for him. These officers advised him that they did not think that their people would understand his inviting this Negro to speak from his pulpit and suggested that the city auditorium would be the more logical place in which to have him speak.

Court houses and city auditoriums meet on equal terms and listen to speakers of different races with much jubilation in political campaigns and prohibition campaigns, and these same folks would call a halt if it were undertaken to hold a soul-saving campaign under similar conditions. Can the race question and the adjustment of inter-racial relations ever be solved satisfactory to the teachings of Jesus Christ as long as the church and the Gospel ministry and the missionaries of all races and people cannot meet on a common level in all Christian work manifesting the same fellowship and spirit of co-operation the men of the world show in secular affairs? Doctor Booker T. Washington in his lifetime, used to tell a story of a Southern planter who said to his Negro servant that the white people of that section were putting on an advertising campaign to induce the moneyed men of the country to buy lands and come into the south. The Negro servant said, "Boss, I am opposed to that proposition." The land owner wanted to know his objection. "Well," said the Negro, "We Negroes have as many white folks down here as we can take care of." Until there is a change of heart and purpose and practice in many of the professed followers of Jesus Christ, the church is suffering today from an over-abundance of church members. The church has lost much of its prestige, not because of the attacks of atheists and infidels, but because of the inconsistency of its own members in dealing with inter-racial matters; and the inconsistency is not all on one side of the house. Until the Negro Christian shall practice love and kindness toward all races, regardless of the attitude of those races toward him, he is not prepared to criticize others for their attitudes. In truth, it is far better to manifest proper Christian spirit toward others than it is to receive this manifestation from others, when in our hearts there is hate and malice. The one who hates degrades himself much more than he degrades the one whom he hates. Love and kindness and goodwill are the weapons by which we shall conquer this country. Our blessed Lord, though often reviled, reviled not again, and His followers will win by following the path He trod. In a recent speech, Mr. Darrow, of Chicago, asked the question, "Why did not Daniel's God and the God that saved the Hebrew children out of the fiery furnace save the colored people of this country from the fires of segregation, of Jim-Crowism and lynching?" I answer, if my people, North and South, or any other people, will be as loyal and true to Daniel's God as Daniel and the Hebrew children were, Jehovah will do all that He did for Daniel and the Hebrew children, and even more. If they will obey the Word of God, if they will be as loyal to Jehovah's Laws, if they will live up to their Bibles and respect the Sabbath and the church and constituted authorities; and live clean, moral lives, God will lift the burdens that oppress them, smite their foes before them, and make their enemies to be at peace with them. God has wrought miracles in our behalf as wondrous as dividing the Red Sea and furnishing water out of the rock in the wilderness. The lifting of four-million slaves out of the cesspool and mire of human slavery, setting them upon the solid rock of American citizenship and clothing them with the rights and privileges of free-men, is as great a miracle as the opening of blind Bartemeus' eyes and the strengthening of the limbs of the impotent man at the Pool of Bethesda. From a race of slaves He gave the world a Frederick Douglass, the gifted Statesman; a Paul Laurence Dunbar, the poet; a Booker T. Washington, the Wizard of Tuskegee; and Richard H. Boyd, who planted the rose of Christian literature for Negro people, whose fruit and sweet perfume have inspired Christian geniuses and Negro authors throughout the country. What God has made of my people in this country is a modern miracle equal to anything He did for Israel in Egypt or the early church in the Roman Empire. Today, He is locking the jaws of the lions, quenching the fiery furnace, and lifting Josephs, Daniels and Esthers to rule on thrones; and I warn you today if you will make the Ten Commandments and the Sermon on the Mount your code of morals, there shall come to you, peace and prosperity and happiness which can never be won by the sword.

The fourth objective is Universal Peace, and as much as peace may be desired, it will never come until corruption and crime and injustice are destroyed and truth and righteousness and purity are enthroned in the hearts of men. The League of Nations failed in its attempt to bring about Universal Peace because God was not considered in the compact and it trusted in warships, in airplanes, and poisonous gases instead of the promises of Jehovah. I call upon you this day to seek world peace by teaching the principles of Him who is declared the Prince of Peace.

I believe you are here for the purpose of making more effective the work of missions, Christian education, and to uplift mankind by putting into operation the Great Commission and uniting our Baptist forces in a program that will make concrete the orders received on Olivet's brow.

Home Missions

Home Missions, the basis of our Convention activities, have been woefully neglected. Till we shall become willing to invest money and men enough in a Home Board to lay a foundation deep and wide, upon which all our other conventional activities may rest, we can never have a very large and lasting Convention. The spirit of missions is the incentive to all denominational achievements. When this spirit grows and glows in our hearts, it will burst forth in new churches established, new buildings erected, increased salaries for deserving Pastors, and the waste places shall be builded up and the desert become a watered garden.

We call upon the members of the Convention and upon Baptists everywhere to so labor to establish a strong mission organization in this country as will make true Ezekiel's prophesy of the holy river where the waters became ankle-deep and waist-deep and deep enough to swim a horse. It shall be easy to maintain all the worthy objects of this Convention when the fires which sent Philip to Gaza and Paul to Macedonia, and Carey to India, and Livingstone to Africa, began to burn in our hearts. God grant that the thousands of loyal Baptists will pray, and pray, and pray, till they are moved to give of their substances in such a measure as will build a strong Home Mission Board, and a Home Mission Program in this Convention.

We should not be satisfied till we shall have a half-million dollar Home Mission Fund used for the purpose of preaching the Gospel in all parts of our common country. The report of the Home Mission Board, which will be read at this Convention, will show that the fires of missions are burning and that this Board has made wonderful strides in mission work this year. I refer you to this report for careful study and consideration.

Education

While our Convention has declared its purpose to establish and maintain a National Theological and Training Seminary for the preparation of ministers, missionaries and religious workers, yet our activities in the field of education should be extended to every state in which there is a Baptist institution of learning. Our first duty should be to liquidate the mortgage debt on our property at Nashville. This should be done at this meeting, and every Baptist here gathered should give his pro-rata to the accomplishment of the task.

We should also give our fullest endorsement to well-established and well-conducted schools and colleges operated by Baptists throughout the country. We should render support to these institutions by holding country-wide educational rallies to secure funds to sustain a strong faculty and to secure the necessary buildings and equipments. We should assist in giving the widest publicity to the work of Baptist schools and labor to fill their dormitories with students. We should support some outstanding college in the East, and the Southeast, the West, and the North. This Convention could furnish students and moneys for these colleges and in turn, these colleges would send promising candidates for the ministry and missionary fields to the National Seminary for training for their work. Education is valuable and conducive to good citizenship only when it is maintained under proper influences. Our country suffers much today and the vilest attacks upon our Christianity comes from some of the most brilliant minds of the age because of an education given under improper influences. Thousands of bright intellects are being trained away from the faith of the fathers and away from the Bible and the church, in institutions of learning controlled by Liberalists and Modernists. Deplore this as we may, we can never overcome these conditions until we are willing to put consecrated men and consecrated money enough into our denominational program to enable our schools and colleges to compete with these non-Christian institutions. I call upon you this day, who are charged with the task of keeping the teachings of our Lord and Master pure and unsullied, to lay upon the altar twenty-five-thousand dollars in this meeting for the defense of the truths we love and for the cause for which we stand.

Church Extension

While our Church Extension Board has done marvelously well with what it had to do, it is obvious to every thoughtful person who has given the church extension work any consideration, that there is need of closer organization, and a stronger business management of this Board. This does not mean that those in control of this phase of our work have not done well; but it is apparent to all that they, nor any other set of men, can do a lasting service in their sphere until church extension is founded on the solid rock of Christian business. We must have a Board composed of men imbued with the one thought of building more church edifices and lifting those already built and debt-ridden, up from under the load under which they groan. This Board should elect a Secretary-Treasurer, and pay him a salary which will allow him to give his whole time to this work. He should be capable of interesting businessmen, bankers, and philanthropists in church extension and establish a church extension fund which would put the Board in a position to finance a building proposition of five-thousand dollars or ten-thousand dollars on short notice.

Under the notice of this Board should come church architecture and the Board should offer suggestions and advice to building committees in order that church buildings erected be adapted to worship and church administration. Much money and embarrassment would be saved if proper advice were given churches contemplating new buildings.

Foreign Missions

As disciples of Jesus Christ advance in the school of missions, it will become more and more apparent that there is no more home missions nor foreign missions but just *missions*. In the Great Commission, Jesus saw the Hottentot, and the Zulu, the Chinaman, the Norseman, the Indian and all the nations of the earth as one community in need of a saving Gospel and said, "The field is the world." The incentive to do foreign mission work must spring up on this side and not in the heathen land, if the work is to be permanent and effectual. That person who is moved by the distressing tale of the heathen and who gives out of sympathy for the benighted pagan, will never render the larger service to the cause. Missionary activities on foreign fields should be inspired by love and loyalty to Jesus Christ, and a born desire to acquaint mankind with the Savior so dear and loving to your own heart. The constituents in this Convention should adopt the New Testament mission plan and beginning at Jerusalem witness for Jesus unto the uttermost parts of the Earth. The wisdom of this program is apparent when we remember the Proverb: "Physician, heal thyself"; and until Christians in America can make America a Christian nation, the heathen will laugh and scorn when we attempt Christianize them. Hence, it is as necessary that we conduct and train our forces at home in the principles of missions as it is that we send missionaries to the foreign field. For in fact, if we send men and women to foreign lands with no trained and prepared supporters behind to sustain them, we send them out to suffer and die. If we attempt to do mission work in Africa, and Japan while we bite and devour one another at home, and while prejudice and hate wrangle in our breasts the one against the other, and while lawlessness and crime flourish here at a greater degree even than in the darkest heathen land, conditions at home will nullify all we attempt to do abroad. Let us keep before us the true spirit and purpose of sending out the Gospel and then we will lay sane plans and render unselfish service.

The plan of co-operation formed between this Convention and the Lott Carey Foreign Mission Society is a step in the right direction, and, if carried out in the spirit of Jesus Christ, without any attempt to honor anybody or any organization but Jesus Christ, will hasten the day when the Gospel shall be preached in every land. The loyal disciple of Jesus Christ does not consider whether he is to be known as a missionary hero or whether there shall come to him distinguished honors for service rendered on the foreign field, but he would be happy in service were heathen lands brought to knowledge of Jesus Christ even though he himself was never known among the missionary workers. We believe that wise, sane and unselfish counselors in this Convention and in our sister organization will work out this plan of co-operation to the redemption of the world and the glory of God. Let us all be patient and unselfish and willing to put our best service into the plan. I counsel the churches making up this Convention to increase their contributions to the foreign mission work, remembering that bread cast upon the waters will return again, and if we build up a foreign mission fund that will sustain and increase the work undertaken in heathen lands, there will be no necessity for scrambling for glory, for in saving a lost world, there will be glory enough for all.

Publishing Board

Our National Baptist Publishing Board blossoms and sends forth its sweet perfume as the bright and consummate flower of our highest aspirations and richest achievements. It is through this Board that we must disseminate among all people, Baptist thought and New Testament teachings. This Board has made known to the world that authors and writers among Negro Baptists and among all peoples, as no other organization has been able to do. It has given to Negro Baptists standing and prestige that challenge the literary world. It has produced authors and writers. It has created a place for thousands of our young people. It has borne upon its back the burdens of the denomination. It has put thousands of dollars into our missionary funds. It has kept the denominational fires burning in every section of our country and in the foreign field. The corps of faithless and discouraged Baptists have seen its light and stood upon its feet. It is no longer an object of controversy; its purpose and character are clearly defined in the charter under which it operates, and the records of Davidson County, Tennessee, show its relations to Negro Baptists in this country. Hence, we have no cause for engaging in bitter controversy, but honest and intelligent persons will examine these records and be willing to stand by them, and the persons who in the face of them insists in making false representations or seeks to misinform the public, or to create false impression among the people, is unworthy of consideration. I need not call upon you to stand by and support this beautiful maiden, fair and pleasant, whose stature is like the palm tree; whose head is like caramel and hair like purple; whose eyes are like the fish pools in Heshbon and fruit like the cluster of grapes that shaketh in Lebanon. The National Baptist Convention will never die as long as Henry Allen Boyd races the country from the Lakes to the Gulf, and from the Atlantic to the Pacific; and sings the song of progress and efficiency as exemplified in the masterful institution at 523 Second Avenue, North, Nashville, Tennessee. A small token of our appreciation can best be manifested in every member of this Convention making at least one yearly purchase of the products of this Publishing Board and speaking a word of cheer and goodwill to those who are giving their lives that it may not fail. If you have confidence in J. P. Robinson, in E. R. Carter, in L. L. Campbell, in J. L. Harding, in G. B. Taylor; if you have confidence in H. Allen Boyd, you are willing to commend the future of this Publishing Board to the loyal support and love of succeeding generations. A young man stood before an old minister bowed with the weight of years and labor, and pointed out to him the defects in the church edifice he had built. When this young man had finished, the old man looked straight into the eyes of the young man and said: "I cannot point out any defects in the building you have built." The world's record will show that those who would criticize and find fault with our National Baptist Publishing Board, not one of them have built a worthy institution of any kind.

Other Boards

Our Evangelical Board, our Benefit Board, and our Laymen's League deserve our consideration. The work of soul-saving and of caring for the aged and infirm ministers and the work of centralizing, controlling and utilizing the manpower in our churches, as represented by our Laymen's League, is by no means to be despised; and we hope our churches everywhere will give the wide door of opportunity to our evangelical staff, and that ways and means may be utilized to make the Benefit Board a real asset, and that we encourage the laymen in our churches by giving them such prominence on the program in this Convention as shall bring a thousand churchmen, other than preachers, to the sessions of the Convention.

I congratulate the churchmen, lawyers, and doctors, mechanics, and merchants, who find time to turn aside from their secular occupations to work with us in extending the Kingdom. Their counsel, their co-operation and the money they give to support the ministry and all church activities should receive our highest appreciation.

Woman's Auxiliary

Our Woman's Auxiliary has proven a source of encouragement, inspiration and financial assistance to the work of this Convention. Without its aid, what we have accomplished could not have been accomplished. Woman is the sensitive flower which responds to the faintest solicitation and which beautifies and sweetens everything she touches. She is true to every trust, loyal in any cause, and walks in the path of service with undying devotion. Jochabed, Hannah, Ruth and Esther won unfading glory in their day and gave to the world the highest example of unselfish service, loyalty, and queenly virtues. They have their prototypes in Madames Georgia DeBaptist Faulkner, M. A. B. Fuller, Anna Washington, William Grimble, J. L. Harding, J. H. Winn, G. W. Alexander, Lula Mae Hurse, S. R. Prince, I. H. Kelly, and a score of others, whose character is as fair as the sun and service as Gibraltic as the Andes Mountain. They deserve our counsel and encouragement. We extend to them a hand of full co-operation in building a national organization and extending the work of the Kingdom.

Stand-bys

The loyal, unswerving, rooted-and-grounded in the truth disciples of Christ are the class upon whom the civilization of the world depends. Our churches and schools and Christian homes, our civilization and the foundation upon which the government rests, look to this class of men of faith and hope and love for their sustenance and perpetuation. Mean jealousies, false representations, slanders and hypocrisies, have never won and will never win a victory for Jehovah. If Negro Baptists in this country would ever triumph against wrong and wickedness, they must come clean with God and clean with their brethren. The humble, the faithful, the pure in heart, have nothing to fear, but a guilty conscience makes cowards of us all. Men skulk in the dark and form unholy alliances overnight and resort to strategy and schemes to accomplish selfish designs, but their feet shall become entangled in their own net they have set, and Haman will hang on his own gallows. But the righteous is as bold as a lion, he shall flourish as the palm tree, his strength is renewed like that of the eagle.

Whatever program may be laid at this Convention must be dealt with as God's plans and purposes and not as mere exigencies and man-made policies for the emergency. God's purposes are eternal. He may be ten-thousand years producing a diamond from a carload of coal soot, but He will be neither hurried in His process nor frightened from His task; and when it is finished, it will be perfect. And so man who would construct a program under God must make his program after God's conception and attributes. The program we would construct must first, by the grace of God, be formed in our hearts. Let God's Kingdom be planted in you and let it grow on as the flowers blossom from the tiny seed planted in the garden walk. A man infected with measles will infect others, and when we become infected with missions, world evangelism and Christian training, others about us will catch the disease. Leaders must use wisdom, judgment and precision. They must not permit their feelings to carry them away from the straight and narrow path of duty. At times, a leader must do the unpopular thing, which will bring down upon his head the wrath of the populace, but he must be true to his God, true to his conscience, and true to the interest of the people. Lincoln's war policy not only made him unpopular in the South, but many of the Northern politicians and statesmen condemned him. However, he, whom they assassinated in 1865, is loved and adored throughout the civilized world in 1926.

Overcome By Faith

The achievements of the leaders and reformers and builders have made real history in the world by faith. "By faith Abraham when he was called obeyed." "By faith Moses when he was come to years refused to be called the son of Pharoah's daughter." "By faith the walls of Jericho fell down." "By faith the harlot Rahab perished not." And the pathfinders of latter days discovered that they could win life's battles by faith and not by genius, and culture, and wealth. By faith Columbus discovered a new world; by faith the Pilgrim fathers, the Quakers, and the Huguenots planted villages along the coast of the Atlantic and laid the foundation of our Republic. By faith Jefferson, Adams, Franklin and Hamilton gave us the Constitution and the Declaration of Independence. By faith Luther led the Reformation and William Carey planted the rose of modern missions in India; by faith Phillips and Lovejoy and Garrison struck human slavery in this country its death blow. By faith the leaders in our race just emerged from the degrading system of human slavery, organized churches, established schools, and laid the foundation for good homes and business enterprises, which make this race of mine the marvel of the civilized world. As much as we may prize and respect intellect and ability, and human instrumentality, our success and attainment will depend upon our faith. "All things are possible to him that believeth." We shall never win in this country by trickery, strategy, and advantage; but if we shall ever build a permanent citizenship, it must be accomplished by faith in the promises and principles of Jesus Christ. Our banks fail, our great commercial enterprises go to pieces, our educational programs flounder upon the rocks, our churches and associations and national Conventions lag behind, not because we have not the money to support them, not because we have not the men with brain and talent to operate them, not because as Baptists we have not the numbers in our churches to sustain them, but because we fail to comply with the teachings of God, who declared, "Upon this rock, I will build my church and the gates of Hell shall not prevail against it." The faith which led Moses across the Red Sea, Joshua around the walls of Jericho, Nehemiah to rebuild the walls of Jerusalem, led Lincoln, Frederick Douglass, and Sojourner Truth to plead the cause of liberty and human rights until freedom reached forth her hand and lifted four-million slaves up out of the mire of serfdom and sat their feet upon the solid rock of freedom and American citizenship. And that same faith will lead my people out of the present bondage of ignorance and superstition into the Promised Land of usefulness and happiness.

Conclusion

And now, my brethren, if we should review the history and achievements of Baptists there looms before us a shining monument of glorious deeds and benefactions. From the days of John the Baptist until now, has the Kingdom of Heaven been preached by Baptists. Paul and Peter and John and Bunyan and Spurgeon and William J. Simmons and Gaddie and Lee and Morris and Boyd and Lott Carey and Luke, and an unlimited number of heroes who have fought the good fight, won the victory and now rest under the shades of the Tree on the banks of the River of Life, bequeath to us their faith, their character, their abilities, and their labors, as a rich heritage. Their memory inspires and cheers our spirits in this sacred presence. May we not pledge to the cause for which they gave their undying devotion our talent and our resources? As twice-born men, under orders from on high, let us perform so well the task committed unto us that their spirits and all the holy angels in Heaven will rejoice at our accomplishments. When for the last time the King of Day mounts up the Celestial Highway, drawn by prancing steeds, whose feet are shod with fire, and Milky Way shall fade, and stars shall tremble and planets burn up, and kingdoms and throne shall crumble and all the works of man pass away, then I want you and me and the faithful soldiers in Christ everywhere who come to appear before our great Commander, laden with trophies won on many a battlefield, to hear our Redeemer say, "Well done, good and faithful servant." Let us labor together here and rejoice together before His beatific throne in Heaven.

Annual Address of Dr. J. E. Wood
President of the National Baptist Convention of America
In Session at Denver, Colorado, September 7, 1927

My Brethren in Christ:

Time's rapid cycle has brought us together in our Convention's 57th Annual Session. We assemble today under conditions entrancing, inviting, inspiring. His omnipotent hand paints the rainbow of His unchanging promises in the mortal skies; His providence records an epoch, the most tragical of which history gives an account, and there looms upon the horizon threatening clouds the most ominous, of His judgment. That soul is dead who while rejoicing in our Father's goodness fails to study the records of His dealings with individuals and nations, or ignores the approaching doom which will follow as a natural sequence the rejections of the teaching of the Man of Galilee.

Agitations and commotions in the social, commercial, political, and religious world awaken in the bosom of every thoughtful student of history feelings of serious apprehension; and no one alive to the problems of the age will be indifferent to the conditions under which the nations are hastening to their destiny, nor fail to heed the voice of the Captain of our salvation, who calls us to guide humanity's ship safely through the turbulent waters of life's restless sea. In the furtherance of this task we assemble in this religious convocation, a militant host of loyal Baptist men and women, whose hopes, and purposes, and prayers are for the redemption and religious development of a lost humanity, and the exaltation and glory of the crucified Christ.

As we review the panorama of startling events and cosmical achievements of this convention year, our spirits are stirred, and as Job's horse paweth in the valley, so the loyal soldiers of Jesus Christ crave a part with the heroes of history who conquer in the field of science, and literature, and religion. And we lift a prayer to God, not that the burdens may be lightened and the tasks made easier; but that we may be possessed of faith and hope and courage and love to labor on. At no period in the Christian era has the opportunity been greater to test real worth, to measure our faith, to weigh character, and to properly estimate true love and loyalty to the King than in this present age. The falling away of many, the acceptance of false teachings and the cowardice of some in the ranks, are a challenge to our faith; and amid the din and cry of debasing unbelief and contemptuous scorn, and apostate desertion, is heard the stentorian voice of our matchless Leader, asking: "Wilt ye also go away?"

The faith of the fathers is our valuable asset in the present day civilization. "The stone which the builders rejected is become the head of the corner." No system of education, no code of morals, no form of government, which ignores the teaching of Jesus, can survive. Our assemblage here today is to emphasize these truths, and to demonstrate their value in rebuilding a torn and bleeding, prostrate society.

May we not regard this coming together here as serious as the assembling of the Magi in Herod's palace? For we seek the way to the newborn Christ, the hope of the world. May we not regard it as far reaching as the continental Congress in Faneuil Hall? For there should go from this solemn presence a fiat which will affect all the future of Negro Baptists in America. May we not regard our gathering here as epoch making as the Diet at Worms? For shall not we send forth a proclamation to the sons of men proclaiming a world's salvation in the blood of Jesus Christ, shed on Calvary?

The time has passed when believers in Jesus Christ can play at kingdom building. A waiting world, a torn asunder church, and a faithless and selfish leadership call for the loyal, fearless followers of Jesus Christ to contend earnestly for the faith delivered once for all to the saints. The loving God, by whose grace we are permitted to gather in this beautiful city, merits our earnest devotion, our unselfish service, and our largest contributions to the extension of the kingdom. We must write a new epoch in Negro Baptist history in letters so bold that he who runs may read of our determined, unflinching purpose to win a victory which will reflect for all time to come the glory of God and the loyalty of the men and women who support this Convention. The exegeses of this convocation test the love, the faith, the heroism of every Baptist affiliated with the National Baptist Convention; and we shall prove to the world, whether we are merely a band of good time seekers or an army of loyal soldiers fighting under the banner of the cross. God grant that you and I may convince the skeptic and doubter that we are truly on heaven's mission.

If we study the history of Negro religionists, we are forced to the conclusion that there is needed woefully, at this time in religious progress, an organization composed of believers in the cross and in the great commission, that are willing to pay the price, to lift salvation's banner high above every other flag or insignia of authority. I believe that this Convention offers such an organization to the militant, Christ loving, self-forgetting Baptists of the world; and we are willing to pronounce our faith, present our cause and rest our case upon the teachings and purposes for which we stand. If we have a just purpose, a worthy cause inspired by pure motives, we have a right to demand the loyalty and support of every Baptist who loves the Lord and desires the triumph of His kingdom; but, if we have no mission and there be no good reason for our existence, then, we deserve to die. Let us face the facts, if there be need for just such an organization as we have undertaken to maintain. What are the purposes for which it exists, and are we moving along safe and sane lines to attain the desired ends? These, it seems to me, are pertinent questions for our consideration. We can never hope to build a great Convention prosecuting a work affecting the human race by mere sentimentality or by pointing out the weaknesses and mistakes of others who have failed; but, if we shall attract to this Convention men and women of intelligence and godliness and righteous hope, we must demonstrate to them that we are rendering mankind a needful service.

There are reputed to be three-million Negro Baptists in America. If these Baptists can be organized for efficient service, and twenty-per-cent of them trained to unite upon a well-defined program to extend the kingdom, there will be accomplished in this country a work in kingdom building greater than anything ever yet accomplished by Negro Christians in the world's history. Our object is to weld together these Baptists into such an organization, and train them to cooperate in spreading the gospel to the end of the world. If six hundred thousand Baptists will bring their talent and money and influence, and lay them on the altar we can finance the local work in every church, sustain the educational work in every state and build a Home Mission program which will give the denomination standing and strength throughout the world and quadruple our activities on foreign fields. However, this can never be done by spurts and jerks. We must get under the load, and by one long, steady pull, all together, go over the top with Jesus. Dr. J. W. Rowland in the Expositor speaks of the "three great verbs of the Christian life." They are "come," "tarry," "go." No disciple of Jesus Christ is fully prepared for service till he has learned the meaning of these three verbs. Jesus said to John and James and Peter and Andrew, "Come unto me." He said, "Come," to Levi and Zaccheus and to all mankind ever since then, "Come." And He not only commands us to come, but to tarry. Too many persons come in the moment of excitement, of high tide, who fail to tarry. The cause of Christ will be sustained by those who tarry in faith and service and sacrifice. And after we have come and tarried till we have learned of Him and imbibed His spirit and become filled with His power, He bids us go. We must go in the graces — "from one degree of grace unto another." Baptists must go in faith and in good works. We must go in the Great Commission to carry the good news to every creature.

Missions

Missions is the foundation of kingdom building. When Baptists hearts catch on fire with missions, our cause will flourish throughout the world. Brother pastors, can Jesus Christ depend on us to enlighten the people in missions? To your knees, O men of God. Tarry in your secret closet till the pentecostal fires begin to burn in your hearts as they did in the early church; and then, with your lighted torch, fire the souls of your constituents. If we can awaken in our membership a knowledge and a love of missions, we shall be able to realize one-million dollars annually for the work of this Convention. But, be assured, we can only interest others when we ourselves have become truly interested. If you and I will let the Holy Spirit use us, the money to finance the kingdom will be forthcoming.

I would put one-half of this one-million dollars, five-hundred thousand dollars, in an endowment fund to be used to assist poor, struggling churches and under-paid pastors. I would use two-hundred and fifty-thousand dollars on the foreign fields; and use two-hundred and fifty-thousand dollars to finance our Educational work. This perhaps would serve to stabilize the work of our Convention. When we shall make duty and responsibility the incentive to work in this Convention and love and loyalty to the Christ the motive for our activities, the whole machinery of organization will move so smoothly and joyously that figures will not hamper the measurements of our giving. But, born a-new spirits, consecrated to God, dedicated to the work of kingdom building, will not limit their contributions to the Lord's treasury.

> "But if I should make some resolve,
> And duty did not call;
> I love my God with zeal so great
> That I should give Him all."

Surely, we should expect a million Baptists affiliating with our

Convention who would gladly give one dollar annually to our work. But, our first task is to enlighten our people in missions — its Author, its design, its scope, its ultimate aim. Under the mission program we should establish mission courses in every church; we should distribute mission tracts, books, and papers among the members; one Sunday each month should be known as mission day.

As much as we should love the heathen, and the lost and outcasts at our door, our gifts should not be based primarily upon our love and sympathy for these; but upon our love to God. When our love to God shall become supreme; when we become dead to self and the world, and all things, and alive in Jesus Christ and His cause, we shall gladly make our gifts of talents, and time, and influence and of our goods to His cause.

The daughter of a noted minister lay dying of the awful disease, tuberculosis. Her father had an engagement to make the commencement address to a Harvard graduating class on the morrow. His daughter noticed the anxiety on his face as he paced the floor. She called him to her and said: "Father, I know what you are thinking about; you are thinking of not going to make that speech tomorrow because you are afraid I'll be gone when you return. Go to Harvard, and look those young people straight in the face and say to them, "If any one of you have an opportunity to do anything for Jesus, jump at the chance." My brethren, missions is the open door which gives every follower of Jesus Christ an opportunity to do something for Jesus. You can give Him some time, in the lowly places in your communities; you can go out in the waste places and across the deep into pagan lands, and lift Him up; you can put your money (and do you know this is the smallest gift you can make) into the mission treasury to support the suffering laborers who have left home, and loved ones, and business, and pleasures — forsaken all to carry the crucified and risen Saviour to a lost world. "Jump at the chance."

When the true mission spirit burns in our hearts, the spirit which sent the Son of God from heaven to earth, the spirit which sent the early church to preach the gospel throughout the Roman empire, the spirit that sent Moffatt and Livingstone, and Wm. Carey and Judson and Lott Carey and scores of others to heathen lands, we shall gloriously support and advance every object for which our Convention stands.

"Do not then stand idly waiting
For some greater work to do;
Fortune is a lazy goddess —
She will never come to you."

"Go and toil in any vineyard,
Do not fear to do or dare;
If you want a field of labor,
You can find it anywhere."

Christian Education

Education is a tool sharp and keen, but its value in forming character, developing worthy useful citizenship and making the world a safer and happier place in which to live, is determined by the hands in which it is placed. The grossest immoralities, crime and lawlessness flourish most in the circles of some of our great colleges. What form of vice from petit larceny to revolting murders have not shocked the decency and morals of society, committed by graduates and college students? We are told that in well nigh every university supported by public funds, may be found atheistic clubs, pledged to the task of discrediting the Bible and undermining in the minds of the youths of those institutions the faith taught by their parents.

This condition in the realms of education is a challenge to the churches, and especially to Baptists to whose heart the teachings of the Old Book are as dear as life itself, to build and maintain institutions under Christian influence in which may be molded the character of our children.

The Western Recorder, perhaps, one of the ablest Baptist weeklies in the South, says: "The satanic teachings which have been emanating from not a few of our American universities and colleges have not happened by accident or under the urge of any new discoveries of science or scholarship."

It is said that atheists, agnostics, infidels and modernists are rarely found among the Catholics. May not this be attributed to the fact that they build their own schools and endow these institutions so handsomely as to sustain them in a princely manner? Shall the children of this world be wiser than the children of the light? It will avail us nothing to make faces at our young people caught in this maelstrom; but the future of the denomination lies in the ability of Baptists to establish and operate efficient schools for their children. The world watches you today to see if we are concerned in the education, the morals, the destiny of the persons who must conduct the affairs in the church of the next generation. When we shall give as much time and money and thought to rearing our children and shaping their future as we devote to the chickens and pigs and blooded horses and automobiles, the future church will stand secure.

The Denominational Paper

Next to the Bible in influence and in shaping and determining the future of Baptists stands the newspaper. In a recent issue of a Baptist paper, Rev. A. P. Turner of South Carolina is reported as saying: "Under God I am a preacher, because when I was a boy my father subscribed for the *Baptist Courier*. I read about Baptists everywhere. I read about the work of missions, the great fellowship of Baptists, the great work of Christians to bring the reign of Christ in all of the world. It all looked far bigger to me than anything else. I prayed God to take me and use me in helping to do that great task. Thus the Lord made me a minister of Christ — in large part through the thoughtfulness of my father in placing my young and impressionable mind under the influence of the Baptist paper.

You cannot know of the activities in the Baptist world if you fail to read the Baptist paper. There is nothing more heartening, and that points with more unerring certainty to the bright future for Baptists than the growing habit among our people to read denominational literature. The Baptist *Union Review*, our national organ, has grown in favor with pastors and laymen at a wonderful rate in the last few years. That Baptist is a back number who does not read this paper. And, you owe it to the denomination, to your family, and to the management which sends forth weekly this magazine of useful information, to pay for it and give it a permanent place in your home and library. It brings to you weekly, general religious information from all parts of the world. It keeps you advised as to the work of your co-workers in different parts of the country; it affords you a school in theology and the latest methods in Sunday School management; it supplies your library with information which will prove helpful in the social, in the commercial, in the political, as well as in the religious world.

Our Publishing Board

More than thirty years ago, Negro Baptists began publishing religious literature to be used in Baptist Sunday Schools. There were, then, among us leaders who doubted the wisdom of the enterprise or the ability of Negro Baptists to carry on to a successful consummation. But even then, there arose in Israel a seer whose prophetic vision saw in the dim future a mighty institution sending forth to enlighten the nations, millions of pages of sound religious literature. He saw the need of an outlet for the budding ideas pent up in the ambitious souls of the thousands of young men and women graduating annually from our schools and colleges. He saw in such an institution an opportunity for honest, industrious young people to find a field of service and become an asset to the race and to society. And, R. H. Boyd, in his own language, "With a stool chair, a ten-cent tablet, and a lead pencil," laid the foundation for the greatest religious publishing concern owned and operated by Negroes in the world. He saw young men and women gifted with the pen, with no resources to back them in their endeavors to give expression to the golden thoughts which blossom in the soul; and he extended a beckoning hand to C. H. Parrish in Kentucky, to J. T. S. Brown in Florida, to W. H. Moses in Virginia, to E. W. D. Isaac and Sutton E. Griggs in Texas, and J. Crenshaw in North Carolina and hundreds of others throughout the country, and said to them, "Write what thou seest;" and the National Baptist Publishing Board became the wing upon which the heart springs, the soul longings of these aspiring sons of Ham are borne to the ends of the earth. And in all candor and sincerity, I believe the facts justify the assertion that but for the National Baptist Publishing Board and R. H. Boyd, the persons with facile pen here referred to would have never been known in Baptist history. And, in whatever field they may choose to labor, in whatever harvest they may reap, gratitude, the loveliest flower that blossoms in the garden of a noble heart, will carry them back on memory's wing to the desert in which they were found; and they can never forget the pit out of which they were digged. And, there she stands the Gibraltar of Baptist thought and teachings and contribution in self-help, and freedom, and independence. She has weathered the storms of a thousand seas, withstood the shot and shell of the most bitter adversaries; and she comes into the safe harbor of glorious achievements with sails unfurled and flippant in the breeze; her bosom ladened with good things—faith, hope, love, and good-will toward all men.

This Board is handed down to generations of Baptists as a rich heritage and deserves the veneration, the support and admiration of Baptists, especially, but of all Negro people throughout the world.

Other Boards

I am not unmindful of the importance of our other boards—the Church Extension Board, the Benefit Board, the Evangelical Board and the Laymen's League. Each of these boards is capable of rendering noble service to the denomination and to mankind. They should have our unreserved support and encouragement. When we shall have become imbued with the true spirit of missions, it will be easier for us to give the needed support to all the objects of the Convention.

Our Women

The leaders among our good women have been active in pushing the claims of the Women's Auxiliary in the different states throughout the year. The reports from that department of our work are causes for rejoicing among Baptists everywhere. Increased number of tracts and pages of literature, enlargement of the field forces, deepened sense of responsibility and deeper spirituality are indicative of the aroused interest and enthusiasm which are seizing upon our Baptist women. Like Jocabed who by faith defied the Pharoah's wife and nursed in her home three months the deliverer of her people, contrary to Egypt's laws; like Deborah who fought by Barak's side and pursued the Moabites till Sisera lay dead nailed to the floor in Jael's house; like Ruth who followed Naomi and refused to be dissuaded till she had attained the dignity of ancestor of the blessed Lord; like Esther, the orphan girl who rose from the slave hut to the throne that she might plead the cause of a doomed race, so have our good women nursed the fortunes of this Convention; fought side by side with the leaders in the battle of Jehovah; refused to turn from following after the people whose God is the Lord, and have risked place and fortune and fame that the cause which they serve may triumph. "Her price is far above rubies." Let us give to their work unstinted support.

Unity Among Baptists

All intelligent, loyal Baptists favor unity and harmonious cooperation in kingdom work. We favor the organization of the whole Negro Baptist denomination in one body if the kingdom can be extended thereby and Jesus receive greater glory. However, we can best show our candor and sincerity in urging unity by first getting together in our local bodies. While we forwent strife and read out of our city unions and ministerial alliances persons who do not think with us on the national issues, we are in a bad road for union. Baptists will rejoice when their brethren will show the Christ spirit the one toward the other everywhere. When all Baptists can work in the unity of the spirit agreeing on worthy objects of endeavor — when they will put their money in a big mission program and support a great education system. When these conditions first obtain among Baptists, it will then appear that steps toward organic union may be considered with profit. Can we unite upon certain schools and colleges which all will agree to support, and in which all may hold interest? Can we agree on a mission program and all put our money into it and lend our influence to its success? What are the evidences of sincerity when leaders talk of organic union? I counsel my brethren everywhere that all acrimony in debate cease; that Baptist ministers everywhere be received as brethren; that the spirit of love and kindness be encouraged; and we allow nothing to enter our lives which will so degrade us as to make us hate and revile our brother. Let us be loyal to the truth and to Christ's kingdom and be willing to forsake all and suffer all things for His sake and every problem shall be solved and rightly resolved.

The Church and Social Conditions

Never since Jesus Christ gave His marching orders to His followers have the sphere and activities of the church been so vehemently contested as they are being contested today. We are told that she is only one of the many institutions which must bring salvation to man. Again, that there are other organizations rendering to mankind greater and more helpful service than she is rendering. And, again, we are boldly and flippantly told that the church has outlived her usefulness and should be scrapped. Some say the Y.M.C.A.'s, the N.A.A.C.P., the Lodges are rendering a greater service to humanity than the church of God.

Those of heroic spirit in the ranks of Christ's loyal followers will not be discouraged or dismayed at this attack upon the bride, the Lamb's wife; nor will they be deterred from the path of a sacred duty to defend her cause till all "thy sons shall come from afar bending before the gates of Jerusalem." We accept the challenge and lift the veil of twenty centuries and point to the achievements of God's church. Whose teachings have broken the spell of paganism in every land; made cannibals devout worshippers, and heathens useful members of well-regulated society? What institution has destroyed the cursed traffic in human beings and outlawed slavery; who was it that led in the destruction of the saloon; and lifted womanhood up from the depths of servility and shame and placed her upon the pedestal of honor and glory? In fact, every useful institution and organization among the civilized nations of the world owes its existence to the Christian church.

But, soldiers of Christ, we must not rest upon past victories; if we hope to maintain our lead in rebuilding the world, we must dedicate our powers and resources to this task. The church must be the salt of the earth in saving society; she must go out into the streets and highways and gather in the outcasts and the neglected. She must lay hold on the law-makers and the administrative forces and uphold justice and right living in the community. We must offer society a saner, a more useful and a happier program of life than can be found anywhere else. The church must teach men to deal with their brethren on earth justly, kindly, and with brotherly love if they hope to live with them in heaven.

Memories

As we enter upon the deliberations of this session of the Convention, the proceedings are tinged with sadness, for there are they whose presence and counsel and support gave strength, and cheer, and sunshine to the brotherhood; but their seat is empty. Campbell of Texas, than whom a truer friend of this Convention, a more dependable leader, a wiser counselor, and more courageous defender of the faith, never imbibed the morning breeze or was cheered by God's sunlight. R. Mitchell of Kentucky, the life lovely whose gentle spirit was as beautiful as the lily and whose love was as tender as that of a woman. C. C. Goins, who stood practically alone among the hills of West Virginia and held up the banner of this Convention till the summons from above relieved him of his post. B. F. Farrell, the beloved of Indiana whose door was always open to his brethren and his hand extended in deeds of helpfulness and good cheer. R. D. Philips, the man of deeds not words, who fell asleep at his post of service in Columbus, Ohio. And, Marshall and Cross and Crawford and others whose labors and influence merit for them a place on the roll of heroes whose names in shining gold are written in heaven. They fought a good fight; they kept the faith; they have finished the race; and went up to join the innumerable hosts who wait in the city of God.

"Soldiers of Christ, well done;
Praise be thy new employ;
and while eternal ages run,
Rest in thy Saviour's joy."

Conclusion

As we face the task of constructing and carrying forth a religious program, a Baptist program, we are overwhelmed at the goodness of God who saves us and uses us in extending the kingdom to the ends of the earth. And, we join with the Psalmist in his exclamation of joy: "What shall I render unto the Lord for all His benefits toward me?" May we not here and now pledge our eternal fidelity to Him. In the name of the millions of weak and helpless and dependent children who look to Negro leadership for deliverance, in the name of our brothers in heathen lands, in the name of the suffering heralds of the cross who have borne the burden through succeeding centuries, in the name of the Christ whose shed blood on Calvary has redeemed us, let us go up at once and possess the land.

Looking through the vista of years, I catch the vision of a new day for Baptists. In my mind's eye, I see millions of consecrated men and women awakened and vitalized and inspired for service. I hear a cosmopolitan gospel as fiery as Elijah's denuncio before Ahab on Carmel's heights, as relentless and uncompromising as John the Baptist's preaching in the wilderness, and as bold and as evangelistic as Paul's defense before Agrippa. I see rising as sphinx from the ashes of a discredited and decaying sacredolism, a church membership and a church worship and a life of service in the community as potent as dynamic and as radiant as yon blazing sun. I see crowning some hill in every rural community a church where a man saved by grace and called to preach Jesus Christ administers to the souls of men. I see gathered into a million Sunday Schools our American population till not a loiter or idler can be found on the streets or upon the highway on the Lord's day; but all by studying God's word to know His will. I, then, see from these religious activities a prosperous people secure in every citizen's right. I see a million well-ordered, well-kept homes, occupied by happy families who honor God and respect the laws of their country. School houses will stand in every community as sentinels to guard the education, the morals, the health, and the life activities of the youth of our land. Then shall disfranchisement, discrimination, mobs, burning alive of human beings, and race riots give place to justice, fraternity, and equality; and Columbia's land shall in truth and in fact be democracy's home and liberty's country. The word of God will be her foundation stone and brotherhood the secret of her strength and security. To secure these ends is my mission and yours.

Then,

"Is this the time, O Church of Christ,
To sound retreat?
To arm with weapons cheap and blunt
The men and women who have borne the brunt
Of Truth's fierce strife and nobly held
Their ground?"
"Is this the time to halt when all around
Horizon's lift, new destinies confront?
Stern duties wait?
Our nation never wont
To play the laggard,
When God's will was found?"
"No! Rather strengthen stakes
And lengthen cords,
Enlarge the plans and gifts, O thou elect,
And to thy kingdom come for such a time;
The earth with all its fullness is the Lord's.
Great things attempt for Him,
Where great things expect
Whose love imperial is
Whose power sublime.

Annual Address of Dr. J. E. Wood
President of the National Baptist Convention of America
In Session at Shreveport, Louisiana, September, 1928

My Christian Friends:

This assemblage of the Lord's hosts presents a picture of beauty and sublimity which lend inspiration to the flinted rocks, cause the hills to clap their hands, and move the trees and flowers to shout for joy. I am rejoiced to greet in this gathering here the gospel herald who through the year flown by, has not ceased to sound the gospel bugle, to the passing multitudes, moving to the judgement; the college professor who has not slacked his task to mould the character of the youth that must make up the future citizenship of the nation; the professional man, the farmer, the mechanic, the laborer. They weave a wreath of love, unity, fraternity and equality which pictures the common weal and the single purpose of the disciples of Jesus Christ who compose this convocation.

Before entering into a discussion of the matters vital to the life and progress of this Convention, and conducive to the success of this meeting, I pause to express to every messenger here assembled my sincere thanks for the loyalty and devotion with which you have supported the work. Looking back over the road we have come during the intervening months between the Denver meeting and this gathering, I am rejoiced when sweet memory brings to me the many kindnesses and courtesies with which my brethren and sisters have showered my pathway. We have traveled the country from the lakes to the gulf, visiting churches, associations and conventions in the states of Illinois, Indiana, Ohio, Pennsylvania, Maryland, District of Columbia, Michigan, Missouri, Oklahoma, Texas, Louisiana, Mississippi, Tennessee, Florida, North Carolina, Colorado, Arkansas and the brethren where ever we have gone, have been sweet and cordial extending us the most generous hospitality. My thanks for these kindnesses cannot be expressed in words. I would not be so egotistic as to regard these acts of kindnesses and brotherly love as honors to me personally, but I know they were the deed of love from hearts devoted to the work of the Kingdom, who sought to honor the work and glorify God by entertaining His humble servant. In His name I express my thanks.

We left Denver last September flushed with the triumphant victory, the most signal ever witnessed by an assemblage of Negro Baptists on this continent. The meeting so far West had caused many to doubt the ability of the Convention to carry a respectable following. But, all were agreeably surprised at the attendance of thousands. Forty-one ministers attended the meeting for the first time and twenty-eight were persons who had formerly affiliated with the Incorporated Convention and one of these had been an officer of one of the boards of that Convention.

On every side the decorum, the personnel, and the spiritual atmosphere surrounding the delegation were most highly commended.

The finances for all purposes surpassed all previous years. More money was raised for Home Missions, more cash was paid on the Theological Seminary debt, and more cash on the indebtedness of the Convention, than was paid in any previous year, of the forty-eight years of our existence. These achievements have not been won by the grumblers, the complainers and the fault-finders. Nor are they the achievements of any one person. But, thank God, there is a mighty host of twice-born men, who in an unassuming, unswerving and faithful manner has "stayed by the stuff" and put the program over. They may not be known for their much speaking and volubility; but their deeds have built a monument as high as the Himalayas, which shall keep their memory fresh, enshrined in the hearts of a grateful people while time shall last. I believe that there is sufficient loyalty to Christ, sufficient loyalty to the work of the Convention, sufficient intelligence among its constituents, sufficient courage and self-sacrifice to carry on the work begun till every foe is put to flight, and our educational work and mission work shall flourish as the Cedars of Lebanon.

There are certain virtues which must characterize every individual as well as every institution if he, or it, will live and bless society. Among these virtues may be mentioned honesty, courage, self-denial. It matters little what else one possesses. If he is wanting in these, he is a failure. This Convention has come through the storm. It has suffered the virulent attacks of supposed friends and has stood the bombardments of avowed enemies. The old ship has at times been allowed to drift into the shallows of doubts and skepticism, but there were safe and loyal sailors aboard the ship, and the flag has never failed, nor the crew deserted the cargo.

Can Baptists Get Together?

No worthy union and cooperation among Negro Baptists can obtain so long as deception, hypocrisy and falsehood hide the hairy hand beneath the seductive smile of flattery, trinketry, and the siren's song. Men high in the councils of Baptist affairs have gone through the land proclaiming Baptist unity and calling for the Conventions to come together; while secretly they sow the briars and thistles of discord and strife. They point to this organization as "splitters," "rebels," "Heretics." The only terms of union they have ever offered is the terms the Master offers the slave; the sovereign offers the rebel. They have flung it to the Baptist world that this Convention does not exist; have pointed us out as a handful of the disgruntled. There can be no offer of terms co-operation till all Baptists are accorded absolute equality and recognized as Christian brothers. Till then, we shall ever question the rights of Czars and Monarchs to prescribe the course we shall pursue. The intelligent religious world is awakening. Thoughtful Baptist leaders and other thinking Christians are asking: "If the incorporated Baptists have the numbers, and the wealth and the wisdom and the piety, why is it that they raise less annually than half the money for Education and Home Missions raised by the Unincorporated Baptists, and why is it that, of all the money they report as raised for Foreign Missions, they send less to the foreign fields than their brethren send? Believing that the virtues before referred to — honesty, courage, and self-sacrifice — form an armor bright, which no poisonous dart of the slandered and traducer can penetrate, we meet the expounder of falsehood and misrepresentation in the arena of public opinion and refute all of his false statements. We speak in the most kindly spirit; we gauge the battle by the eternal truths of God; we make the Bible our standard of brotherhood and the Golden Rule our code of ethics; and we appeal to Baptists everywhere to compare our accomplishments with other anywhere and judge our right to the commendation of intelligent public by what we have done.

And yet, we come in no boastful spirit. We cry: "Not unto us; not unto us, but unto Thy name be all the glory." We are humiliated and hide our faces when we consider how great things He has done for us and how little we have done for Him. I am mistaken in the spirit, the gratitude, the thankfulness of the persons who make up this Convention if we fail to put into the Lord's treasury at this meeting, the largest contribution we have ever made to the causes for which we stand. What God has wrought through us should move every Baptist here to rise up and honor Him in His deeds.

We cannot rejoice at the shortcomings of others; we cannot measure our progress by others failures; we must measure our gifts by God's blessings. How much shall we give since He has done so much for us? If each one here will measure his donation in this meeting by the Lord's favors to him, we shall have funds sufficient for all our causes.

The Baptist World Alliance

This gathering of World Baptists from every nation met in Toronto, Canada, June 23 to 27, 1928. A very elaborate program was arranged and much information and inspiration were gained by those who attended its sessions. As President of this Convention, we issued credentials to all persons desiring to attend the Toronto meeting. We heard that one person to whom credentials were issued was not registered under the credentials. We know several who were registered under them.

Your committee met the Executive Committee of the Alliance in King Edward's Hotel, Sunday afternoon, June 24, and presented evidence showing we were a duly and regularly organized Baptist organization in that body. There has been objections raised to our admittance and the matter was referred to a committee for final disposition.

In July, we received the following letter from Dr. J. H. Rushbrooke, Secretary of the Alliance, dated July 21, 1928:

> Rev. J. E. Wood,
> Danville, Ky.
>
> Dear Brother Wood:
>
> I write as General Secretary of the Baptist World Alliance to notify you formally that the Executive Committee has entrusted to a special Sub-Committee, consisting of Dr. Gray, Dr. Maddrey, Dr. Abernathy, Dr. Van Ness, and Dr. Scarborough, the responsibility of further investigating the question raised by your application for membership in the Baptist World Alliance. You are fully aware that this Committee is appointed in no unsympathetic spirit, but with the hope of finding an entirely satisfactory solution.
>
> With kind regards,
>
> Yours very sincerely,
>
> Signed: J. H. Rushbrooke

The correspondence touching the matter of the Alliance is herewith submitted.

Replying to Dr. Rushbrooke's letter above referred to, we wrote:

Dear Dr. Rushbrooke:

We are glad to acknowledge your favor of July 21st apprising us of the appointment of a sub-committee to further investigate the relations of the National Baptist Convention (uninc.) to the National Baptist Convention (Inc.) We should be glad to have this committee visit our Convention in its annual session at Shreveport, Louisiana.

Appreciating the spirit manifested in your letter, and with all good wishes, I am
Yours sincerely,

J. Edmund Wood,

President National Baptist Convention

Our Boards

The provisions in our constitution creating boards to look after certain definite phases of the work are the out-growth of the wisdom and judgment of the fathers. They felt if all the work of the denomination were vested in any one board many phases of the work would suffer. Therefore, they established an Educational Board to take charge of the educational work; a Home Mission Board to have charge of the mission work within the United States and her territories; a Foreign Mission Board to supervise the extension of the kingdom in foreign lands; the Evangelical Board to create and stimulate interest in soul-saving throughout the world; a Church Extension Board to build churches and assist in building churches; to establish a loan fund for the purpose of helping struggling congregations to build church edifices and to pay off church building debts; a Benefit Board to provide a fund for worthy ministers in their hour of infirmity and old age; a Baptist Young People's Board to publish literature and establish societies for our young people, provide them with capable, competent lecturers who will instruct them in the doctrines, policy and history of the denomination; a Publishing Board to create and publish sound and helpful literature and disseminate Baptist sentiments among the nations. No one board is the Convention, but every board an integral part of the Convention. Every board owes the Convention something. It should be loyal to every phase of the Convention's work; it should show the spirit of harmony, and fellowship, and service to all. The Convention owes much to these boards. To manifest preference and a spirit of favoritism for certain boards is as a mother showing partiality toward a favorite child. It leads to jealousy and hate on the one hand and pride and arrogance on the other. It will be a sad day for this Convention when our boards begin to strive the one against the other; and to beat and devour one another. These boards were created to do a definite work in extending the kingdom. Love, pure and undismayed is necessary to the performance of that task. We may have talent, culture, and refinement; but if we have not love, not only will we be unfit to help others, but our own enterprises will shrivel and perish. There is not a board in this Convention so powerful and resourceful that it can live on and grow great, but taking the advantage of her sister boards. There is not a man in this Convention who can advance very far and endure very long who seeks to climb to prominence and honor through jealousy and spite and insincerity. Love is the only fair maiden that will lead to unfading glory, and she always leads by the way of the cross, down through the valley of humiliation and the dungeon of self-denial. Two brothers planted a wheat field, and harvested the wheat and gathered it in shocks. They divided the field and set an equal number of shocks on either side. That night in bed, they began to think, each of the other. Said John, "Brother Will has a wife and seven children to support. I have no one but myself. He needs more than I do. I shall go and take some of my wheat and put them on his side of the field." Will was thinking in his bed, and he said, "Brother John has no wife and children to comfort him; he must be lonely and cheerless. I shall comfort him by taking some of my shocks and put them on his side of the field." So they both started at the same time to give his brother some of his shocks, and they met on the dividing line each with an armful of bundles for his brother; and their neighbors erected a monument on the spot where they met and dedicated it to fraternal love. God give us love which "vaunteth not itself," "seeketh not her own," and "beareth all things."

The Call To Duty

Never before has such a challenge been made to the true followers of Jesus Christ. The world asks of the church: "Show us that you have a better life program than is offered by other institutions — the fraternities, the Urban League, the industrial unions, politics, the sororities." Five-thousand and five-hundred students at Syracuse University have organized their own church. No university officers or persons connected with any outside church have anything to do with it. No prayers except silent prayers are offered in the services, and they refuse to meet in any church house though several local congregations offered their edifices. They select their own preacher, usually a different one for each service, and pay him by personal offerings lifted in the congregation. This action on the part of more than five-thousand intelligent young men and women emphasizes, among other things, the failure of our church worship to grip the soul of the sincere seeker for truth and the lack of a program to which the budding manhood and womanhood may look for a solution of our spiritual and social and civil problems. How long will the masses be held in a church when all which can be said of the services is the sermon was scholarly, the music was fine, and the worship was orthodox? There are certain Baptist gatherings the only virtues of which they boast are their big crowds, their old stand-pat leadership, and their ability to manipulate phases so as to conceal their true character and disguise their intent and purpose.

We must give the people a program of purpose and achievements. We must give them more than a dead skeleton of theories and meaningless phrases. We must clothe these skeletons with flesh and blood and sinews of performances and breathe into them the breath of vital accomplishments til they shall stand upon their feet and live. If you have not faith enough in your own proposition to risk your money, and your reputation, and all your future in it, you are simply camp followers and may never be depended upon to fight the battles of the hosts.

The world cries to Christ's followers, tell us what your faith has accomplished? Has it made you happier and braver, and a greater burden bearer and a better and more useful member of society? A National Convention or any other religious organization is of little value unless it is known among men as a factor in winning men to the useful and helpful life and inspiring higher Christian ideals. To this cause are you called and to this task we must dedicate our all.

Christian Citizenship

When the Great Teacher said, "Render unto Caesar the things which are Caesar's and unto God the things that are God's" He laid upon the believer in Jesus Christ the obligation of supporting good government and maintaining a clean, wholesome administration of the law. While it is not my purpose to enter into a discussion of the political problems which claim the attention of our citizenship today, yet, the on-rushing tide of crime, lawlessness and disrespect for constituted authority which threaten to engulf the nation demand that the alarm be sounded and that all Christian citizens who love the government founded by Washington, and for which Lincoln died, aroused to arms to beat back the foes who would tear down our bulwark of liberty, destroy the citadel of the traditions of the fathers and drag into the mire of broken pledges and unkept promises the stars and stripes for which our fathers died.

My appeal to you is to study the problems which today agitate the nation, seek the wisdom which comes from above in choosing the course to pursue in this crisis, and when you are called upon to cast your vote, vote as you pray.

The preacher is not primary a politician. He is not a ward healer, a money grafter, nor an office seeker. He is a Christian statesman, like Elijah warning the people against corruption which threatens a nation, or a Joseph who in Egypt paved the way to preserve life and peace in the years of famine, or a Daniel who saved Babylon against her own voluptous living, pleasure seeking and blasphemy. Living the Christlife in the community — humility, kindness toward all men, peace, self-control and righteousness — will prove more powerful in winning favor and respect, then bayonets and rapid firing guns. We are going to win in this country by industry, honesty and helpful, useful living among our neighbors. "The fruit of the spirit is love, joy, peace, long-suffering, gentleness, goodness, faith, meekness, temperance: against such there is no law."

In This Sign Conquer

In Jesus Christ, through Him and with Him, this Convention shall win. I am not half so much concerned as to whether the rich, the learned, the vast numbers shall be with us as I am to know that the King of the heavens, the Ruler of nations is on our side. "It is better to trust in the Lord, than to put confidence in princes." If we have faith in Jesus Christ, as much as we have in farms, and oil wells, and banks and insurance companies, we shall win the day. "Not by might, nor power, but by My Spirit," saith the Lord Almighty.

I have seen the spread eagle orator sway the multitudes by a recital of our achievements in the world of commerce and finance. He lifted his hearers to heights of ecstasies when he told them of their holdings in homes and real estate, and factories and bank accounts. We live in the richest country in the world; and we as a race have made unparallelled progress since our emancipation.

I saw somewhere recently that we produce 40 percent of the iron and steel of the world; 20 percent of the world's wheat supply; 40 percent of the silver; 50 percent of the zinc; 52 percent of the coal; 60 percent of the aluminum; 60 percent of the copper; 60 percent of the cotton; 75 percent of the corn; and 85 percent of the world's supply of automobiles. America stands at the head in her production of wealth; how does she stand in the production of treasuries in heaven? If you and I are unwilling to consecrate our holdings to the Lord to be used to redeem and bring back to Him a wayward and sin-polluted world, failure, vanity of vanities will be the suitable epitaph for our sepulchre.

I would close my Bible today, and step down from the sacred rostrum, and never again lift my voice in defense of the cross, if I could believe that railroad stocks and government bonds, and Congress and the Supreme Court and the Constitution could save and perpetuate this United States. If this nation is to stand as the leader of nations, and perpetuate the principles of liberty, charity and fraternity it must be done in the name and spirit of the crucified Christ. *In hoc signo vinces,* is the battle cry of the army of the Lord and in His name we shall win the world.

I rejoice with all patriotic citizens in the achievements of the American people. I glory in the history of the Negro group. Like a golden thread running through the warp and woof of the nation's progress from Jamestown to the day when Perry pinned Old Glory on the North Pole, the Negro's part is interwoven with the nation's history. In industry, in education, in military service, in religious development, he has been identified with the best traditions and service of the nation. We are told that he has been given to us to teach her religion. When I think of America's religion, I am reminded of the country boy who went courting a city girl. He asked his mother how he might win this girl. His mother said to him, "You must seek to win her mother first. Speak complimentary of what you see and praise the acts of the mother." At dinner, butter was served in individual dishes. The boy, being reared on the farm, had seen the butter served on large plates, so desiring to say something complimentary, he said: "This is mighty good butter, what there is of it;" and, noticing from the expression on the faces of those at the table he had not said the proper thing, he amended his remark by saying, "and there is plenty of it such as it is."

When I study America's religious program today, I insist that there should be more of the New Testament religion and that it should be of a better brand. Let the light of love and loyalty to Jesus Christ burn in our soul till we are moved to bring our talent, our earthly goods, ourselves and lay them all on the altar to be used of Christ our King to bring the world under His rule.

Recommendations

1. I recommend that here and now red-blooded, upstanding Baptist men and women, rise up in this meeting and lay upon the tables money to wipe out the debt of our Theological Seminary on the property at Nashville. If this cannot be done; then, I recommend that the debt be reduced to the minimum and the Board of Trustees advised to provide for carrying the remainder at a reduced rate of interest.

2. I recommend that every board of the Convention organize as soon as the new members are elected in this session; and hand to the Recording Secretary of the Convention the full list of members, including the newly-elected officers of the board.

3. Believing that the Theological Seminary should be kept before the public throughout the year, I recommend that the Trustees of that institution to be called upon to consider the advisability of electing a President at a creditable salary who will devote his time to soliciting funds and advertising the school till such time as the school may be opened for classes.

4. We recommend that the Foreign Mission Board investigate the status of the charter under which the board was organized, and to ascertain if said charter is still in force and report its findings to the next session of the Convention.

5. We recommend that one field man be placed on the field in the territory of this Convention to awaken interest in our Foreign Mission work, and that the churches be appealed to for a more liberal support of our foreign missionaries.

Conclusion

We stand today midway the mountain slope. At the base below are thousands who started on the journey but have fallen by the wayside. In that unsightly and discouraging multitude are the "I cant's," the "I won'ts." We look ahead to the mountaintop, and on its summit we see millions who pressed on in the race till they reached the goal: John the Baptist, Paul, John of Patmos; Chrysostom, Huss and Savonarolla; Carey, Judson and Livingston; George Lilse, John Jasper and Wm. J. Simmons; R. H. Boyd, C. T. Walker and L. Lee Campbell; and myriads of others forming a company which no man can number. They scaled this mountain height, won the race and have taken their stations among the world's notables. They beckon us from their eminence. Shall we catch inspiration from the holy picture they form in the skies, and with renewed strength go forth to victory in the name of our Lord?

Annual Address of Dr. J. E. Wood
President of the National Baptist Convention of America
In Session at Norfolk, Virginia, September 4–9, 1929

Dear Brethren in Christ:

We assemble today on soil made sacred by the blood of pioneer Baptists who planted the rose of the gospel centuries ago which continued to blossom and beautify and perfume Virginia's citizenship, until the civilized world has been attracted and enriched by her rare virtues. Sweet memories of her gospel heroes rush upon here as we think of Lott Carey, the man of faith; of Jasper, the man of power; of Jones, the sweet angel in the church; of Holmes, the father and counselor in Israel; of Hayes, the golden mouthed whose oratory stirred men's blood and made the corpse of dead institutions stand upon its feet and live. These sainted spirits lend enchantment to this occasion, subdue and mellow our spirits, fit us with the frame of mind to wait and listen until Jehovah speaks. And men of God who come from almost every state in the Union will catch the fires which inspired those holy toilers to build churches and schools and preach a soul saving gospel until Baptists cover the earth as dew.

Virginia is not only the mother of Presidents, but she is the mother of preachers; and her sons have come home to demonstrate their fraternal love and how well they have lived out the lessons taught at mother's knees. And no unguarded words rashly spoken, no act of commission or omission shall rob the occasion of the most perfect happiness, nor mar the joy of the mother heart that welcomes us home.

Baptists from the four corners of the earth gather in this beautiful city of Norfolk, in holy convocation, under the blood-bespangled banner of Him who has commissioned us to publish His name among all nations. The eyes of the world are upon us. From Atlantic's storm shores to the golden strand of the Pacific; from the tall pines of Maine to the everglades of Florida eyes are watching the actions and deportments of the men and women here assembled today. But, more important that the eyes of the whole world that scrutinize our deliberations is the all-seeing eye which has guided us through the years. When I remember that He who has a bigger interest in the kingdom than any other person here is present and will work out a program which will bless us all and glorify His holy name, I am content to do my duty fearlessly, courageously and faithfully, and leave the results with Him.

Our Opportunity

The opportunity of Negro Baptists at this time is rare. The aching heart of the poor, the ignorant, the oppressed cry out of their distresses for deliverance. At this time when the Old Book is being attacked, when truth is compromised for gain and world glory, when men in whom we once confided as safe defenders for the gospel of Christ give uncertain sound, and the masses are restless and seek for the old paths, it is an opportunity for the sincere followers of Jesus Christ to sow the seed of the gospel and cultivate it with Christian living. If we shall be wise enough to use the restlessness of the dissatisfied as an opportunity to impart to them the truth which they so much need, we shall win for Christianity a victory imperishable. Earth's sufferings, race clashes, strife between man and man are the opportunities for Christ's followers to hold Him up as the Light of the world, the Adjuster to whom all difficulties may be brought for adjudication. Congress, the President, the Supreme Court have failed to meet the cry of the common people for redress. Some of our leaders insisted that the elevation of Mr. Herbert Hoover to the Presidency of the United States would usher in an era of goodwill and prosperity and happiness. Mr. Hoover is in the White House, and crime, lynchings, segregation, defiance of law move on as in years gone by. We have put millions of dollars into our secular schools. Educational institutions are being richly endowed and yet crime and law violations have not decreased. These conditions are an opportunity for the church to offer its program to the world as a solution to the social, moral, and industrial problems of the generations.

Our Convention was born and is being sustained by a constituency that believe religious institutions exist to perpetuate spiritual things and not primarily to advance the worldly glory of personal gain of men. It should be the high purpose of the men of this Convention to interest men in kingdom work until they will put their time and money in the cause of missions and Christian education. You and I want the world to say of us, those men at Norfolk had their minds set on Jesus and what they did was for His glory.

The problem of mankind is essentially a gospel problem. "Ye shall know the truth, and the truth shall make you free." This generation shall suffer intellectual slavery, physical slavery, and moral slavery until we shall agree to live by the word of God. And, it is the mission of religious institutions to carry this truth to earth's pining nations. What is needed most in this country and in all lands is a knowledge of God's word and a willing obedience to His will.

The biggest opportunity any religious organization ever had is given to the National Baptist Convention of America today. I want the members of this Convention to demonstrate in their lives the Christ spirit by consecrating themselves unto the Lord, by giving unto Him their talent and their money, and by making such sacrifice as will win the victory we seek. It is reported that we are a race of poor and ignorant people, and we often find men and women in the race who use this allegation as an excuse for our failure to do a man's job. I hold that there is wealth enough and Christian training enough and wisdom enough in the aggregation of Baptists here assembled to carry forward the work of this Convention in a handsome, yea, glorious manner.

The real and permanent advancement of a people must be advancement in morals and intellectual attainments. Greece and Rome attained a high degree of art, literature, commerce, and military power; but their civilization was transitory and their glory has long since faded. We delight to point to the Negro's history in this country. In material things his progress is without a parallel. His farms and commodious homes, his banks and insurance companies, his factories and mercantile institutions stand as monuments to his industry and genius. But I wonder sometimes if we have grown in love, and faith, and good works as we have grown in manual training and physical strength. Do we think as much of our Bible schools, our missionary work, our church worship as we think of our sheep and cattle, and are we devoting as much time to the making of fine Christian men and women as we are to the task of raising fine horses and fine chickens? I plead for a class of followers of Jesus Christ who will make world-surprising, devil-frightening contributions to kingdom work. If some man or woman of faith would rise up in this Convention and write his check for ten-thousand dollars to be used in training minister and Christian teachers, and some would write his check for ten-thousand dollars for missions, Satan would become alarmed; but so long as church members will invest fifty-thousand dollars in prize fights and Sunday baseball and give fifty-cents to redeem the heathen world, the rulers of darkness will not be disturbed. God grant that you and I will devote less time trying to make big men and big speeches and more time making big sacrifices and big contributions to the objects of the Convention.

Our Auxiliaries

The work of this Convention is fortunate in having as its loyal supporter a strong Woman's Auxiliary manned by a corps of efficient officers whose report to this body will convince the most skeptical that they are with the brethren, heart and hand in their endeavor to extend the work of the kingdom. The President, Mrs. M.A.B. Fuller has been incessant in her labors to stir the Baptist women of the country to greater activity in missions and Christian education. Her appeals have been convincing, and I am sure will yield much fruit. In her program, she is supported by her entire cabinet; and we are expecting great things of them in this session.

Our Laymen's League represents the manpower of the denomination. Some of the most capable and consecrated laymen in the denomination head up this organization. Prof. W. H. Fuller of Austin, Texas, the President, and Mr. L. Landers of Nashville, Tenn., the Corresponding Secretary, have been busy throughout the year trying to arouse interest among the laymen. They are the minister's friends; and if we give these workers the proper encouragement, they will prove a valuable asset to this Convention. We hold these auxiliaries in full fellowship to share in our struggles and rejoice in our successes.

The Boards

You have established boards to care for the different objects of the Convention, and I believe for the most part their reports will show that they are alive to the task assigned them. These boards have done more in the last year, in their respective fields to inspire Baptists and others to give to the cause, than was ever done in previous years. The Foreign Mission Board has sought to arouse a deeper interest in Foreign Missions and has given to carry out the agreement with the Lott Carey Society to cooperate in sustaining the work on foreign fields. The Home Mission Board continues to increase its operations and has added to the number of its field workers, has helped churches and mission stations, and has contributed very much in making sentiment for this Convention. The Evangelical Board has kept the work of soul saving alive and has enlisted many men and women in the cause, who hitherto had given little, or no attention to this phase of our work. The Benefit Board still cries to the brethren for help, and the cause which it represents is deserving of our consideration.

Our Publishing Board

The peculiar position which the National Baptist Publishing Board occupies in the work of the denomination and the service which it is rendering the Baptists and humanity demands special consideration. What would be the standing and progress of Negro Baptists in America today had there been no Richard H. Boyd and no Publishing Board? I am no hero worshipper; but Richard H. Boyd wrought a work in the religious world that shall lend inspiration to the ambitious youth of the land and enrich Baptist history throughout succeeding generations. From his fertile brain the National Baptist Publishing Board sprang like Minerva from the brain of Jupiter and gives a field of service to a hundred and seventy who earn a livelihood under religious influence. This Board supplies fifty-thousand churches, Sunday Schools, and B. Y. P. U.'s with wholesome literature and sends forth Baptist teachings and Baptist sentiments to the four corners of the earth. We thank God for this board and its manager, Henry A. Boyd.

The Theological Seminary

The year in which we were elected to the Presidency of this Convention, the Trustee Board of the Theological Seminary was reorganized. The Seminary debt was reported to be twenty-three-thousand dollars. The new Board has labored incessantly to payoff this debt; and at our last session in Shreveport, this debt had been reduced to eleven-thousand dollars. Considerable repairs have been made on the building and the insurance and interest have been paid to January 15, 1930. These men on the Board have given liberally of their personal money on this debt and made appeals to the constituents of the Convention to contribute to the liquidation of this debt. It is expected that at least five-thousand dollars will be paid on this debt at this session of the Convention.

The Educational Board has cooperated with the Trustees in this work and is a valuable asset to our educational work.

Our Entrance Into The Baptist World Alliance

In December, 1927, we wrote the Secretary, Dr. J. H. Rushbrooke, signifying our desire of becoming a member of the Baptist World Alliance. He advised us to file our application with the Executive Committee which would meet in New York City in January, 1928. This we did. We sent to the committee a copy of our latest minutes with a letter setting forth our regular meeting and the nature of the work we were doing. After the adjournment of this committee meeting, we received a letter from the Secretary stating that the committee had no evidence before it to show that we were a separate National Organization from that presided over by Dr. L. K. Williams. Considerable correspondence followed when the Secretary advised that we meet the Executive Committee in the Toronto meeting, June, 1928, with what ever evidence we had to show that we represented a National organization. Dr. D. E. Over and myself met the committee. We met there brethren of America who vehemently opposed our entering the Alliance. The committee decided it would not have time to properly consider this question while in Toronto, and the matter was referred to a sub-committee with power to act. This committee met in Detroit, Wednesday, May 17. We were in the hospital at the time and had been there for several weeks. However, we asked our daughter to come to us and prepare the papers for the committee. She secured a leave of absence from the bank of Chicago in which she was employed as bookkeeper and came to our assistance. We lay in the hospital and dictated the statement of evidence and the rules upon which we made the application. We sent for some brethren to meet in Lexington and go to Detroit to meet the committee. Dr. A. A. Graham came to Lexington, and we gave him the facts we had assembled; and he met Drs. J. W. Hurse, E. H. Branch, and M. P. Parrish in Detroit. They went before the committee of the Alliance, presented their cause, and when the committee saw the documents, they were surprised that we had such an organization and are doing the work which our minutes showed we were doing. We were voted into the Alliance, practically unanimously. The following letter from Dr. J. H. Rushbrooke explains the situation.

> The Rev. Dr. J. Edmund Wood
> President, National Baptist Convention of America
> Danville, Kentucky
>
> My Dear Dr. Wood:
>
> The members of the Executive Committee learned with regret that illness prevented you visiting Detroit on the 17th last. They sincerely trust that you are making a good recovery.
>
> It is my privilege to inform you that after full consideration, the Executive Committee, by a practically unanimous vote, adopted on the motion of Dr. C. H. Parrish recommendation from its sub-committee in the following terms:
>
> That the applicant body (frequently described as the National Baptist Convention Unincorporated) be admitted to membership of the Alliance under the

designation "National Baptist Convention of America."

You will be glad to learn of this decision, and I am also glad to transmit it.

The Executive Committee was gratified at the evident interest displayed in the Alliance by the members of your delegation and appreciate the promise to contribute to the annual budget the same amount as is expected from the National Convention already in membership. Since our fiscal year ends June 30, I think your contribution should commence with the new fiscal year (July lst, next), and I will write you further on the subject.

Meanwhile, I extend to you and your brethren, on behalf of the Executive, a hearty welcome into our fraternal fellowship and rejoice that you enter under such happy conditions.

With all good wishes,
Fraternally yours,

Signed: J. H. Rushbrooke

Seven-hundred and fifty dollars per annum is our quota which may be paid in quarterly payments of one-hundred, eighty-seven dollars and fifty cents in July, October, January, and April.

In July we made the first quarterly payment. We asked some brethren to send us ten dollars each and the following named brethren responded: C. H. Clark, E. H. Branch, A. A. Graham, A. A. Banks, S. S. Jones, E. R. Carter, J. N. Jenkins, J. H. Winn, Dr. Henry A. Boyd sent us a check for one-hundred and eighty dollars that we might make the payment in the month of July when due. The following letter shows that the money was received in Dr. Rushbrooke's office and we were given credit for same.

Baptist World Alliance Office
4 Southampton Row
London, W. C. I.
6th August, 1929

Dr. J. Edmund Wood
National Baptist Convention
Danville, Ky., U. S. A.

Dear Sir:

Dr. Rushbrook is away in the country, and in his absence, I have to thank you very much for your letter of July 24th, enclosing checques for $187.50 as quarterly contribution towards the funds of the Baptist World Alliance. I have pleasure in sending herewith the official receipt.

Dr. Rushbrooke would desire me to send you his kindest regards.

Yours faithfully,

Signed: M. Nisted
Secretary to Dr. Rushbrooke

I reported to you that the National Baptist Convention of America is a bona fide member of the Baptist World Alliance in good and regular standing.

An Appeal for Miss Burroughs

Last spring while lying the Lexington hospital, there came an appeal for help from the National Training School for Women and Girls. When I received this appeal, I asked the Lord to open the way that the President of that institution might receive the money so much needed to carry on the work of the Training School. I asked my daughter to write a small personal check for this work. I then had her write a note to the officers of my church to take an after offering the following Lord's day which they did. I then said to myself every church in our Convention can do as my church has done. So I sent out an appeal through the columns of the *Union Review* for that work. I felt if Baptists can contribute to Y.M.C.A. work and Urban League work and N.A.A.C.P. work, surely, they will give to a great Christian institution for the training of our girls though it be not under the immediate control of our Convention.

A number of the Trustees of this school are members of the Convention. Among them may be mentioned Dr. J. P. Robinson, Dr. Charles Hawkins, the late Dr. David E. Over until his death, and your humble servant.

The young women this institution has sent out who are honoring the race in useful vocations merit a contribution not only from every Baptist, but from every member of the Negro race in this country. And while every pressure conceivable has been brought to bear to force the President and Board of Trustees turn over this school to a particular group of Baptists, they have stood like the rock of Gibraltar and refused to be moved, maintaining that the school belongs to all the Baptists. Let no pastor and no church refuse to give support to this institution and its President, Miss Nannie H. Burroughs, for it is the only school of its kind among Negroes of the world and is doing a work in Christian womanhood without a parallel in history.

Some Progress

At the Fort Worth meeting in 1923, the reports for education was $724.30; for Foreign Missions, $535.00; for Home Mission, $101.25; and for Conventional expenses, $1633.89. As an indication of the growth of the Convention, we give a partial statement of the finances at Shreveport. Collected for Education, $3129.04; Foreign Missions, $1865.89; Home Missions, $400.00; Expenses, $2414.60. The finances at Denver was even better than Shreveport.

The first year after you had elected me your President, I met Dr. C. S. Brown, President of the Lott Carey Missionary Society, in the Vincennes Hotel in Chicago, the month of February, 1924, where we discussed plans of co-operation between the Lott Carey Society and the National Baptist Convention. Growing out of this conversation, I took the initiative and appointed a committee of brethren to meet the Lott Carey Convention in Washington, D. C., in August. We addressed the Convention in favor of uniting in the work of Foreign Missions which was heartily endorsed by that Convention, and a committee was appointed to meet us in Chicago the following month. The Committee met our Convention in Chicago and a commission was appointed to meet in Indianapolis the following November where the plans of co-operation between the two Conventions were formed which are in force today. After negotiations for eighteen months, we succeeded in having this Convention enrolled as a member of the Baptist World Alliance and she stands today the equal of any Baptist organization in the world.

We have succeeded in paying an eleven-hundred dollar debt of the ex-President; a printing account of nearly three-thousand dollars, and incidentals amounting to fifteen-thousand dollars. While these accomplishments were being wrought, the Seminary debt of twenty-three-thousand dollars was reduced one-half. I believe this history of achievement will compare favorably with that of any religious organization in this country.

There will be some persons who are dissatisfied with the progress we have made. I, myself, am dissatisfied with the work we have done. But, in every organization, there are two classes of dissatisfied folk. One class is dissatisfied and grumbles and finds fault; but the records do not show that they ever do anything worthy to improve conditions. The other class is dissatisfied and gives their time and influence to make conditions better. Again, we have them in this Convention who are bearing its burden and have paid the price to make possible the record we have disclosed.

Recommendations

Ten years ago, Dr. R. H. Boyd brought to the Convention in this city the Boscobel property as a home for the National Theological and Training School. Many of the wisest men in the Convention who were enthusiastic for the school in Nashville ten years ago, today, question the wisdom of undertaking to operate a school of high order in the community of towering colleges as are in Nashville.

1. Therefore, I recommend that a commission of twelve discreet and forward looking men be appointed to canvass the situation and report its findings to this Convention.

2. I recommend in its investigation this commission will call into consultation the Trustees of Virginia Seminary and leaders in the Virginia Convention and consider the feasibility of this Convention adopting the Virginia Seminary as our institution for the training of denominational and race leaders.

3. Too long have we played at erecting the Boyd monument. The life work of this great and good man demands that Negro Baptists memorialize his work by the erection to his memory a suitable memorial. I recommend, therefore, that the Boyd Memorial Commission be instructed to take steps this year to erect a memorial.

4. We recommend that the Church Extension Board be so organized and re-inforced as will enable it to become a real help to the poor struggling churches in their endeavor to secure suitable places of worship. Aid to these churches is imperative, and we must not allow them in communities where churches are needed to be forced out of existence from lack of proper assistance.

5. There will be held in the City of Chicago, in 1933, a World's Exposition commemorating the one-hundredth anniversary of the founding of that city. This, it is said, will be the greatest exposition ever held on the American continent. Already forty-four nations have asked for space on the exposition grounds. The children of this world are usually wiser than the children of light; may it not be so in this instance. We recommend that this Convention appoint a commission composed of one member from each state in the Union to take charge of suitable exhibits and displays for the National Baptist Convention. This commission shall have power to make suitable reservations, to provide for suitable religious services throughout the exposition, to secure and have on display exhibits of churches, houses, schools, and Baptist institutions; to secure data and publish a Baptist encyclopedia in which will appear every Baptist preacher, professional and businessman and woman in America, each person paying a reasonable sum for his space. That this publication be completed and on display at the opening of the exhibition.

6. That the Convention hold its 1933 session in Chicago.

The Departed

Our hearts have been sad by the taking away of some of the most useful, heroic, and loyal men in this Convention. We look for an Over, the scholar and logician; for a Drane whose spirit was as brave as a lion and as gentle as a dove, for a Tait whose soul was as pure as the driven snow and whose words were as sweet as honey in the honeycombs, and they are not here. And others now in the glory land who shall be missed for their seat is empty.

Life is but a pilgrimage; we are travelers to our Father's house. They who have gone before are beckoning us come; and some sweet day we shall sit down with them in the home of the soul.

Conclusion

It is said of Captain C. B. Miller of the British Navy that when the cruiser Nottingham was torpedoed during the World's war, and he saw that the ship must go down, that he called his men to order, and ordered them to slip over the rail into their lifeboats. He stood on the deck until the last man had left the ship; he then leaped into the sea in full uniform and encouraged his men as he swam about them and was the last man to be rescued. Baptist leaders, let us not desert the crew, but, may we support and encourage those who fight for the cause as long as there is a man on deck of the old ship.

The victories we have won forecast greater victories in the future. We have won the expanding west, the rich and fertile east felicitate with us in this assembly; our Lott Carey brethren and members of this Convention are being welded into one great religious force which is destined to become the most powerful organization for kingdom building in the world.

The darkening clouds lift, the morning light appears, and men of all nations and classes rally to our banner.

> "Here we raise our Ebenezer,
> Hither by thy help we come."

The world looks to Baptists for some things it can find no where else. An open Bible, free speech, personal faith in the Christ, a regenerate church membership, democratic form of government are our trophies. We cannot calculate the results of our labors if we will live out these principles. But to shout these principles from the mountain top and then fail to live them out is open mockery. What shall be the fruits of the labors and activities in this Convention? What contributions are we making through this Convention to the world's advancement? Are we making these gatherings the means by which men find themselves and work out the will of God?

As we go from this assembly, may we carry the happy memory of a rich fellowship, of a full co-operation in good works, of a fixed determination to use this Convention for the glory of God and humanity's good. This I crave and pray; and attaining this, I ask nothing more.

This year has been a test of our faith, our courage and our ambition. Never before have we been so definitely called upon to trust God, to trust our friends and to believe that our mission was heaven appointed. And, when we were sick nigh unto death and five physicians stood around our bed and discussed our case, and loved ones and friends were anxious, the presence of the Christ gave courage in that dark hour to meet the crisis bravely, do our duty and leave the results with God. Then there glowed in our soul the flame of a radiant ambition to carry on the cause to which our life has been consecrated to make Christ King of all the earth and to awaken among Negro Baptists the determination to spread His gospel in every land.

We stand before you today having passed through the furnace of afflictions, and we can never cease to love and praise His great name for all He has done for us. And whatever of reverses or successes the future may hold in store, the flowers which beautify and sweeten may strew our path, or thorns which prick and tear may hedge our way, but, yet, our faith in the Jehovah shall not be moved; and the joy which comes through companionship with His shall abide forever.

"I know not where His islands lift
Their fronded palms in the air;
I only know I cannot drift
Beyond His loving care."

John Wesley Hurse

John Wesley Hurse (1866-1935) was born on July 10, 1866 at Colyerville, near Mason, Tennessee. He spent the early part of his life on a farm near Mason and did not have the chance for much formal schooling. He united with the church in Colyerville at the age of fifteen.

Up to the age of thirty-two, when he felt the urge to enter the Christian ministry, his scholastic standing was scarcely that of a first grade pupil. W. G. Mosely wrote of him in the *Kansas City American*, "His explorations of books and literature extended no further than McGuffey's First Reader and initial pages of the Blue Back Speller. From boyhood to manhood, he learned to read the newspaper and the Bible."

In 1886, he moved to Kansas City, Missouri. He worked on various jobs including coachman, asphalt worker, and packing-house worker. He enrolled with the Washington School of Correspondence and at the end of six years, had his first degree conferred upon him, Doctor of Divinity.

In the summer of 1898, he entered the Christian ministry at the age of thirty-two. He preached on the street corners in "Bellevidere Hollow," one of the most sinful and spiritually-deprived sections of the city. It was predominantly composed of Blacks and Italians and was known as "Hell's Half Acre" and "the Bucket of Blood."

He was first married to Janie Frye in the early 1900's. They were the parents of five children: John, Jeneva, George, William, and Josephine. Following the death of the children's mother, he later married Miss Lula Mae Butler, who was considered the greatest Gospel singer of her generation.

He pastored Pilgrim Baptist Church and thereafter, founded and pastored Saint Stephen's Baptist Church in Kansas City, Missouri, for thirty-two years (1903-1935).

Dr. Hurse served eight years as First Vice-President of the National Baptist Convention of America. He became President in December, 1929, following the death of Dr. J. Edmund Wood.

He died early Monday morning, October 14, 1935.

Annual Address of Dr. J. W. Hurse
President of the National Baptist Convention of America
In Session at New York, New York, September 10–18, 1930
Jubilee Session

We are assembled at the Metropolitan City of the world, the great city of New York. Brethren and co-workers and gospel yokemen, heaven's brightest lights of all the world: Greetings:

I bring to you today the old banner with a double triple-ration printed in gold, Eph. 4:5, "One faith, one Lord, one baptism."

Through the providence of God and our constitution, the duties of President of this great religious body were conferred upon this, your humble servant.

Dear Christian co-workers, looking over this vast, beautiful and intelligent august body, my heart is made to abound, my spirit is given new courage, my soul is happier. For I know after looking in the faces of your Christian characters that God's work is safely entrusted into your hands; that here among you are the gospel buglers, bugling God's message to the utmost corners of the world. Standing up like mighty oaks, brave, fearless and courageously telling the world that there is only one National Baptist Convention, Unincorporated of America, and that this Convention sitting in the most wonderful city of New York is by the deeds accomplished, letting the world know who and what we are and for what we stand.

We suffered a great set-back in the death of our sainted President J. Edmund Wood, a man who had led us on to victory for a number of years, and who is now with the aid of his sainted spirit leading us on. God called him home, but He in His mighty wisdom kept J. Edmund Wood with us until we were lambs, not sheep, able to stand on our feet and go about our Master's work. Here let us pause in silent prayer, thanking God for our late President.

To prove to this world what we are, depends greatly upon the support given the one man chosen to lead us. Regardless of the man's ability to lead, he cannot make a success unless he has your support.

We must take our thoughts off "self" and try to find the Joshua — a Joshua that has our cause at heart, one that will front for us, plead our cause, and will give his time, his assistance to the least one of us. When we find him, let us all give him our hearty support.

Let me appeal to your better selves. Let us stop back-biting, bickering and clamoring for office. This Convention, fellow messengers, is not a political convention nor an organization of the world. We are God's chosen elect, with a mission ahead, a goal set, and a reward to work for. Not for the pitiful few dollars that we may earn, nor the man-made honor which comes our way. Let us put the Convention first, last, and always, feeling that beside the Convention, we are naught.

Dear co-worker, let me pause to thank you, yes, each of you for your consideration, your loyalty and your hearty co-operation. I want to thank those who did not rally to us, for you played a large part in whatever success that I have made as your President. Had you not opposed me, I could not have overcome. For my pathway would have been smooth sailing. To you loyal brethren who have given me every assistance, who put your shoulder to the wheel and pushed, not to make Hurse's regime a success, but the National Baptist Convention a success. I thank you.

We have been sought to join the incorporated Convention, tactfully we have refused — refused because we knew that we are stronger numerically, financially and educationally. We have within our fields the only Negro owned and controlled publishing house in the world. We are free from our white brethren, our schools are among the leading schools of this country. Let us fight to keep it so — to keep our Convention on the heights where our incorporated brethren have placed us. Let us strive to continue being their star, always wanted but just out of reach. To obtain and to hold this element will require the untiring strength and support of each of you. The Convention needs it, duty demands it. May we count on you?

When we left the most exquisite city of Norfolk, Va., last year, we left behind us a record that is hard to surpass. We had an A-1 attendance, with an addition of brethren from the incorporated Convention. Today, I see new faces among us. To you brethren we welcome you into our midst.

The finance of this meeting is excellent. Our boards, various departments and individual messengers rallied as never before.

A year's program was mapped out, and to the best of my ability I have carried out the plan with your assistance. For to accomplish our aim the support of all is needed. I am delighted to say that we were not found wanting. You came to my support like twice born men. Yes, men we knew, preached and believed that there is a God, and that His work had been entrusted into our hands. For when He issued the call to "Feed my sheep," he was talking to us. We have not let the slackers which we find in every organization cause us to weaken.

This spirit shown is the true Christian spirit. With this we want to add honesty, courageousness, sacrifice and the feeling that each of us is an important cog in the machine. We want to say to ourselves, "If each member in our Convention was just like me, what kind of convention would it be?" We not only want to ask ourselves the question but live up to its principles, for in that way we can make it the kind that it should be.

At last we are members of the World's Alliance, you know the fight our late President made to secure our membership. You know the fight that was launched against us. Therefore, I am appealing to you to make it possible for this Convention to keep up its dues, to make the meetings, to love and abide with all requirements. For when the world has ceased to be, we want to be found members of the Baptist World Alliance.

The Educational Board, Home Mission Board, Foreign Mission Board, Evangelical Board, Church Extension Board, B.Y.P.U. Board, Benefit Board, and all other boards, let us continue to work in peace and harmony. Always remember the great commandment: "Love ye one another." For in doing this, we believe success is yours.

To the Woman's Convention, we extend our greetings. We love this Convention; we thank you for the support, the strength, the encouragement, you have given us. We count on you at all times. Your Home and Foreign Missionary work is a credit to you. We earnestly pray for your continuance.

Our aim, dear co-worker, is to baptize the world, to convert our heathens, and to make the world a better place for our being here. We want our actions and our achievements to live long after we are forgotten.

Let us study the needs of this Convention, of our churches, educational facilities, and foreign friends. Study the ways and means of bettering them. Then proceed like soldiers to battle, never looking backward but ever pressing on, looking forward to our goal. In this is our method of success.

Recommendations

1. I recommend that we sell the school property at Nashville in order that we may not become the laughingstock of the world and throw all our educational strength to our great school in Virginia.

2. I recommend that all expense bills of the Convention be brought before the Convention on Saturday and passed on by the Board on Monday. I do believe that the people who bring the money here ought to know the going of it.

3. For lo, these many years of my connection with this religious body, there has been a continuous clamor among the delegates asking for an itinerary of office. I, therefore, recommend the four years itineracy for the President and that he be elected every year, but not to exceed four years.

4. Owing to the extreme cold weather in January, I recommend that our winter meetings be held in the month of March prior to the fourth Lord's Day. In my opinion, this will enable all of the boards to be present, and we will be able to raise some finance.

5. I recommend that for the good of the field that the Secretaries of the Foreign Mission Board, Home Mission Board, Church Extension Board and Evangelical Board give their entire time to the field.

All of which I humbly submit for your prayerful consideration.

Conclusion

In conclusion, I want to quote this verse:

> "Life is like a mountain railway,
> With an engineer that is brave.
> We will make the run successful,
> From the cradle to the grave
> Always mindful of obstruction,
> Do your duty, never fail.
> Keep your hand upon the throttle,
> And your eye upon the rail."

When quoting that verse I always think of the sainted dead for it reminds me of their noble lives. It so wonderfully expressed their sentiments and their theme of life. For they are: J. Edmund Wood, R. H. Boyd, E. C. Morris, Wm. Beckham, Dave Over, C. T. Walker, L. Lee Campbell, George Lilse, B. F. Farrell, R. D. Phillips, Drain, Hawthorne, Cross, Marshall, Crawford, Mitchell, and a host of others made the run successful, always with their hands on the throttle, making a brave and courageous run; giving this old world great institutions, organizations, religious education and the one and only Negro Baptist Publishing House owned and controlled by Negroes in the world and this great Convention unincorporated.

Yes, to you great men who imitated the wonderful Son of God in giving your lives for the cause, we bow in memory. We honor your greatness. We are striving to, in this Fiftieth Anniversary of our great Convention to leave a record that you could be proud of, that the world is proud of, and we are proud of; we are leaving the city and the Convention with you in our minds; with your immediate lives before us; with the determination to push onward and departing, leaving behind us footprints on the sands of time.

Green L. Prince

Green L. Prince (1870-1956) was born in Princeville, Gonzales County, Texas, August 15, 1870. He was a twin brother of Samuel Prince and one of a family of twelve children born to Samuel Prince and his wife, Sarah.

He was educated in the public schools of Texas. He entered the Christian ministry after twenty-nine years as a school teacher. During that time, he served as President of Sanjo College for three years; principal of an Indian school in Muskogee, Oklahoma; and principal of a high school in Tulsa, Oklahoma. In the fall of 1944, he became President of Mary Allen College, Crockett, Texas, which was owned and controlled by the Missionary Baptist Convention of Texas. He established the G. L. Prince Hospital in Crockett.

Dr. Prince was married to Laura F. Prince for many years. They had four children: two sons and two daughters. Laura died February 20, 1939. In June, 1940, he married Gertrude Naomi Johnson of Fort Worth, Texas.

Dr. Prince pastored in San Antonio, Texas; First Baptist Church, Tulsa, Oklahoma; Central Baptist Church, Muskogee, Oklahoma; Francis Street Baptist Church, St. Joseph, Missouri (ten years); Greater Zion, Denver, Colorado; and Avenue L Baptist Church, Galveston, Texas for twenty-three years.

He was elected President of the National Baptist Convention of America in Chicago, Illinois in 1933. He served as one of the vice-presidents of the Baptist World Alliance. He traveled extensively throughout America, Europe, Asia, and Africa for the cause of Christ.

Dr. Prince died Thursday morning, November 29, 1956 at 4:30.

Annual Address of Dr. G. L. Prince
President of the National Baptist Convention of America
In Session at Kansas City, Missouri, 1950

To the National Baptist Convention of America:

Unto God, our heavenly Father, and Jesus Christ, His son and our Saviour, we give thanks for the opportunity to meet again in another annual meeting.

The nations of the earth are in a state of fear, trouble, and confusion as to what the future will bring. Christians should not allow themselves to be confused or fearful, but keep in mind that Jesus said, "For all these things must come to pass, see that ye be not troubled."

What is happening to cause the world to be in this condition should be the hopeful sign of the approach of the establishment of the kingdom of Jesus Christ on the earth. According to the scripture, as the world moves toward the end of Gentile-rule, the condition of the world will become worse.

Our meeting here should be characterized by a sincere desire to do what we can to make this Convention a more useful organization in performing Christian service. All selfish motives should be relegated from our minds. We should with courage face the task set before us. We should examine our accomplishments to ascertain what can be done to improve them. We should never be satisfied with what has been done. When satisfaction becomes a mental condition, progress ceases.

Boards

The constitution specifically states in its preamble why this Convention was organized:

> "We the members of the Baptist Foreign Mission Convention of America and the National Baptist Convention of America, do unite ourselves together for the purpose of doing missionary, educational, and all religious work among ourselves and throughout the world."

In order to have its purpose executed, the Convention has established boards. To the boards the Convention has entrusted the execution of its work; as such they become agents of the Convention.

The constitution states that "Each Board shall be subject to the

Convention in all it does at recess or during the meeting of the Convention."

It is the right of the Convention to investigate and inspect the work of the boards, that it might ascertain what has been done and how it is being done.

It is very necessary that each member of the Convention sense the importance of the work of the boards. I will read what the constitution states about the work of the Boards.

Our Foreign Mission Work

We have at this time a better opportunity for doing Foreign Mission work in Africa than ever before. Much has been said about the situation there since Sister Jessie Mae Hicks visited there. It would be well for us to keep in mind this scripture, "Render therefore to all their dues; tribute to whom tribute is due; custom to whom custom; fear to whom fear; honour to whom honour." Rom. 13:17.

It remains for the President of the Convention to clarify this whole matter, for he has the documentary facts.

First, the President did not send Sister Hicks to Liberia to spy on the work of the Corresponding Secretary of the Foreign Mission Board.

Secondly, the Corresponding Secretary of the Foreign Mission Board asked Sister Hicks to pay a salary to the Rev. O. S. Davis' wife. She was inclined to do it, but said she would like to go to Africa to see what was being done before she agreed to do so.

Third, she conferred with me about it. She said she would pay her expenses, and did.

On her arrival in Liberia, she discovered conditions as they were and made her report to the President.

By searching the records in Liberia, she found that no land had been granted the National Baptist Convention of America and that the land where Mrs. Fuller had located the mission and where Rev. Davis was carrying on missionary work for the Foreign Mission Board and being contested and that Mrs. Fuller had contracted to buy 102 acres from one of the contestants for $500. (Five-hundred dollars, and had paid $125.00 on it). Sister Hicks saw the uncertainty of obtaining 102 acres; she began negotiating for 1000 acres with the Office of the Liberian Government. President Tubman promised to help her get title to it for the National Baptist Convention of America.

Sister Hicks was notified that the President of Liberia had called an extra session of the legislature to convene on the 3rd of April 1950 and that it was possible to get a petition through the Liberian Legislature, granting the 1000 acres of land to the National Baptist Convention of America, but it would be necessary for someone to be in Liberia at that time. I then commissioned Sister Hicks and Sister Fuller, who volunteered to go with her to Liberia to secure title to the 1000 acres of land selected by Sister Hicks. They were successful in getting a title to the land.

Christian Attitudes and Solution of All Problems

Christians are in the world but not of the world. All questions relating to the welfare of humanity on earth whether they are racial, social, economical, industrial, governmental, or religious can be solved by application of Christian principles. The world today is trying to solve its problems by world methods. The world system is of the devil. "He has organized the world of unbelieving mankind upon his world principles of force, greed, selfishness, ambition, and pleasure." The Christian system is based upon love for God and for man, so human beings who are regenerated are subject to the will of God.

Christ in His prayer said, "I pray not that thou shouldest take them out of the world, but thou shouldest keep them from the evil, they are not of the world." John 17:15-16

Many so-called Christian leaders instead of leading according to Christian principles have accepted the world methods of leadership. Men of the world are employing all the secular instruments of the world to solve the world problems, because they do not believe that the application of Christian principles is the most effective method for the solution of the world's problems.

Let us remember the word of God to Zerubbabel saying, "Not by might, nor by power, but by my spirit, saith the Lord of hosts." Zech. 4:6. Christian leaders should lead the people to trust in God for the solution of all their problems. "I will lift up mine eyes unto the hills from whence cometh my help. My help cometh from the Lord, which made heaven and earth. He will not suffer thy foot to be moved; he that keepeth thee will not slumber nor sleep. The Lord is thy keeper; the Lord is thy shade upon thy right hand. The sun shall not smite thee by day, nor the moon by night. The Lord shall preserve thee from all evil; he shall preserve thy going out and thy coming in from this time forth, and for evermore.

Baptist World Alliance

I regret very much that I was unable to attend the Baptist World Alliance, but was happy to hear that many of you attended it and benefited by so doing. From what I have heard of what was done by the Alliance in regard to segregation and discrimination, the Alliance did that which proved it is a Christian body. Any organization that believes in and practices segregation is not a Christian organization. The biggest problem in America is the race problem. So long as this problem is not solved the Negro cannot believe that our government is sincere in its fight for world democracy.

Unspiritual Ministry

Ministering to be what it should be must correspond to the nature of man. Man is a trinity. He has a spirit, a soul, and a body. I Thess. 5:23; Heb. 4:12. It would be a good thing for every one who tries to minister to man's need to ascertain how each part of his nature functions for his good, then base his ministry accordingly, any other method of ministering is unsound.

The chief purpose of evangelical preaching is to so preach the gospel that people will believe in Jesus Christ and be saved. It is not an effort to stir up the emotions of people or please them.

Spiritualizing people is not the work of men but is the work of the Holy Spirit. The Holy Spirit acts upon the whole man, spirit, soul, and body.

Pooling Our Own Resources

It matters not what progress is made to get rid of segregation in the educational institutions of this country; you and I will not live to see the day when there will not be race segregation in the United States of America. The question then is, "What should we do for ourselves in a segregated society?" We should continue to contend for all the rights and privileges that are due us as citizens of this country that any other citizen enjoys. But since we know that other citizens will not provide for us adequate institutions for our welfare, then we should pool our own resources and build them for ourselves.

Annual Address of Dr. G. L. Prince
President of the National Baptist Convention of America
In Session at Richmond, Virginia, September, 1956

To First Vice-President Dr. Pettaway, Second Vice-President Dr. Sams, Presidents of the Auxiliaries, Officers, Members of the National Baptist Convention of America, Greetings:

Through His mercy and by the wise providence of God, I am now permitted to bring to you my Twenty-Third Annual Address on this Seventy-Sixth Annual Session of the National Baptist Convention of America.

As we meet here in this historical city of Richmond, Virginia, let all of us who were with this Convention twenty-three years ago, let our minds run back and see the mighty host who started with us at that time but are now gone to meet the Great Judge of all the earth.

Many who met with us last year in Chicago, have gone to give an account of their stewardship during their sojourn while here on this earth. Let us be mindful, many of us here today will not be allowed to meet this Convention again, we too will have gone to give an account to our Master.

We meet today in a very troubled world, a most challenging hour, nations against nations, crime, murder, robbery, assault, liquor and juvenile delinquency all are at their zenith. In spite of all our new inventions and comforts, there still remains the devastation and sin never before witnessed in the history of the world.

We meet at a time when men live and boast in vain glory, when man lives in his vaulted pride, when he boasts of his physical power. We are living at a time when man feels that he has captured the physical universe. A time when man has been able to unravel many of the deepest mysteries, at a time when he has pushed back the foothills of ignorance and solved the most intricate problems. We are living in both an atomic age and an electronic age, for all this, man lives and rejoices.

Let us not be misled in the great accomplishments of civilization in the world today, this is not the supreme need of the world. The world's chief lack is not in material goods, but abundant Spirit Life. The men and women who stand in God's presence should carry the consciousness that we are not speaking for ourselves but that we are speaking for God, and with the authority of God.

Unfortunately, men's hearts and minds all over this nation are disturbed as never before over the "Civil Rights" issue. Remember, God that made the world and all things herein . . . hath made of one blood all nations of men to dwell on all the face of the earth, and hath determined, all men are brothers: this is not a statement of a pious hope nor an idealistic goal. It is the statement of a fact, when men fail to act as brothers, they violate the Laws of God, regardless of race, color, or creed. Men who deny true kinship with their fellow men, and that means all men, find themselves at odds with their own destiny.

It is the purpose of God to make our personal character approximate our high calling in Christ Jesus, which means that holiness is obligatory upon every one of us who has been redeemed. When we have truly been redeemed, regardless of public opinion or any other opinion, we are willing to rightly interpret the teachings of the New Testament and be guided by the Holy Spirit.

True Christians are the guardians of the truth that all men are the sons of God and cannot but be brothers, hence they should sense the true significance of man's "inalienable rights" to life, liberty, his right to live in peace and dwell in safety. They would realize that there is a standard set by God's creative Love that all men are each other's brother. Men are not tools for other men. What serves one at the cost of others' welfare, cannot be the Will of God who loves them all.

Remember Christ died for us that He might live in us. Men who profess to be Christians ought to live and act like Christians. The appalling conditions under which we are living now should shame all Christians who have the power to take the Christ stand against it, and fail to do so.

Prejudice is taking a particularly vicious form in the world today. Let us be very mindful less we too, find ourselves filled with it. When we allow our minds and hearts to be overcome by prejudice, we suffer wasted potentialities, warped personalities, lowered economic standards, conflicts and tensions which are obstacles to progress. Crime, disease and death itself, are just a part of the price we or anyone who allows prejudice to overshadow his heart and mind must pay.

As your President, let me admonish you to take the Christ Way. The Christ Way is the right way. Let us as a body of Christian believers realize the inescapable responsibility which rests upon us to seek peace, justice and freedom for all mankind. Let us be reminded that our conscience lives not in our own strength or reason, but in the power that comes from God. Impelled by this faith, all our actions will be humble, grateful acknowledgment that He has redeemed the world and He can and is able to redeem us.

Spiritual regeneration is the only hope of our world today. We are not responsible for being a separate group racially-speaking, from all other groups in the United States of America, neither are we responsible for the segregation and discrimination imposed upon us by those who have the power to do it. Even the scientists declare that all men are one species, and offer no defense for prejudice. In the midst of all this, the Negro has thrown out a challenge to the world. There is not another race on the face of the earth that has made the progress the Negro race has made in these ninety-one years of partial freedom.

Our faith in our own capability is founded on the outstanding achievements the race has made in fields of science, education, economics, architecture, engineering, agriculture, sports, and last but by no means the least, religion. Time nor space will permit me to name many we know in person that have made enviable records in these named fields and other fields as well.

The Negro has demonstrated to the world that he has physical and mental ability equal to any other race with the same opportunity. The present condition through which we as a race are passing should encourage us as a group to take every advantage to assert our claim and right to full status of first class citizens in this country for which our sons have bled and died. The day of "Uncle Tom" is gone forever.

In the outset, I mentioned that this was my twenty-third year to attempt to bring you an annual message. To give a brief resumé of my stewardship during these twenty-three years as your President, I think is quite in order. You will please consider facts are just facts and one is not considered being selfish or self-centered in stating true facts.

When I became your President, this Convention was not a true representative organization. It's membership consisted of persons who paid the annual fee of five dollars ($5.00). Because of this policy of raising money, the Convention was unable to meet current expenses, and the Convention was deeply in debt. Its Boards were paralyzed so that they could not do effective work in their various fields.

God gave me the wisdom to see this could never be a great Convention unless its membership was composed of Baptist organizations such as churches, district and general associations, and State Conventions. God be praised, you accepted this plan as a Convention, and through your fine co-operation, this National Baptist Convention of America has grown mightily, numerically, financially, and I hope I can truthfully say, spiritually.

When I became your President, there were only two bodies, the parent body and the Senior Women's Convention. We now have, through your co-operation, five well-organized religious bodies doing work for God. Many of you have not fully accepted some of them, but I am praying that you will fully accept and give them the full right away from your churches.

It was through and under the leadership of this President that all discrepancies of our membership into the Baptist World Alliances were removed. Each time you have honored your President by sending him to the Alliance, I have seen to it that the heads of the Auxiliaries had the opportunity to go and the Convention paid their way, too, as well as the President. (In spite of the unmerited things that have been said about this President, not allowing you certain opportunities in the Alliance. I have given each of you the opportunity you had not had.)

Your President was elected to the Executive Committee of the Alliance and served for five (5) years and was then elected as one of the Vice-Presidents. I have served on programs in the Alliance three (3) times, was on program when it met in Ohio but the automobile accident prevented my serving.

Your President was on program last year in London. Please pardon me. There is a reason for telling you this. Each time the Alliance honored the President of the National Baptist Convention of America, it was honoring you as well.

As your President, everything has been done that could possibly be done to dignify this Convention, not only with the world organizations, but above all, I have stressed our supreme obligation to God, in our homes, to our fellow men, and our conduct as we attended these meetings. I have ever stressed it is just as obligatory for an organization to be honest in the sight of God as it is for an individual to be honest.

I have ever spoken out against padded bills, against the idea some seemed to have had that the Convention was organized to fatten a few and leave the Great Cause for which the Convention was organized: To carry the gospel to the uttermost parts of this world, to suffer. Lest we forget all of us who have had to do with the monies collected in and through this Convention and it was entrusted to us and we failed to let it reach its designated source, not-may-be-so, but must give an account to God for our stewardship. That is going to be an awful day for some of us.

A moral life will automatically follow a spiritual life. It is of vital importance that this Convention will at all times carry on in such a way that what it does will advance the work of Christianity in the world.

Our Educational Work

The greatest mistake ever made in fostering Christian education was made in mal-administration which resulted in the loss of Boscobel College in Nashville, Tennessee. Hence when this President came to office, this Convention was not doing any tangible thing for Christian education. I didn't feel it safe for us to undertake the responsibility of trying to operate and maintain another college, so I recommended that this Convention make liberal donations to eligible Christian colleges. You accepted the plan and more than ten (10) different religious colleges have been helped.

As a Convention, we must realize the great need for effective moral and spiritual training in education. God and the Bible must be the source and the dynamic back of moral teaching if it is to be effective in building Christian character in our boys and girls. They must be taught with positive emphasis on spiritual living for God.

Under this administration, the following organizations have come into being and are doing a great work:

The Junior Women's Convention, the Brotherhood Convention, The Youth Convention, The Benevolent Department. All have added tremendously to the work of this convention.

All Christians must be alarmed over the appalling and ever-increasing crime wave of our youth today. Your President felt that if youth could nationalize crime, why not give them a chance to nationalize Christ? They can and will if enough time and patience and guidance is given them.

J. Edgar Hoover, Director of the Federal Bureau of Investigation, our best authority on crime says, "Major crime in youths went over the 567,000 mark in 1955 in youths below 18 years of age, many even below the age of fifteen years."

There are many contributing factors in juvenile delinquency. Parental duties neglected in the home, fathers should be men of prayer and power to properly teach and lead a son or daughter. Mothers are charged with the most sacred trust ever committed to human hands: the molding of previous lives; what patience and tirelessness, what love and tack; what wisdom and wealth of resource a mother needs to do the task that God has assigned to her hands. She should above all, be a praying mother.

Not only are the mothers and fathers responsible for the right example being set before the youth of today, but all Christians are held responsible for making Christ known to human ears, not by telling only, but by living it daily. The youths need to feel that they are getting advice from those who know and have experienced the power of God.

God's eyes are on world conditions and He cares with a concern beyond the understanding of man.

When we read where graft and corruption have stolen their way into city, state, and national governments, we have been shocked and our confidence severely shaken, to read the list of betrayers of trust, but this makes us know something of the devastating, demoralizing, and destroying power of the forces of the Devil.

Our Dead

While deeply aware of our losses, for the valiant servants of Christ, we as Christians must proclaim with Apostle John: Blessed are the dead who die in the Lord from henceforth; Yea, saith the Spirit that they rest from their labors and their works do follow them.

A Christian Body And Not A Political Body

This is a Christian organization and I am appealing to you as a Convention to keep it so. Political methods of attaining office is not in harmony with Christian principles. The Holy Ghost should have something to do with the selection of Christian leaders.

Caleb Darnell Pettaway

Caleb Darnell Pettaway (1886-1968) was born December 18, 1886 in Concordia Parish, Ferriday, Louisiana, to Cage and Louise Pettaway. He attended public schools in Natchez, Mississippi. He moved to Little Rock, Arkansas in August, 1910. In 1917, he voluntarily enlisted in the United States Army and went to Fort Des Moines, Iowa, to officer's training camp as a candidate for Captain.

He married Jennie E. Vagner, June 12, 1918. Two children were born to this union: Paul and Louise.

He enrolled at Philander Smith College as a fifth grade student. Despite the fact that he was much older than most of the students in his class, he was determined to complete his education and realize his dream for the future. While a student, he held odd jobs as houseboy, chauffeur, stock clerk at Missouri Pacific Round House; clerk at Mail Terminal; and railway mail clerk.

He responded to the call to the Christian ministry and was ordained March 25, 1920. He pastored the following churches for a short while: Pleasant Valley at Scott; Liberty Hill, Little Rock; Shiloh, North Little Rock; subsequently, he was called to Shiloh Baptist Church, Little Rock, in 1927; Saint Luke, in 1946; and First Baptist Church, Wrightsville, 1947. He resigned as pastor of First Baptist Church at Wrightsville in 1966, while remaining as pastor of Shiloh and Saint Luke.

His first wife having died, he was married to Cleola Hampton, June 5, 1952.

He was First Vice-President of the National Baptist Convention for fifteen years and became President following the death of Dr. G. L. Prince in 1956. He was elected to the position in 1957 and served for ten years, until he resigned in 1967 and became President Emeritus.

He was a trustee of Arkansas Baptist College, and received a Doctor of Divinity from that institution. He received the LLD from Arkansas State College in Pine Bluff. He was President of the General Missionary Baptist State Convention of Arkansas. He was founder and President of the United Friends of America, a fraternal society organized in 1918. He died Tuesday, August 20, 1968.

Annual Address of Dr. C. D. Pettaway
President of the National Baptist Convention of America
In Session at San Francisco, California, 1961

The Rising Tide

The word *tide* refers to those alternating relative motions of the matter of a planet, a satellite, or star, which are due to the gravitational actions of external bodies. In this class of motions, we have two terrestrial examples besides the familiar tides of our oceans and seas. These terrestrial examples are called earth-tides of our oceans and seas. Earth-tides consist in the alternating slight change of shape of the solid body of the earth due to the gravitational action of the sun and moon, and the atmospheric tides are due to the alternating slight motions of the atmosphere which is due to the same cause. There is, however, a still wider use of the word, tide. It is based on the descriptive and kinematical, instead of on the casual and astronomical ideas and takes for its criterion that the motions in question shall have certain features in common with ocean-tide.

But my purpose, my dear friends, is not to discuss the word *tide* as it related to the ebb and flow of the ocean waves. In that sense, it would be only a metaphor. But rather, I wish to use it as it refers to the ebb and flow of human hearts, human conduct, and human behavior, from the beginning of history up until now, the record shows undoubtedly that man has wonderfully advanced scientifically along the line of human progress. His physical advancement, however, has out run his spiritual advancement by far, because man has put more emphasis on the physical than he has put on the spiritual.

History shows clearly that no one race, one nation, or one country has been the front-runner all the time. Therefore, no one country has been on top all the way through or all the time. But the changing tides in the cycle of time have arranged it so that the nation which is on top today may be on the bottom tomorrow. It may be replaced, and its position occupied by another nation. Need I to remind you of the history of the past — ancient, medieval, and even modern? Where are the golden days of the ancient past? of Greece, of Rome, and their top ranking stars such as Homer, Hesiod, the Caesars, etc. Greece was the seating of learning, the center of culture, the home of philosophers and statesmen. But look at them now. Greece, where the Apostle Paul once stood, is now only marked by a snaggled stone on a hilltop; and Rome, the home of the Caesars and the one time mistress of the world, is now only a tomb. While the shores of the Bosphorus which long ago used to ring out with the peals of Byzantium, have lost their significance, moved over and made room for the rising tide of the twentieth century.

And so the world moves on and the tide keeps rising in spite of all that can be said or done. Up and up goes the tide but down and down go the nations which had eyes but refused to see; ears but refused to hear. They were like the dinosaur of old, big, powerful, frightful, and frightening. But the dinosaur failed to make the necessary adjustment for the continued existence of its life and it had to fold up, go out of business, and become extinct. He is now only a legend of the past, and so are most of the great nations that held sway in the past.

But we have come only from the ancient through the medieval up to here; but we haven't touched the modern. That's where we are now (in the modern age of the twentieth century). Looking back on history seeing their mistake, I wonder if we will take heed to our ways and set our house in order before the curtain is rung down? After the modern, then I wonder what next? Who knows? Who can tell? Who will be left? Who will be here? — the tide is rising. It is sweeping on to oblivion everything that gets into its way that will not conform to righteousness nor make proper adjustment in equity and justice — our conduct and our attitude toward our fellowman. There are some people in high places right now who can do anything and everything they want, right our wrong, and get away with it if they belong to the favored group. They are the elite; they are on top right now. But wait awhile, let's see what will happen. Then there are some other people who belong to our group. But remember always the tide just keeps on rising. It will continue to rise until it covers every mountaintop of sin and selfishness. "Yes, it will rise on," said the prophet, until it fills up every valley of depression and gloom. The rich and the privileged live on the mountaintop of splendor and plenty, while the poor and the underprivileged must live in the valley of gloom and despair. But remember, the prophet said, "that every valley shall be exalted (that means you and me) and every mountain and hill shall be made low (that's the group that's up there now), and the crooked shall be made straight and the rough places plain and the glory of the Lord shall be revealed, and all flesh shall see it together," for the mouth of the Lord hath spoken it. The voice said, "Cry," and he said, "What shall I cry?" "All flesh is grass the godliness thereof is as the flower of the field. The grass withereth, the flower fadeth, but the word of our God shall stand forever." Let's take a glimpse now of the modern age and the twentieth century. Have you ever seen or heard of as much confusion, turmoil, and strife in the world among men as there is today? Notwithstanding all the wars that have been fought — and there have been many — there was never as much hate and confusion as there is today. Heretofore, wars and conflicts have been somewhat on a local plane or on a somewhat limited scale. But if war comes now, this time it threatens to engulf the whole world. I don't think either side desires to unleash a full scale war and employ the full powers of destruction that both sides have. Because I believe that both the United States and Russia have enough power right now to destroy the world. And I also believe that each one knows that the other one has it. And there is no such thing as either one of them being able to completely destroy the other before the other can retaliate in kind and destroy him, too.

So what would either side gain? Neither one would be left. I believe both of them know that and neither of them wants it. But I believe they are stalling and bluffing to see which one will back down. But the very premises of such reason is wrong to start with. Suppose they do aim to fight a limited war if they do fight at all? Who knows after they get started, but that the limited war may become an unlimited war? Why fight any kind of war anyhow? Russia doesn't live in Germany and neither does the United States. So what? Why is all of this? What has brought it on and what's the cause? As I said before, sin in little places, sin in big places; sin by races and sin by nations; sin by individuals and sin by groups. From our present condition, it would appear that the peoples of the world have been eating too long and too many sour grapes and they have thus set the world's teeth on edge.

Take Africa — the largest, the richest and the most underdeveloped, and underprivileged country in the world. All of it was owned and controlled by foreign powers except Ethiopia. Then in 1935, Mussolini went on in Africa, jumped on Ethiopia, subdued it, and added it to Italy, thus ending the last and only sovereign independent native country in Africa. But, this did not stand. Ethiopia was and is restored. Mussolini is dead, and Italy today, in the strict sense of the word, is only a second rate nation when it comes to world power. Thus, in the meantime, the tide keeps rising. However, South Africa (the meanest place in the world to our people right today) and Liberia had the nearest thing to self-government or home-rule of any of the African countries. South Africa was a member of the British Commonwealth but lately withdrew, while Liberia continues to be a protectorate of the United States and is run by colored people or Negroes. Prior to 1956, or just five short years ago, a country of more than 11 million square miles was run and overrun, managed and mismanaged, ruled and ruined by foreigners. While the natives were exploited, treated mean and unfair in many cases, and in some they were even massacred and slaughtered while all the big powers winked at it but kept silent, there was not a hand raised in their behalf. There was not a voice raised to plead mercy for them, not even the so-called church of Jesus Christ. But, thank God, there was an all-seeing Eye: an all-powerful Hand, and an Almighty and just God looking down from above. He got tired and sick at heart (so to speak) at the way things were going and in one full stroke within five short years, He struck the shackles from the hands and feet of millions, and lifted the burden from the backs of the people of 22 countries and set them free. (Wish I had time to name them). So that today the voice of the black man is heard in the highest council on earth — the League of Nations.

So you can see, my dear friends, that the tide is still rising; the worm is beginning to turn; even so, let it be; come, Lord Jesus — Amen. Let not your chariot wheels delay. But ride, ride, bring on the welcome day when my shackles too will be broken and I, as free American Citizen, can stand up anywhere, anytime, and in any crowd, and sing both truthfully and proudly, "My Country 'Tis of Thee, Sweet Land of Liberty, of Thee I sing, Land where my Father died; Land of the Pilgrims pride; from every mountainside, let Freedom ring."

Men and women of National Baptist Convention of America take courage, do not despair, lift up your heads, our dawn is breaking. Let us gird up our loins for the fray, let us do something worthy of our chance and of our day — boards? Let us be good citizens; first-class citizens, and let us be satisfied with nothing less. If we are right, God will fight our battles. If we are not right, let's stop right now and get right. Let's set our own house in order. Hate nobody, but love all men. We can then be assured that God is on our side. And if God be for us, who can be against us? I do not know what you may do. But as for me, I shall work; and I shall pray. I shall listen, and I shall wait.

"The world moves on and the tide keeps right on rising. It rises in spite of anything that man can do because the dollars of a rich country or the powers of the press cannot stop the rising power of the tide. The tide is directed by the hand of omnipotence no matter what we say or do, no matter who we hate or love, if God says it is, it is, and if God says it will be, it just will get out of the way."

"The tide keeps rising, coming now to the modern age. We see much; we learn much. Nobody is so blind as people who refuse to see. Nobody is so deaf as people whose ears deliberately refuse to hear. I wonder if America should take heed and set her house in order. Churches are on every corner and right today we are riding high horses; injustice, unfair pay, hate, rampant. In our government in Washington, a few men there try to do honorable things but their colleagues cry them down."

He told of a question put to him earlier, "Would you be a freedom rider?" "I am a freedom rider, and I am a freedom speaker. God doesn't want me to take away my life ignorantly . . . wants me to cry aloud and spare not."

"I am not a coward. I am not afraid to die, but I want my life to count. I wonder, therefore, if our country will open its eyes and be fair and recognize the tide that is coming. I do not want to be granted any special favors nor to be taken in their arms and jump me up and down. But I want the rights, the privileges that the Constitution of the United States grants me. I want the right to ride on anything on wheels and in air if I have the money to do this."

Spoke of housing in south — no room at the inn (Jesus' birth). "A man can have $100 in his pickets in the south and looking for a place to stay. They won't say we don't have any room; they will simply say I can't take you in, your color bars you. I am proud of my color. God knew what is the best color for me. God wrapped me up in the best color of skin I could best serve Him. Some people right now in this country can do anything and everything they want to do and get by with it. Some people in high places right or wrong will get by with it; but, we must wait awhile. I see the white caps way out yonder; the tide is sweeping them in."

"Have you ever seen so much hate confusion as there is in the world today? What's the reason, the causes? The only reasons, the only causes of this monosyllabic word, one little word is sin."

Talks of Russians and Americans: Russians say, "You kicked me around but that won't work any longer." They used to kick me around, too, but that won't work anymore. The Russians are saying they want peace and a comfortable world. The United States say we are peaceable, loving people. We spend millions of dollars on the other side and right here at home they won't make white folks treat me right. Charity begins at home. I am for helping other people, but I feel like they ought to treat me right first here at home.

Rev. W. Hershel Ford of the Southern Baptist Convention mentioned earlier how well-dressed the group was. "We are ambassadors of Christ and should be well-dressed." He spoke of Christ's garment, how it was sought after. "If you want to get ahead in this country, you had better look like somebody." He continued by saying that we will be treated to a large degree by the way we look.

Annual Address of Dr. C. D. Pettaway
President of the National Baptist Convention of America
In Session at Houston, Texas, September, 1965

Vice-Presidents Dr. Sams and Dr. Byrd, Officers and Members of our great Convention, Ladies and Gentlemen:

I want you first to know how happy I am to be here in your midst today. During these last few months, I have been brought very low by the Lord, but He has seen fit to bring me back thus far and has enabled me to assemble in the annual Convention. And I thank Him for my affliction, because it has helped me to recognize even more fully the great power and love of God. I thank Him for my two Vice-Presidents who are and have been to me as Aaron and Hur to Moses. My hands were "heavy and they took a stone of faith and confidence and love, and put it under" me, and I "sat thereon; and they stayed up my hands, the one on the one side and the other on the other side." I thank Him for you who have been so kind and so gracious to me. And I thank Him for the work He has enabled me to do and for the good I've done in His name and for His sake during the long life He has given me.

In the words of the Psalmist, I wish to speak to you today, out of my heart, my experiences, and my love for God, for this Convention and for you. "Out of the depths have I cried unto Thee, O Lord. Lord, hear my voice; let Thine ears be attentive to the voice of my supplications. If Thou, Lord, shouldest mark iniquities, O Lord who shall stand? But there is forgiveness with Thee, that Thou mayest be feared. I wait for the Lord, my soul doth wait, and in His Word do I hope. My soul waiteth for the Lord more than they that watch for the morning; I say more than they that watch for the morning. Let Israel hope in the Lord: for with the Lord there is mercy and with Him is plenteous redemption. And He shall redeem Israel from all his iniquities." (Psalm 130) If I were able, and for a brief period, I'd like to speak from this subject: "Out of the Depths."

In this Psalm quoted, the writer is a devout Israelite who feels very keen the misery of his circumstance. I consider myself to be, or at least I try to be, a devout Christian, a servant of the Most High, and I feel very keenly today the misery of my circumstances. What were the depths out of which the Psalmist cried unto God? Generally, the Israelites believed that just as prosperity was the reward for goodness, adversity was the punishment for sin. But as we read a little farther, we can sense the voice of experience—a result of walking and talking with God—the voice of a calmer and stronger faith, which recognized that no one is righteous in the sight of God, that beneath God's pure and searching scrutiny, the fairest of our lives will show foul. But with God is forgiveness for our imperfections and our weaknesses.

What are the depths out of which I have cried unto God? Ah, my friends, if you only knew! On May 19 of this year, I was plunged into the depths of affliction. I went to bed, I thought, a reasonably well man. But somewhere between the midnight hour and the break of day, like Jacob, I received a thorn in the flesh and when I attempted to get up, I was unable to walk, unable to stand. But because I know God is able, because I know there is mercy with Him, I know I can trust Him. Out of the depths of my soul I cried unto Him like this: "Lord, you know I've tried to make you a good servant since 1902. I've been right sometimes, and sometimes I've been wrong, but I have tried always to keep in close touch with you so that I could feel your presence and feel your spirit in my heart. If my work here is finished, I'm ready to come home, but if you have something yet for me to do, I'll keep on toiling until my day is done."

The depths is a good place for all of us sometimes. Unless you have cried unto God out of the depths, you have not cried unto Him at all. There is no way out of the pit but to cry to God who has let down the fullness of His forgiving love in Jesus Christ our Lord. Through faith we are lifted up "out of the horrible pit and the miry clay," and our feet are set upon a rock.

I couldn't lift this hand (left); I couldn't move this foot (left). Wherever you put this hand, it stayed right there until I moved it with my other hand or someone came and moved it for me. Wherever you put me, I stayed right there until someone came and moved me. But today, by God's amazing grace, I can move this hand about; I can scratch my head, touch my ear (and you really have no idea how great it is to be able to do even these little things for yourself), and I can walk—a little cripple yet, but I can walk. At first I couldn't even bow down on my knees to pray. And so from my sick bed, lying prostrate and helpless, out of the depths I cried unto the Lord, "Silver and gold have I none, but such as I have, I give thee." Such as I have! I'm saying to you today, everyone of us has something, and we ought to use that something to the glory and honor of God. As Peter and John went to the temple to pray, and saw the lame man begging alms at the gate, Peter said, "Look on us. Silver and gold have I none, but such as I have, give I thee; In the name of Jesus Christ of Nazareth, rise up and walk." How infinitely better was that gift—the gift of God—than the mere alms the lame man asked, and expected to receive.

How infinitely better is the gift of God's love, His grace, His mercy, His power, to us than many of the things we ask and pray for. Sometimes when people ask us how we feel, we say we're "down in the dumps." Have you ever said that? What we really mean is that we're down in the depths of some problem, whether physical, mental or spiritual, or financial and we just don't feel happy. But I would tell you today, and hear me if you will, whatever your plight, whatever your circumstances, be not dismayed, God will take care of you. All you need He will provide—Nothing you ask will be denied. So cast all your cares upon Him for He careth for you. He who fed the prophet by the brook, who kept the widow's cruse of oil from being empty, who watched over the Israelites in the wilderness, who clothed the lily of the field and sees every sparrow that falls; and bless your soul, He who heard my cry and brought me, C. D. Pettaway, out of the depths, will not fail you.

But you can't cast your cares upon Him unless you submit yourselves wholly to Him through prayer, through meditation, through song, and through service. When life is sunny and everything is going along smoothly, we can't cry unto God like we can when we face great danger and grave situations in life. God is able, ready and willing to hear our cries. "I know in whom I have believed and am persuaded that He is able to keep that which I have committed to Him against that day."

Our nation needs to cry out to God out of the depths of prejudice, of evil and hatred, of riots and rioting, of injustice and ignorance, and of sin. We are the most powerful nation in the world (so we say) but our power must not be our wealth, our education, our missiles, our space program, our race to the moon, but our power must be in the words of the Prophet Micah: "To do justly, to love mercy, and to walk humbly with God." The "big three" are not Russia, Great Britain, and the United States, but God the Father, God the Son and God the Holy Spirit. If we would have peace in the world these must be the reigning powers. In these days when despair and futility threaten to overcome us, when we are tempted to believe that the threat of bombs and missiles is the symbol of ultimate conquest, let us remember that good must triumph over evil, life over death, hope over despair. Life's victories do not come on the battlefield—on earth, on sea or in the air—but by God's love and His power in the hearts of men.

Our Convention greatly needs to cry to God out of the depths. We are God's ministers; we are God's spokesmen; we are God's watchmen on the wall. As free men, we must proclaim the gospel of peace throughout the world. God's Word is truth and if we know the truth, it will make us free. At such a time in the history of the affairs of men, we must proclaim anew our faith in God, in our fellowman and in ourselves. We must denounce evil in all of its forms. We must not compromise. We must not be afraid.

We meet here and there in Annual Session year after year for a simple purpose—to enrich our souls with the preaching and teaching of the gospel; to promote fellowship and associational and conventional ties between our ministers, our sisters, our brothers, our youth, and our churches; and to espouse and promulgate the causes which we represent through our various Boards and Commissions. We cannot expect here in the few hours of the few days we spend to solve all of our problems and the problems of the society in which we live. Nevertheless we can, perhaps, put into motion some plans and ideas for future solution of the particular problems within the purview of our objectives. And as the spiritual leaders of the nation in our connection, we do have great and grave responsibilities. It is we who must abort another "Watts Episode" in California, another "Smaw Incident" in Alabama, another "Metcalfe Explosion" in Mississippi. It is we who must perpetuate some system for caring for our senior citizens who are indigent, and provide a pension fund for our ministers who have labored hard and long in the vineyards of Christ.

We must continue to uphold the traditions of our Convention by supporting financially and spiritually our work, and those who are placed in responsible positions should take care that they will well their offices. The Eye of God is upon us; the eye of man is upon us, and we must not fail either of them. Those of long ago who held the same positions that we now hold sacrificed and wrought well. Shall we, who have even greater opportunities for service, do less than they?

In the words of Booker T. Washington, I am determined that we, as the National Baptist Convention of America, be able to say: "Tell them the sacrifice was not in vain. Tell them that by way of the shop, the field, the skilled hand, habits of thrift and economy, by way of industrial school and college, we are coming. We are crawling up, working up, yea, bursting up. Often through oppression, unjust discrimination and prejudice, but through them we are coming up, and with proper habits, intelligence and property, there is no power on earth that can permanently stay our progress. . . We are to be tested in our patience, our forbearance, our perseverance, our power to endure wrong, to withstand temptations, to economize, to acquire and use skill, our ability to compete . . . to disregard the superficial for the real, the appearance for the substance, to be great and yet small, learned and yet simple, high and yet the servant of all."

In a recent issue of *Time* magazine, I found these vital statistics: "There are eight Negro federal judges, 100 county and state judges, four U. S. ambassadors. Thurgood Marshall, who recently resigned from the federal bench at the urging of President Johnson to become United States Solicitor General, represents the United States in the most important litigations before the Supreme Court. Carl Rowan, onetime Ambassador to Finland, only recently resigned as director of the USIA where he was chiefly responsible for projecting the U.S. image abroad. Edward W. Brooke, attorney general of Massachusetts, is the highest elected Negro state officer in the United States. Leroy Johnson, two years ago became Georgia's first Negro state legislator since Reconstruction. Episcopalian John M. Brugess, son of a dining-car waiter, is Suffragan Bishop of Massachusetts; Dr. Middleton H. Lambright, Jr., grandson of a slave, is President of the Cleveland Academy of Medicine. Leslie N. Shaw is the first Negro postmaster of Los Angeles. Historian John Hope Franklin is a professor at the University of Chicago.

Individual Negro incomes went up 54% from 1950 to 1960, and family incomes soared by 73%. The number of Negroes living in standard housing compared to census-defined substandard housing, doubled in the same period. Negro-controlled insurance companies have doubled their assets since 1951; Negro commercial banks have increased their assets from $5 million to $53 million since 1940.

I thought the above statistics might be interesting for you to note. In the light of these facts, you can see that our Convention needs to take its stride and gain momentum with each passing year. We need to expand our horizons. Let us enter another year of our work with a new sense of our responsibility to God, of its ability, under God, to hasten in some tangible way the coming on earth of the Kingdom of God.

As I said in the offset, I have been afflicted since May 19, but I am thankful that God has seen fit to make me better and leave me here a while longer. I am grateful for my affliction for it has made me a better and, I think, wiser man. Paul spoke of his affliction as being light—in labors more abundant, in prisons more frequent, in deaths often, three times beaten with rods, stoned once and left for dead, shipwrecked three times, night and day in the deep without hope; perils of water, sea, robbers; perils of false brethren, weariness, painfulness, hunger and thirst, cold and nakedness—all of this beside the care of the churches. May the Lord forgive us that we should ever murmur because of any affliction that has been laid upon us. Our wait may seem longer than we think it should be, but it is only momentary when we discern the cross Jesus bore. In the words of Christ, we should say, "Father, if it be possible, let this cup pass from me; nevertheless, not as I will, but as Thou wilt."

I thank you for the many prayers which you offered in my behalf. And believe me, I felt the power and the efficacy of those prayers. They sustained me through the long hours of the night. The letters, telegrams, telephone calls, and those who came to see me, I shall ever remember those golden moments which cheered my waning spirits and provided warmth and cheer for me.

I have talked with some of the brethren from time to time with regard to the continued leadership of our Convention which is a very important matter in our equation today. What I said to them, I say to you today. And that is, whatever you feel is the best thing to do today with regard to that continued leadership and progress of our Convention, feel free to do so. And I shall be happy to abide by your decision. The choice is yours.

"Out of the depths have I cried unto Thee, O Lord. Hear my voice; let Thine ears be attentive to the voices of my supplications." The writer of the song caught the spirit of the Psalmist when she penned these significant words:

Out of the Depths

Out of the depths of my soul I cry,
Jesus, draw nigh, Jesus, draw nigh;
Lord, lend an ear to my earnest plea,
Jesus, draw nearer to me.
O Lord, hear Thou my pleading,
Speak to my soul, Cleanse and make whole,
Let me forever in Thee abide,
Lord, let me walk by Thy side

Lord, let my life consecrated be,
Hidden in Thee, Hidden in Thee;
Let me forever Thy Word obey,
Lord, draw me closer each day.
Oh Lord, I want to labor,
Faithful each day, In this true way,
Telling the world what a Saviour I've found,
Spreading the Gospel around.

Out of the depths of my soul I plead,
Jesus, hear me, Jesus, hear me;
Let me steadfast in Thy Word e'er be
That no sin might be seen in me.
Increase Thou my faith
Lord, deeper in Thee, Let me e'er be;
So that no sin might be found in me,
Lord, draw me closer to Thee.

This is my message to you today. My recommendations will follow later.

James Carl Sams

James Carl Sams (1909-1985) was born February 19, 1909, the third child of Charlotte and Lonnie Sams, on a one-horse farm in Cochran, Georgia. There are five children. Others include Louis, Algertha, Handy, and Minnie.

James Carl was nicknamed "Buddy." He was regarded by the other children as "Mama's boy." At an early age, he learned to plow and perform other duties required of him on the farm.

He attended the County Public School in Blakely County, Cochran, Georgia; Stanton High School, Jacksonville, Florida; Florida Normal High School, St. Augustine, Florida. He received the Bachelor of Science degree from Florida Memorial College, becoming one of the first graduates when the college became a four-year institution. He also attended Florida A & M University, Tallahassee, Florida. His graduate studies include Garrett Theological Seminary, Evanston, Illinois; Columbia University, New York City.

He received the following degrees from the following institutions: Union Baptist Theological Seminary, Birmingham, AL, D.D., LL.S.; Independent Baptist Theological Seminary, Philadelphia, PA, D.D.; Central Baptist Theological Seminary, Indianapolis, IN, D.D.; Edward Waters College, Jacksonville, FL, D.D.

At the age of nine, James Carl Sams became a Christian convert and identified with the Long Street Baptist Church in Cochran, Georgia. He served as a member of the choir and Sunday School teacher. He was ordained as a deacon under the pastoral leadership of his brother-in-law, the Reverend G. W. Jenkins.

He announced his call to the Christian ministry and preached his first sermon at twenty years of age in the Little Rock Baptist Church. He married Miss Cornelia Jenkins, who remained his faithful wife for fifty-six years. He was called to his first pastorate, the second Sunday in February, 1935, the First Baptist Church of Oakland, Florida. He led the congregation twenty-three years, six months, and fourteen days.

In August, 1958, Dr. Sams was called to the pastorate of Second Missionary Baptist Church, Jacksonville, Florida. He faithfully shepherded the flock for twenty-seven years. For thirty-seven years, he served as President of the Progressive Missionary and Educational State Convention of Florida, one of the largest state conventions affiliated with the National Baptist Convention of America.

Dr. Sams was elected Second Vice-President of the National

Baptist Convention in Denver, Colorado in 1953. He served in that position for four years (1953-1957). He was elected First Vice-President and served for ten years (1957-1967) in that position. He captivated attention by the firm and positive manner he presided over Convention sessions.

In September, 1957, Dr. Sams was elected to succeed Dr. C. D. Pettaway who did not seek re-election because of ill health. He remained at the helm of the National Convention for eighteen years. During his leadership tenure, giving by churches to the National Convention doubled, giving for foreign missions increased more than five times, and an orange grove was purchased in Florida.

For fifty-six years, Dr. James Carl Sams served as pastor and President. He distinguished himself as prophet, priest, administrator, builder, teacher, friend, and brother.

He died July 10, 1985.

Annual Address of Dr. J. C. Sams
President of the National Baptist Convention of America
In Session at San Antonio, Texas, September 5, 1968

To the Vice-Presidents, Dr. Byrd, Dr. Price, Officers and Members of the National Baptist Convention of America, and our many friends:

Greetings

The clock of time again has struck from the mantlepiece of the convention walls, and by sound is saying it is time to give an account of this year's stewardship for the many activities and duties for which we have been entrusted with since we last met in the sacred walls of Shiloh Baptist Church, Dr. C. V. Jetter of Indianapolis, Ind., as pastor. Many have fallen since then, we must admit; many are upon their beds, but for some reason the good Lord has again spared us to share this fine fellowship such as we have here today.

I should like to thank each pastor, church, district workers general association, moderator, together with each of our state bodies for your loyal support. You have been most loyal in every respect.

Our world is at a point in life now known as the intersection, the "five points" in the highway of life. This age, this scientific age, when every thought of man is to discover that something that will destroy humanity from the face of the earth. Bombs, missiles, satellites, rockets, the atom, and flying saucers are all alike to the end, to destroy. Humanity is not satisfied walking on earth, instead, he wants to take a peek at the moon. God knows that His world is like it is, only because He left it in the hands of man. He (man) messed up the earth; and if he can ever get to the moon, he will do the same. Man is in hope to get away from himself. Until we learn to live here together, it is nonsense to try yonder.

Our Convention

One year ago in Indiana, you elected me as your chieftain, to lead you onward and upward in the work of the Lord through the agencies of this our conventional structure. For this I want to again thank you for the opportunity to serve. I am sure you had in mind that you were electing a man as President, not for his convention, but for your convention. We can do; we must do a bigger and better job than what was done by our silent fathers, the most of whom now sleep in the quietude of God's eternal rest. Therefore, we are faced with a challenge for the best that is in us. Will the causes be blessed more than I am here (you)? We have a great opportunity to do a real good job for God; if we will become disturbed about God's business, O brethren, God has made an investment in each of us, and each of us is responsible to prove our worth to God in whatever our assigned task may be. The great need for this, and all conventions we have in this world, is to put back the emphasis, interest, and concern in God's work. What are the causes? Mission, Education, Evangelism, and etc. These are agencies God wants to use man as a helper in looking for his lost brothers. "Is there a price tag attached?" is the first question. What do I get out of it? Can anyone evaluate the soul of his brother?

We thank God for every one whom God has allowed to share in this great convention. Just some seventeen days ago, we funeralized our late president, Dr. C. D. Pettaway. This man of God gave his all while he shouldered the leadership of this our convention. I thank God I had the privilege to share in his ministry with him and also our late president, Dr. G. L. Prince who now sleeps. I thank God for having made history during my years; for it has been mine to have served from the floor to Second Vice-President for six years, First Vice-President for ten years, and President for one year.

I have traveled during the past year more than forty-thousand miles for this convention's interest. I want you to know it has been a pleasure. We must be keepers of our words; for we pledged during our Winter Board that we would re-open the school at Jamaica. This, we must do. We must screen our educational work and do more. I will work with the boards individually more in the year ahead. Each board must have a program, and that program must need to be planned and worked out during the convention year. We must not come to the convention to raise money; we come to make reports.

Our Nation

In this our America, we the black people of God are the target of the world. We are fought against, denied, deprived of our rights on every hand. We as a convention can never hold our peace; we must lift our voices against all evils that are being hurled against us in these times.

God looked the cities over in yester-years and couldn't find one city preacher. So He took a trip to the country and found a country preacher by the name of Amos. His message was to all, from the king to the peasant. "You are wrong!" Our youth today all over this nation are testing the strength of our Constitution by saying, "We are tired of going to the back door Mr. America! We want to be just people. We no longer want what we have paid for in blood and sweat around this world through the back door. We are sitting down, will you serve us? We know $1.00 is too much for a cup of coffee; $1.50 is too much for a hamburger, but serve us, we will pay the bill. We and our fathers and sons bled and died side by side with yours in every war. If we bled together, died together, then the question comes now! What for? We fought, bled and died for the American way of life. We did not want to be slaves for another nation, then are we not slaves for you, Mr. America?"

The church must make it known that we are proud of our race, but we are dissatisfied with the practices of our fellow comrades. We have pride; we have intelligence; we have character; we have common sense. We want to be who we are, treated differently than we have been in the past. We are satisfied with our wives, our sons, and daughters. Our biggest trouble with you, Mr. America, has been that you don't want us marrying your wife's daughters; but you don't mind us marrying your daughters.

The Negro woman of America is the most beautiful specimen that represent femininity in the whole world. If you don't want us at your house, why don't you stay away from ours? We can never hope to win the battle by physical force, but by prayer, honesty, justice, common sense, pride, manhood, womanhood, character, education, men and women who are industrious, courageous, competent, efficient, and patient. It is to be remembered, if and when we will have come into our upstairs in many positions of nobility, that there are many of our brothers and sisters downstairs, many more who are in the basement of life's unusefulness. The message of the convention must be to encourage our boys and girls to hold on. There is a better day coming...days of fullness, days when every man will be respected as a man, and dealt with in the light of the Golden Rule.

The Church

You hear so much about the church. What is the church and where is it? According to my understanding, the word church came from a Greek word (ek-klecia) meaning called out, separated from the world, filled with the power of the Holy Spirit. The spirit that not only wills but helps us to do. Where is the church? I can never forget the definition given by the late Dr. Davis who said, "The church is across the borderline of carnality. That is, on the other side of all that is carnal; things, thoughts, beyond tangibles, but in the presence of the intangibles." So then, if we are members of the church, there must be a reason. Why am I a member? What is the purpose of Christ for having saved me? He has a purpose. It can never be merely for making a living. If we would allow God to come in our lives, and take hold of the reign, He will see to it that each and every one of His would have a living, and even a better living than what we have now. We are helpers of Christ, in mission, evangelism, education, medicine, and in very respect, both spiritual and physical.

God has a purpose in every one whom he has called to leadership, and we can never hope to hurry God. Whatever God has in his purpose for you and for me, he will bring it to pass in his own time. It must ever be remembered that the emphasis is not on the man in leadership or the man in fellowship, but the causes of Christ Jesus whose interest is on the man who is out of fellowship with the Eternal Salvation. We must hear again the words of our Master, "Lift up your eyes and look on the fields; for they are white all ready to harvest, but the laborers are few." Pray to the Lord of His harvest that he will send forth more laborers into His vineyard.

The church is the bride of Christ. The Gospel preacher is God's Day man, to proclaim, guide, counsel, to lead His little ones to the higher ground of safety, and betterment in this life. We must stop spending so much time putting on our program and work God's program. It is all worked out, nothing to do, but do it. Teach them the Word as it is given. Jesus said, "I must work the works of Him that sent me, while it is day; for when the night cometh no man can work." The program for doctrine is in the Book; the program for evangelism is in the Book, for finance, education, all are in the Book. The church must fight for, and against. The Negro has his best opportunity in these times to prove or be the best example as a Christian above all the races of the world.

Our need in the church is to preach, so says Dr. P. S. Wilkinson. If we want help from Christ Jesus in our struggles, we who are called by the Lord Jesus Christ must now, as never before, preach. This preacher must become disturbed. Trouble will come, preach. Men will fail and seek to do you harm, but preach. Preach until the ungodly will become disturbed. Preach until the white man of this nation will know that Jesus Christ is the hope of the world. Preach until justice will run in human hearts like mighty waters in ocean ways. Preach until Mississippi, Georgia, Alabama, Virginia, South Carolina, and Florida and Texas know that God still sees and cares. Preach until the African will no longer hide behind his devil bush in Africa. Chinese will bow no more his knees to Buddha nor Japanese no more his gods of power. Preach until Communism will loose its grip, and Christianity will hoist high its flag of victory with our Captain in lead as we approach the environment of the haven of rest. We will hear a voice, the voice of Him who spoke first, "Fly wide ye everlasting door and the King of glory shall come in." Somebody will ask the question, "Who is the King of glory?" I want to join the chant, "The Lord strong and mighty, the Lord mighty in battle."

The Boards

Our Boards of the National Baptist Convention of America have been entrusted with the work in the fields of this nation and the world. Let me call your attention to one point we will need—honesty in our endeavors. He who deals honestly with God need never have any worries. Honest with himself, honest with his fellowmen, honest with God's money, with God's time, honest with God's knowledge, with influence. You have seen, as well as I, men with all of these but they work contrary to this end. Where are they now? Some are asleep; some are still living but dead. "Do my will and keep my commandments, ask what ye will, I will grant it."

Annual Address of Dr. J. C. Sams
President of the National Baptist Convention of America
In Session at St. Petersburg, Florida, September, 1969

To the Vice-Presidents of the National Baptist Convention of America, Dr. B. O. Byrd, Dr. Moses Price, Official Family, Messengers, State and National Guest, our many friends, Christian Sisters and Brothers in Christ Jesus:

At the close of the session last year in San Antonio, Texas with our dear beloved brother Dr. P. S. Wilkinson and the members of the New Light Baptist Church, many things have found their fulfillment in time and we have all to thank God for. We enjoyed one of our most outstanding experiences there with our brothers and sisters in Christ.

In February, we sojourned to Phoenix, Arizona and shared another great experience with Dr. Hall and our National Senior Women's president, Sister Fannie Thompson, the pastor, and membership of each church in that area. Too much can't be said about the State of Arizona. They are among the most courteous group of Christians that it has been mine to share with. We can fulfill the purpose of Christ when we have this type of togetherness and unity that is found among us.

Greetings

God in His unlimited mercy and grace has again allowed us to meet face-to-face in this our Eighty-Ninth Session of this our National Assembly; for which we have all to thank Him for. It is known very well among us as believers, He has brought us, His children, from a mighty long way. We have come thus far by faith. The journey has not at all times been smooth, but we are here. Misfortunes, seen and unseen, have attended our way. Loved ones have passed on to the Great Beyond, troubles in home life, church life, problems with our children, problems in our cities and states, our nation and our world. All have been ours to encounter. We have not always known which way to go, but thanks be to God, who has shown us the way, here we are today. It may be helpful if we sit quietly long enough to hear the voice of our Master when asked the question in the forest land, to one of His senior prophets, Elijah, "What doeth thou here, Elijah?" In other words, "What are you doing here, Elijah?"

We have gathered here in the "sunshine city of America", St.

Petersburg, Florida, in the State that is better known as "the playground of America," in the State that has as its heritage, the Rocket Space Center at Cape Kennedy which has sent the first men to the moon, and now the American flag stands in the deep sand of the moon, with its stars and stripes as the true evidence that man has been there. This is nobility to the highest degree in every man's thinking. But men of earth, "What doeth thou here?"

The question is not asked for the sake of the Almighty, but for man. Look at yourself. It is like a parent and his child. Your child may be outside playing in the sand and finally gets into mischief. You begin to think, "Where is that child?" You walk to the door and see him doing something that he has no business. "What are you doing, Sonny?" Nine times out of ten, he will jump and say, "Nothing!" You see him and know what he is doing, but you want him to become conscious of what he is doing.

Today's World

Today, we find ourselves members and citizens of a lopsided society, one that seems to have lost its equilibrium. We share today a philosophy that has caused a short-circuit in the lines of communication man-with-man. Our line of brotherly love has been broken. Respect one for the other, decency, true character in manhood and womanhood has diminished. Children of our today's world have lost respect for parents, teachers, and even ministers of the Holy calling to the Gospel. Where there is a broken wire, you will see sparks protruding, indicating live wire. This is true in human lives, in our home life, in institutions of learning, high schools, colleges and universities; president, trustees, teachers, preachers, and everyone who is trying, and has tried across the years, to build the highways and the lines of communication so that we might restore in every person the ability to care for other's well-being.

It must be made known that the better way of life didn't just leap in their places; for behind every building there is a builder. Behind every productive farm there is a farmer. Behind every evangelistic church there is an evangelist. Behind every shoe there is a shoemaker. Behind every creature, there is a Creator!

The old saying of our fathers of yesterday, "Nothing from nothing leaves nothing!" Young people, remember God has been as good to you as He has been to anyone else in His world. If you want to be somebody you have to get up, get ready, get out, and get going. You can't do it by sitting around crying and demanding what rightfully belongs to another. We need to get away from so much welfare help. You have never known a nation to get very far which has to operate on welfare and government handouts. We the black people of America must check our location and answer the question of courage, "What doeth thou here, Elijah?" Am I here because I am lazy, unconcerned about life and the many opportunities she has to offer?

Our Convention

We, the called believers of Jesus Christ, the witnesses of Jesus Christ, are different. We are not of this world, although we are in the world. It is to be remembered that we have been called out of darkness into the marvelous light of the glorious Gospel of Jesus Christ.

Jesus first called us when he said, "Come after me and I will make you fishers of men." "Come unto me, all ye that labor, and are heavy laden and I will give you rest." "Take my yoke upon you and lean on me; for I am meek in heart: And ye shall find rest unto your souls. For my yoke is easy and my burden is light."

It is my thinking that we spend too much time attempting to prepare our individual programs that we give too little time in the program that has been given by Jesus, the Great Commissioner. Foreign missions, home missions, evangelism, and education are all included in the Great Commission: "Go preach, go teach." This is all of it.

I want to discourage every missionary, every pastor, and every helper of ever doing anything concerning the ministry with the question, "What am I going to get?" Your question should be, "How will the folk benefit from the trust that God has put in me?" For if you give them what they need, you have a promissory note signed by the President of the Universal Bank of Heaven. "I will supply your needs. Do my will, keep my Commandments, ask what ye will in My name and I will grant it unto you."

I said to you last year in San Antonio that if the Lord would help us, we were going to Jamaica and start plans for re-opening the school. Dr. Branch and your President did just that. Today the school is open with a strong faculty and administrative staff and more than 475 students enrolled with a bus for transportation. We went to the bank and set up a system that makes sense for real honest business. My brothers and sisters, if you could have seen those people of slave backgrounds as we have, coming out of the valleys and mountains with bunches of bananas on their shoulders and across the backs of donkeys, working for ninety cents a day, it would make your heart sob.

I realize that we still have poverty here in America, but it's not the same as our brothers and sisters in other countries. It is also worthy of taking note that when the Master called missionary Baptists, He did not send us only to our own people, but He said, "Go ye therefore, and preach the Gospel to every creature: he that believeth shall be saved, he that believeth not shall be damned." We are indebted to every creature: white, black, yellow and brown alike!

We have the personnel, we have the know-how, and we have the money and the time. To quote a statement made by one of the officers of the Second Missionary Baptist Church, "Let us not become so busy doing church work until we forget about the work of the church."

Auxiliary Bodies in the Work

I do want to thank you for your loyal support during my first year as your leader and President. This is no honor that comes to your President, but to you. You broke all records last year in San Antonio. We had the pleasure of giving more to the causes than any year during the history of our Convention. This can only be a continuous reality as God can find in each of us a zest and zeal to be honest in all we do in His name. Don't come up year after year and you know you have people who have never been able to account for what has been entrusted in their leadership. Don't do anything for God because you are afraid of someone putting you out of your office, but do it because it is right to do so.

I want to give God special thanks for allowing Sister Fannie Thompson to head our Senior Women's Convention. As soon as she was elected, she came to her President and had me to know she wanted to do what was right the way God would have her to do it. I am in a position to say to you today that the department made last year its banner report. I am only saying to each of us to do what is right. If you will be fair in your report to God and this convention, He will never leave you and I will never leave you at any session until I know everything and everybody has been treated rightly. Always remember, the causes come first. We need more money for Christian education and the causes of mission.

I want to thank you for having accepted the Benevolent Board's recommendation to be underwritten by Allstate Insurance Company.

Some of us live too long and too well to find ourselves in the condition that we are often found in. Brothers and sisters, we are not going to be young all our days. We grow older every year, whether we admit it or not. Pastors, give a little thought to your wives while things are going well with you; for it makes no difference which church it is, they don't call wives, they call the preacher. Now you tell me what church, after the pastor has gone to his reward, will say, "Sister Sams, you don't have to worry, as long as you live we are going to take care of you and you can remain in the pastorium?" It is only common sense that a man makes provision for his wife. If he should leave first, she is going to have to live elsewhere. I think it is foolish to have two or three cars for two people and not one house.

What Doeth Thou Here, Preacher?

I don't want to say what this preacher said if he had an answer, but I believe he would have said, "Lord, I am here because I am afraid. I am here because I was chased here by war-like men from the voice of a wicked woman." He became afraid. He lost courage, lost faith. His line of communication was broken. You may run, but you can't hide. I can hear my God say, "Come on out!" Do you remember where you were? On Mount Carmel. Did you call me? Did I answer? What are you doing here? I want to run, but not out of fear, but of love.

A father speaks to his son: "Wherefore I put thee in remembrance that thou stir up the gift of God which is in thee by the putting on of my hands. For God hath not given us the spirit of fear; but of *power* and of *love*, and of a sound mind."

Annual Address of Dr. J. C. Sams
President of the National Baptist Convention of America
In Session at Shreveport, Louisiana, September 10, 1970

The Adventures in Faith

To the Vice-Presidents of the Convention, Dr. Byrd and Dr. Price, Officers, and messengers of the National Baptist Convention of America, our national guests, and many Christian sisters and brothers from every section of America and foreign lands:

Greetings

By the eternal purpose of Him who has all eternity in His hand, we have been allowed to come face-to-face here in the 90th session of this our Convention. Since we met last year in St. Petersburg, Fla., the Sunshine City, the flower garden of America, with the Mt. Zion Progressive Baptist Church, Dr. L. S. McCree, host pastor, at the Bay Front Center, many have been our experiences and therefore today they have been compiled in the likeness of another segment in the history-making of many of our brothers and sisters who walked with us in 1969. If they were called today, they would refuse to answer. In all of this, we do remember that we are the creatures of the Creator of all persons and things.

Baptist World Alliance

Just a few weeks ago, during the month of July, many of us were sent, and many went on their own to Tokyo, Japan. This was a great experience for everyone who made the trip. We come today to say thank you for having made it possible for our Convention to have been represented in such fine numbers. I say, again, we must stand together as a body, so much so if we find it necessary to go to the left or right, we must need be together. During our voyage some of our experiences were good and some not so good; but if we stay together, we can and will be respected more by any power that may be in business. Our Convention gave us an opportunity to select an agency to work through, and this was done. As your President, if there were those who didn't get your money's worth, you may be assured you have my deepest concern and at all times I am writing to help in all matters pertaining to our Convention to help make it right.

I am most grateful to the Lord for having each of you as a leader in this Convention. It is without saying, had it not been for you and your support, we would not have the type of Convention that we have today. It is not all in its monetary values, instead, when Christians can meet together in Christian unity and have fellowship one with the other and bring and give inspiration; togetherness in programs, prayers are among the many things we need today. We need to study ways and means how we may expand the program of Christ in evangelism and training, that we may be and become the true picture of Christ our Lord. This can be done best when each of us as a Christian will give ourselves totally committed to Christ in service wherever we may be.

We can only do for Christ and His work in proportion as we envision the need and join hands to help. Anybody can talk about the program and its needs, but it is another thing to find men and women to do some of what they are talking about. There are some people in each group present here today who feel they could and would do a better job than anyone of us in leadership, but he never has anything to offer while someone else is leading but talk.

Our Convention's Work

It is to be remembered that this Convention and its work is not James Carl Sams' Convention and work, but in every respect it is Christ's work through this Convention. I am only one among the many of you who believe this and are striving daily to help the purpose of God to find its fulfillment through us.

We admit that there are some seven or eight segments here among us as auxiliaries, but there is only one Convention. Also some seven or eight boards, but only one Convention. In preparing this address, I made an attempt to count the departments and boards. You will find, according to the records, that we have fifteen, but there is only one Convention. By the same token, we will need to stop somewhere a while and take a look at the many departments; for if we are not careful, we will have fifteen different conventions unless there is a unity in every one of you as a leader of these departments. That is, willing to take orders for the Convention from its constitutional basis. You can never hope to be an asset, but instead, you will become a liability. We must never hope to make our Convention little or small.

I was invited to bring words of welcome to an African Methodist Episcopal Conference. The many of our city was also to bring welcome. There was the presiding bishop and some three out-of-state bishops in attendance. In the pews were hundreds of pastors from every section. All were wearing round collars. So, the mayor gave honor to the presiding bishop whom he knew, and looked with amazement, and said, "To all you bishops, I don't think I have seen so many bishops in all the days of my life." We, Baptists, must watch this all the way from our local churches, districts, states, and general associations; by the time you get to the top, most of the essence may be gone.

Boards and Auxiliaries

We are making progress through most of our departments. The only way to do this is through love and unity. No preacher can do the job in the church that the Holy Spirit has made him overseer by trying to be a "boss man." One cannot argue his way to success. It makes no difference who he is. Every board must study to know its work, and do it. You can't do your job and your brother's at the same time to save your life.

I come today standing before you for my third annual message. I thank you again from the depths of my heart for having given me the opportunity to share the leadership of this great national body; one of which many men covet, some who are asleep and many who are still alive. Believe me, brethren, there is nothing wrong with anyone who aspires for a position in leadership; for any man who doesn't have an inspiration to go higher than where he is might find himself to have poor vision. But at the same time, one will need to use common sense about the position he desires; for there are two or three questions he may need ask himself: (1) What am I doing with what I have? (2) What would be my attitude toward others? (3) Where could God find me when He was ready for me?

Oh, my brothers and sisters, there are many people in all churches and conventions who wish so many of us would take our leave so they could take our places, but ever keep in mind while you wish someone else would move on and out, there is someone behind your door wishing you would move on and out. I am only trying to say thank you! It is not a question of how long one serves, but how well! But I am forced again to say as long as I am President, I will be President.

I trust you understand when a convention elects a President, it is similar to a church electing a pastor. He is to give oversight. He can't do well trying to be superintendent, caretaker, President of the brotherhood, or choir. In all of these, he is to give leadership, but he has to have help. Let everyone just be one. Let the church be the church. Many members, but one body in Christ Jesus.

The Need of Each Department

We need men and women who have vision, patience, love, and concern for the cause and others. I am not sure many of us have come to know some of the things that some of us know. You don't have to move in fear, talking about "I got to look out for myself. When I am old and worn out nobody will be concerned about me" or "These young people will never know what I have put in this thing."

God's way for everyone of us is already fixed. I hear the prophet of my Bible saying, "National Baptists, I once was young, now I am old, but I have never seen the righteous forsaken nor his seed begging bread." If you spend your life for God in your youth or young life, He will not put you on the begging list when you grow old. Our times demand from each of us adventuring faith, the type that moves not knowing where you are going. Pull up stumps, move mountains, scoop out valleys, keep moving. It matters not how long the journey. Keep walking — all He has for me is in the way.

The Message to the Church

"And Isaac spake unto Abraham his father, and said, 'My Father;' and he said, 'Here am I, my son.' And he said, 'Behold the fire and the wood; but where is the lamb for a burnt offering?' And Abraham said, 'My son, God will provide Himself a lamb for a burnt offering' so they went both of them together."

This is the need for our time. We need to go up together. Togetherness is our great need. Both went up together facing death itself, but they went together. We are forced to cry, but we ought to cry together. Often we find broken planks in the bridge, but we need to talk together. Walk without fear and unity. Faith is the railroad track on which the train brings the cargo in for the soul — the ship that masters the bosom of the mad waters of the oceanway loaded with goods for the soul, and will be delivered at the port of Promise by the Keeper of all things and persons.

"Be not dismayed whate'er betide,
God will take care of you;
Beneath His wings of love abide,
God will take care of you.

God will take care of you,
Thru ev'ry day,
O'er all the way;
He will take care of you,
God will take care of you."

In God's own time, He provided for Himself a Lamb. He touched Isaiah 53:7 about 750 years before His coming: "He was oppressed and He was afflicted, yet He opened not His mouth; He was brought as a lamb to the slaughter; and as a sheep before her shearers is dumb, so He opened not His mouth."

Annual Address of Dr. J. C. Sams
President of the National Baptist Convention of America
In Session at San Francisco, California, September, 1971

To the Vice-Presidents, Officers, members, and messengers, visitors and friends from the nation and abroad—Greetings!

The Lord has so arranged it that we, the people of God, have been spared to assemble again in an annual gathering of the National Baptist Convention of America to share our mutual vows and spiritual fellowship one with the other. We have assembled here on the Gold Coast of California, one of the beauty spots of our nation; the state whose trails were blazed by the pioneers of yester-years, as their eyes and hearts were set in this direction. They watched the golden sun rays as they blended their majestic power with the belching waters of the Pacific, and no longer styled itself as a dual system, but formulated into a system of unity.

It was here where the eyes of the known world focused their attention. Some came for one thing, and others came for other reasons. This state, like all others, has made and is making its history. It is not mine to say how proud any of us might be about what has been, and is being written in the chapters of our history, in this our nation and our world.

We, the witnesses of Christ, are the lightholders for a lost, disturbed and confused world. We must face up to it and find an answer for our stewardship.

I. Why Cometh Thou Here?

II. Lift Up Your Eyes and Look!

III. Where From Here?

I come today to say thank you for your loyal support in so many endeavors in the work and ministry of our Lord Jesus Christ through this our Convention. You have been loyal and untiring in your support. It is to be remembered again, that this ministry we share is the Lord's work. Each of us is a helper in the unfinished task of Him. I hear these words as they fell from the lips of the Savior:

> "Lift up your eyes, and look on the field;for they are white already to harvest but the laborers are few. Pray to the Lord of the harvest that He will send forth more laborers into His vineyard."

The field belongs to Him. The land belongs to Him. The crop is His, and we are His helpers. We are workers with Him.

> "Behold, I send you forth as workers, then I promise you I will come again, and pay every man according to his work."

Where are we in the work of the Lord in this our Convention? Are we fulfilling the purpose of Christ in our work? I can hear many silent answers, "no." Then, why? I have made it known many times, before now, that we need men and women in leadership of our churches and conventions who are honest people. Born-again people who are not afraid to trust God when they begin to get a few years behind them.

Let me tell you young men now, there is no need waiting until you reach 50-60-65 years of age and wake up and try to get a hold of something. Then try to do in five, seven, or ten years what you should have done when you were thirty or forty years of age. It has been my experience that if you are to be somebody, you can't wait until you are an old worn out person, then jump up early one morning and decide you've got to look out for yourself. Give your youth to the Lord. Get some sense, take your time and think things through, do right by your family, church, needs, and poor. Give your best to the Master and He will let you stay around for a while, and He will give you success. Be faithful, true, love people, and be trustworthy. Be one who can be trusted with whatever people will trust you. When one has proved himself to be honest, people will give far more than you will ever get wrongfully.

Do We Stop Here?

If your heart is as steadfast as mine, we share the expression of old: "We can't stop now!" If you were assigned to the task by the same One as I was, you will join the chant, "We can't stop here!" If the child would stop growing at the age of one, we would always have children but no men. If saplings would stop growing, the forest would be filled with saplings but no trees. If chicks stopped growing, we would fill all the coops in the world, but there would be no fryers, hens, or roosters. If education ended with the ABC's there would be no place for educators. If converts were the desired end results, there would never be helpers in the Kingdom work. Discipleship—If Heaven wasn't reality, all would go to Hell.

Why Cometh Thou Here?

We all will admit that we are here in California. This is a fact. But remember, this is not the question. Why am I here? For what did I come? Why cometh thou here? Did you come just because it is California, to see old friends, or to prove economic social ability? Why are you here? Did it cost God's church a thousand dollars to send you to bring one-hundred dollars, five-hundred dollars, three-hundred dollars, or to bring thirty-five dollars? In other words, is your being here costing ninety-percent more than the causes we have come to support? God forbid!

National Baptist, it is time, and high time, that we stop playing church and admit that if we don't do better, we ought to give up. We should come out and admit that we have failed in the program of Christ, our Lord. Why cometh thou here? Did you come to have a good time? Right now, there are men and women all over this world who are hungry, naked, ignorant, molested, unlearned, and forsaken. Do we care? Does anyone care?

What seeth thou, O Man? Do you see, do your hear young people of the world and this nation crying daily that they can no longer trust us as mothers and fathers of our times? Do you hear them saying to us, "You give birth and hire nurses to take care of us until we are old enough to dress ourselves, then you send us off to school to be taught, then at 18 years of age we are inducted into the world of conflict to give our lives for a little more geography, money, the things of material, all for what?"

America, America, and National Baptists, we might as well face it. Things, and things alone don't make men. Instead, men make things. Do you see this man of our times as he sees life in his way? The average man wants two or three cars in his family, he can't preach unless he has a crowd, he will not preach if the church gets behind in his salary.

What Do You See?

I see a famine, a spiritual drought, a spiritual lake all dry. There is no longer a yearning for souls. Nobody wakes before day crying about the church and humanity. We are more concerned about getting the members in the church now, that is, so many hundreds or thousands instead of trying to get Christian, born-again men and women. You don't have trouble with Christians. Our troubles come out of the numbers.

Ninety-percent of the average pastor's time is spent trying to keep peace and harmony among those in our churches; and ten-percent for all the work of his ministry.

Where From Here

> "Go ye therefore into all the world, preaching the Gospel to every creature. He that believeth and is baptized shall be saved, he that believeth not shall be damned.
>
> "And they went forth and preached everywhere and the Lord working with them with the Word, and signs following."

Human and divine co-operation is a must in the spreading of the Gospel.

Our attention is called as Gospel preachers. The Lord called those of us whom He called to preach. I am not talking about it as we have made it, but as He left it. He didn't send us to be members of the barber's union, the NAACP, to head government agencies, nor teachers in public school. I am sure of what He said to me: "Go preach." He told me if you preach, I will be with you always. If you preach, everything you need is included. If you want a house, preach; if you want more houses, preach; if you want more money, preach; if you want old-age pension, preach; social security, preach; cars, boats, preach. All is wrapped up in one package: Preach! If you want a larger church, preach; if you feel you ought to have a better church, preach.

Let Us Rise And Build

Build, for old buildings have served their usefulness. Tear down and build. Our times call for new building. Christ Jesus is the need of today. Build on Christ, the True Foundation.

> "On Christ the solid rock I stand;
> All other ground is sinking sand.
> I dare not trust the sweetest frame,
> But wholly lean on Jesus' Name."

Build on Christ! What can I expect if I build on Christ? Your house will *stand* when the storms of life are raging. It will *stand* and you will have strength to know that, "I know in Whom I have believed, and am persuaded that He is able to keep that which I have committed unto His hand against that day."

Ernest Edward Jones

Ernest Edward Jones (1931-) was born May 3, 1931, in DeRidder, Louisiana, the third child of Rev. David Jesse Jones and Daisy Hatcherson Jones. At the age of seven, he was baptized by his father in the Sweet Home Baptist Church.

Considered by his peers as deeply religious for his years, he was voted the "Most Religious Member" of his high school class. He demonstrated outstanding leadership skills which so impressed his classmates that he was elected Class President for four consecutive years.

His tall, lean, and graceful frame possessed an agility which made him specially suited for basketball. He enrolled in Grambling College in Grambling, Louisiana, where he played varsity basketball for four years.

In 1949, he accepted the call to the Gospel ministry. Two years later, he became pastor of Mount Harmony Baptist Church, Ruston, Louisiana. A year later, August 31, 1952, he married Leslie Alexander, his college sweetheart, who had the distinction of being "Miss Grambling."

For seven years Rev. Jones served as teacher and principal in Morehouse Parish. He received degrees from Bishop College and the United Theological Seminary. Several times, he has been honored with the Doctor of Divinity degree.

He pastored several churches in Morehouse Parish area. At the age of twenty-seven, he became pastor of the historic Galilee Baptist Church in Shreveport, Louisiana. Since that time, the Galilee church was experiencing astounding growth and development. More than five-thousand souls have accepted Christ during the twenty-seven years of his pastoral leadership. A new and commodious sanctuary, valued at more than $1,000,000, has been built and dedicated free of debt. The church owns thirteen acres of land in the heart of the city, including the old church building and rental properties.

Currently under construction, is a 202-HUD Project, "Galilee Gardens," which will be the living quarters for the handicapped and elderly, at a cost of $1,700,000.

Dr. Jones moved rapidly on the ladder of denominational leadership. He became moderator of Mount Hermon District Association, serving with distinction for sixteen years. He was elected President of the Baptist Missionary and Educational State Convention of Louisiana, Incorporated.

In the National Baptist Convention of America, he was elected to chair the Social Justice Commission and served faithfully for eight years. The Constitution was revised, making it possible for Dr. Jones to become the first "Third Vice-President" in Convention history.

He was elected to the position of Second Vice-President following the death of Dr. M. L. Price of Texas. After serving a year in that position, he was elected President of the Convention, following the death of Dr. James Carl Sams of Florida.

Dr. Jones assumed the leadership of the Convention, September 5, 1985, in the 105th Annual Session. It was an occasion when he was doubly honored, serving as host pastor in Shreveport, Louisiana, and President of the National Baptist Convention of America.

Annual Address of Dr. E. E. Jones
President of the National Baptist Convention of America
In Session at Shreveport, Louisiana, September, 1985

Introduction

Vice-President Lockridge, Presidents of Auxiliary Bodies: Dr. Fannie Thompson of the Senior Women, Dr. Hattie L. E. Williams of Senior Mission II, Sister Francis Worthey of the Junior Women, Sister Ruby Lockridge of the Nurses, Brother Charles Walker of the Ushers, Rev. Brother Curtis Lee Carter of the Young Men for Christ, and Brother Previn Carr of the Youth Convention; Officers of the Parent Body, all Auxiliary Body Officers, Board Secretaries for Foreign Missions, Home Mission, Evangelism, Education, Benevolent, and Baptist Training Union: Drs. Robert H. Wilson. O. B. Williams, Freddie Dunn, Wallace Hartsfield and J. Royster Powell — Board Chairmen: Drs. J. W. Toomer, Luke W. Mingo, Potter and Wiggins, J. B. Adams, W. M. Bowie and A. Bernard; Commission Chairmen: Drs. Frank K. Sims, R. W. McKissick, Committee Chairmen, Dr. F. Benjamin Davis and others, Messengers and friends who have come to share this 105th Annual Session of the National Baptist Convention of America . . . Greetings in the name of our wonderful Christ.

You have assembled in a great city. Great because it is a city of churches, many communions, and many sinners. The challenge to evangelize is ever present here. Great because there are some good people here in Shreveport. Great because this is where I live, not just exist. On behalf of all our pastors, churches, political and civic leaders and this city in general, I personally want to thank you for being here. I trust that the hospitality that you have received is acceptable.

Twelve months have swiftly rolled around. Many outstanding voices have been hushed in death. We have been shocked, grieved and still mourn the homegoing of five of our top officers, namely: Dr. J. C. Sams, our President, Dr. M. L. Price, our First Vice-President, Dr. John Francis, Jr., our Treasurer; Dr. J. L. Richards, our Statistician and Dr. C. W. Williams, our Chairman of the Committee on Bills and Accounts. The efforts of these great men will not be forgotten as their deeds live on. I feel a sense of humility, pride, and joy when I realize the Lord allowed us to walk with giants.

"And are we yet alive to see each other's face?
Glory and praise to Jesus give for His redeeming grace;
Preserved by power divine to full salvation here,
Again in Jesus praise we join and in His sight appear."

"What troubles have we seen? What conflicts have we
passed?
Fighting without, and fears within, since we assembled
last;
But out of all the Lord hath brought us by His love,
And still His grace afford, and hide our lives above."

"Then let us make our boast of His redeeming power,
which saves us to the uttermost, till we can sin no more;
Let us take up the cross, till we the crown obtain,
And gladly reckon all things loss, we may Jesus gain."

I am called upon to give account of my stewardship as the presiding President of this convention for this past year. Every other person in leadership is called upon to report to this body, also. Last year in Los Angeles, California, we elected a full slate of officers. The Grim Reaper—Death, has constantly visited us this year. We are powerless to slow down or stop this inevitable appointment. Our concerns weighted with our griefs have caused us to anchor ourselves deeper in Him who knows all things and is constantly working for our good.

Two days after Christmas, 1984, Dr. Sams fell with a stroke that impaired his speech. January, 1985, I visited him in a Jacksonville, Florida, hospital. He was quite cheerful, but I dared not burden him with the affairs of this convention. Upon leaving, it dawned upon me that our mid-winter board meeting was in February and that there was a possibility he would not be able to attend. Judgment dictated to me that I had an unusual responsibility of guarded responsibility of guarded leadership; that of moving our convention forward and operating within the realm of respect and acceptance of our President. For me that was not a difficult task. Thanks to God, Dr. A. E. Chew and others that through prayers and much thought, we put together the Biloxi, Mississippi meeting. It was a success in every measure of the word. Let me again thank the program participants and the wonderful pastors who responded to our call.

In Biloxi, we heard some of the best preaching that could be heard. More than $75,000 was raised in that meeting. All loans, debts, enrollment in the Baptist World's Alliance, our appropriated share of finance into the National Congress of Black Churches, donations to Boards increased nearly 100% and a $5,000.00 love gift to our

President were just a part of our financial doings. Believe it or not, we had enough left over to cover $2,800.00 in bad checks from that meeting.

In Denver, Colorado, in June during the National Baptist Congress, we held our summer board meeting for a half-day. Churches, convention, and associations contributed $14,460.00. Personally, I felt that we did poorly. However, it represented about a $5,000 raise over the previous year. We received from the National Baptist Congress the convention's share of the receipts, which amounted to $17,250.00. In Denver, our total amounted to a little better than $32,000.00.

During the brief session, Dr. Wallace Hartsfield electrified us with a powerful devotion message that almost sounded like a sermon. But, who cared, it was superlative. Then, that mighty preacher, Dr. Robert H. Wilson preached as if it was his last time. Following his sermon, we raised better than $600.00. Any man who preached as he did deserved the offering. So we gave it to him.

Strangely and oddly enough we would have brought into this conventional year about $20,000.00 if the hot checks have cooled off.

In Denver, I proposed a challenging plan whereby this convention can have at least $1,000,000.00 working for us. This amount ($1,000,000.00) will be placed in certificates of deposit at the highest possible rate of interest. When we have reached our goal, I expect more than $100,000.00 in interest. This interest will be used to subsidize the action boards of our convention. We must be witnesses in doing to the reality of Christ. The message must go out. Struggling churches must be helped. Widows of pastors must be seen after. We have the juice, as Albert Chew says, to do it, and do it we must. I have come prepared to make sure this $1,000,000.00 venture gets started. On behalf of a great church, Galilee, here is $1,000.00 followed by a great state convention with another $1,000.00 and from a hosting committee for 1985, $2,000.00 and from Leslie, our four children and seven grandchildren, our $1,000.00. Now I know the fund is started. Others of you have come prepared to follow suit. Following the message, you will have that opportunity. Don't feel bad if you do not have it. Make your pledge today and send it in as quickly as you get it within the next twelve months. Please, no hot checks, but we will accept cold cash.

This fund will be set up where it cannot be cashed in by anyone other than the convention by your consent. Three of four signatures will be required then. This little nest egg will only demonstrate what we can do for the Master's cause. Any concern needs money to operate. But, you need it for more than operations. It helps you feel better about yourself. It helps others feel better about you. It also helps others to respect you.

You will receive direct communication from the convention in the form of a quarterly newsletter. Periodically, we will print in the *Union Review* the report so that all may know what is being done. It is possible non-involved churches will become involved at this point.

I was so proud of you as I saw you rally to the Ethiopians. I do not know the exact figure you gave, but I know it was over $100,000.00 because I presented a check to Africare for $100,000.00 on the day we left to go to Ethiopia. Dr. Wilson, Dr. & Mrs. M. L. Thomas, Dr. Obie Williams, Dr. A. C. Bowie and a young minister Mel of the East Mt. Zion Church of Cleveland left by air to go to Africa on a brief fact-finding trip. From New York to Frankfurt, Germany, to Saudi Arabia, then to Addis Abba, Ethiopia, we flew. We had a number of conferences with health officials, food distribution officials and the director of African relief from Africare in Washington (a black organization). Our fact-finding trip carried us to Murkelle in northern Ethiopia. We saw people in droves like animals moving here and there. We saw the naked, the starving, the toothless, the homeless. We saw crude farming equipment. The average income in Ethiopia is $150.00 a year. The land was dry. The forest is gone. People are dying unmercifully. The ladies cooked in holes outside of their tents in a designated area. There is no such thing as running water. There are no toilet facilities. Flies are swarming, lighting on the sick frames of the people. The smell of human excretion is in the air. Hospitals are pup tents. A shotgun house would be a palace for many of our black brothers and sisters there. I left from Africa, but Africa will never leave from me. We must go back through our gifts, somehow we must get some more gospel into that country. There is a need for medical staff. I left Africa, but it will never leave me.

15th Baptist World Alliance

I found much to be desired for this meeting. By the same token, I found a great fulfillment as principally all nations on the earth gathered in Los Angeles, California, to share a common fellowship in Christ Jesus. Several things made the meeting a success.

(1) Our own Dr. Fannie Thompson was one of the presidents. Dr.

T. J. Jemison was elected one of the vice-presidents for the next five years. Dr. Albert Chew and myself were elected as board members.

(2) The New Mount Calvary Baptist Church Choir of Los Angeles, California, marched nearly 300 choir members on the stage and brought the house down. That church is a member of our Convention and has a Sunday School attendance of better than 500. I want you to see that pastor. I am asking him now, to lead a seminar in Corpus Christi and tell us how to do the same.

Let's start getting ready now to attend the 16th session in Seoul, Korea in 1990.

The Posture and Position of Our Convention

Those who are inferior must first feel that way within. God has not intended any of us to be less than another. Nor, has he intended that any of us would feel ourselves more than the next person. Some are more talented in some areas than others. Some have more comprehending minds than others. Others have more common judgment. Some experience more earthly success than others. Some suffer more than others. However, we are equal in two things - we live and we all die.

This convention is 105 years old. We have been at it a long time. Naturally, we have experienced peaks and valleys, but isn't that the way of life? Whatever our yesteryears held for us in history, history is good for two things:

(l) We are reminded of what we were then and,

(2) We have a platform to step upon for brighter things ahead.

Today we stand upon the giant shoulders of those who paved the way through blood, sweat, and tears. Today, we must be committed to stand as mighty soldiers of the cross with shoulders even broader and stronger. There are generations following us who will occupy the high places.

God does not want this convention to shrug along with dropped shoulders. We are God's army and His army is a mighty army. National Baptist Convention of America must become proud of our past, praise God and work for our possibilities. We have the resources, the brain power, the personality, the adaptability and sure enough, an abundance of the Spirit of Christ to cause this nation and this world to be conscious of whose we are.

Some of the best churchmen in this nation are in this Convention. The richest black man in Louisiana is in this Convention. Some of the greatest missionary work in the world is being carried on by this

Convention. Some of the preachingest preachers are in this Convention. We need to thank God for what we have because He has a whole lot more to give us. These bones will live.

National Baptist Convention of America has two very strong points, dynamic preaching and unparalleled fellowship. Thank the Lord we have this! Both are strong and needed in order to have a great Convention.

We are not as strong as we can be in the encouragement of churchmanship in the local church. Many of our pastors and lay people are products of great Christian institutions and universities. They are born again and they have knowledge that should be shared. These resources must be tapped and harnessed for kingdom building throughout our Convention's domain. We must develop programs that are researched, tried, proven and transformed into the black experience. Our great need today is to teach more, this is not to say that we should preach less. Our teachings must be intensified. We are called upon, with the caliber of people we minister to today, to inform and inspire them. Many of our so-called church fighters are carryovers from the school of "us" run the church and you just preach. Others are worldly transplants that need to be born again. While still others know just what has been passed on to them from other generations and would do better if they knew better. This is where teaching comes in.

As a denomination, we are not taking the time that is needed in serious Bible study. Sure, read and study all of the books at your command on how to do, but you had better first learn who you are doing it for. That is found only in the Book, the Bible. I want to exhort you to go back home and begin somewhere. You may not have but five persons interested, but I would rather have five Bible-informed people than have 500 ignorant of "what thus, saith the Lord." *Can these bones live?*

Too many of you take too lightly the scope of the church, associations, and convention. The looseness of the Baptist church in denominational affairs breeds apathy in fellowship, errors in slowfulness in support of worthy causes and death for would-be thriving churches. If the bishop in an Episcopal structure can summon the preachers and churches of his diocese to report annually, how much more should the bishops of the Baptist church want to summon themselves to report and enhanced the Kingdom's cause. *Can these bones live???*

My observation is that we have too many Conventions in this one

Convention. For the most part you do what you want to do with or without the sanction of the Convention. This is wrong and must be corrected!!! The National Baptist Convention of America is an umbrella and every single entity of it must come under that. The truth of the matter is everything that you do in your auxiliaries must support the aims and the objectives of this Convention. Our prayer must be that of the Lord's, "Make us one." My question is *"Can these bones live?"*

The Boards of our convention are set up to carry out the yearly task of our Convention. This Convention must expect the leaders of these Boards to give through prayer, research, and work into the development of plans and programs for their respective areas of work. The Boards operate for the Convention and not the Convention for the Board. They must always be reminded that we are dealing with the King's work. I am asking State Presidents and General Association Presidents to send strong men, praying men, planning men, and inquiring men to these Boards. National Baptist Convention can be no stronger than these Boards and our auxiliary bodies. I am a firm believer in being liberal with the Lord, and I also know He holds me responsible for being conservative and thoughtful about how His money is spent. A portion of the integrity of this Convention rests with how these Boards appropriate money. *Can these bones live?*

Several of our commissions are weak. This must not be. Commissions must work as commissions. National Baptists must define these areas and expect commissions to work on behalf of this Convention. Commissions must work in the area of their assigned task and not extend themselves beyond what they are commissioned to do.

Social Action

Far too many of us are awaiting Dr. Martin Luther King's dream to come true. Dreams just don't come true. We dream great dreams, but we must make them work through human efforts. We are not at a time of lunch counter sit-ins, or library sit-ins (frankly, I wish that black people would stage some library sit-ins, we need to know what is happening in our world today). You can eat anywhere you have money. Economic development is our problem.

We must exhibit skills in negotiating with businesses, especially those who have high black clientele and no blacks employed or just a few shallow window dressing. If businesses of this kind cannot hire black people, who are responsible for their livelihood, stop trading there and let them know.

Blacks that are in business must provide equally as good a service as anybody else. Receptionists who cannot be kind and courteous must be fired. Blacks who want to draw salaries but don't want to work, must be terminated. Don't allow employees to work for you looking any kind of way. God bless OIC and other organizations that are training young people to work. We must recapture Dr. Sullivan's idea. The government has cut back on funding these programs, but we must open the doors of our churches and the trained within our memberships must help the untrained become self-supporting. "Give and it shall be given to you, etc." (Luke 6:38)

Dr. A. L. Bowman is seated here on the platform today at my request. He set up a plan to help 20 men in the Union Church in Denver save $5,000.00 each. Those men saw their possibilities and extended that program to include a number of other meaningful self-help ventures that are now worth millions of dollars. Don't cry over spilled milk, find another cow and milk her. That group in Denver, Colorado, owns a shopping center. They have formed a Black Women's Mortgage Corp., and operate an accelerated school program. If Al can do it, you can do something. (Philippians 4:13)

Black people are often accused of waiting for pie in the sky. I am expecting my pie in the sky but I like pie down here also. I want to walk those streets of gold, but I also want to walk on Fifth. I am looking forward to my golden slippers, but I want to slide my feet out of a pair of Johnston Murphy's to try them on. I want my long white robe, but I also enjoy Hickory Freeman suits, here!! I want my starry crown, but I will know my size if I wear a Stetson here. Jesus said I have come that they may have life and have it more abundantly. The Lord will not penalize you for having something here on earth. All that He asks you to do is pay him the 10% and above, comfort the feeble-minded, and share your blessings with others. I am a witness that He will bless you.

We must become concerned as a Convention about the whole man. Unemployment among blacks and the disadvantaged is high. Especially, we must become concerned about black youth unemployment. We must recognize some of the problems that are with us.

1. This present National Administration is not sensitive to the plight of minorities.

2. We do not have enough thriving enterprises among us.

3. Churches must lead the way in hiring our youth.

This present administration is a conservative one that seems bent on balancing the budget at the expense of cut-backs, cut-outs, all at the expense of the poor. We spend billions of dollars in defense. I maintain that we should have a strong defense against poverty here in the richest country in the world. Shall we be destroyed by nuclear war or will we be destroyed by living in substandard housing, starving to death, improper diets, or freezing in the winter?

Black people must come to trust each other more in business. Middle-class black America must realize that we owe a debt to our brothers and sisters who are less fortunate than we are. Business-minded people must pool their financial resources to build stronger businesses and hire people who really want to work. Our black professionals must stop soloing in business and join hands with others of their professions and build medical clinics and strong law firms. They must hire bright young college-trained people, with pleasing personalities to work. They must pay them well.

Churches must stop talking about what they can't do. Too many of our churches are shut tight from one Sunday to another. There is no secretary, no janitor, no full-time musician; no Director of Christian Education, no social worker, no ministerial help, not much preaching. Our churches are suffering from understaffing. Staffing is not an expense, it is an asset. Shame on you if you think this cuts down on your effectiveness. This ain't the horse and buggy days, this is the computer age. Everybody else will have gone off and left you. Maybe you don't understand the computer, but this is not the first thing that you did not understand. You don't fully understand your new birth, but you know it is so. Don't curse modern technology. Make it work for you. Nearly everything that we touch today is computerized.

The summer is an ideal time to put your young people to work. Set up a summer work program. Make some jobs. Members of your church need baby-sitters, house cleaners, grass cutters, car washers, and window washers. Hire our young people to aid on office work. They have been to school. Let them type your sermons, work in your office. Do some telephoning. Every church owes it to their young people to do more than pray for them and criticize for hanging out on the corner. You will be surprised to see how your church will rally to this cause. *Can these bones live?*

This administration has quietly dismissed the idea of quota hiring. Jobs that many whites turned their noses up at a few years ago are now their source of livelihood. The war for equality is still on. We must be soldiers.

Sermon Text

"Can These Bones Live?"—(Ezekiel 37:3)

A fragmented, dissolute, displaced heart-broken people are existing at the level of hopelessness. The skies of prosperity are muggy. The daybreak of deliverance seemed so far away during this long captivity. There was nothing to be excited about. God's chosen people felt stuck in the morass of human hopelessness. Rightly so perhaps, as they remembered how hard-headed, how disobedient, how stiff-necked they had been. It appears that they had passed the stage of repentance. How were they to cope with their helpless selves in a hopeless situation? God has a prophet!

As recorded in Ezekiel 37:1 & 2, "The hand of the Lord was upon me, and carried me out in the spirit of the Lord, and set me down in the midst of the valley which was full of bones, and caused me to pass by them 'round about: and behold, there were very many in the open valley; and lo, they were very dry."

Several things strike me hard and heavy.

1. The hand of the Lord was upon the prophet-preacher. I cannot help but feel that one of our problems is operating without the hand of the Lord being upon us. Our churches, our members are filled with accumulated knowledge of how to do things, but we miss one valuable ingredient - the hand of the Lord being upon us. Our Convention and associations are so wrapped up in egotism, graft, and bigness until we would prefer to not have His hand upon us. One needs little imagination to see why our valleys are filled with lifelessness and hopelessness. My brother preacher, wherever you preach, or pastor, make sure the hand of the Lord is upon you.

2. Rest assured you will not be going anywhere until His hands are upon you. Dress well, holler loud, drive exotic cars, but until the hand of the Lord is upon you, you will not be carried anywhere. Those of us especially who preach must remember this gospel we preach, these churches we pastor don't belong to us; we are and they are the sole possession of God. He carried us out in the spirit of the Lord. When one is carried it does not mean he goes where he wants to go. The destiny and destination of the one being carried is in the hands of the carrier. I am not in Shreveport, Louisiana by choice. The Lord brought me here. Because God is God, He alone reserved the right to place me wherever.

3. Ezekiel had no choice in the matter. God had His hands upon him and carried him out in the spirit and set him down in a dead church. Whoever heard of bleached, dried, lifeless bones paying tithes, or singing a hymn, or praying a prayer, or visiting the sick. Ezekiel did not even see a decaying body—nothing but dry bones. Nobody can expect an amen from dry bones. All the preacher could do was look. All he saw was bones and more bones. And the Lord had the audacity to ask him, *"Can these bones live?"*

What kind of an answer would you expect Rev. Ezekiel to give. It seems I can hear him thinking, "Lord, I was minding my own business over on the banks of the River Chebar. I didn't want to be in Babylon in the first place. This ruthless crown brought me here in 597 B.C. and I was wailing and weeping with the other Jews. I was about to hang my harp on the willows until you put your hands on me and brought me here. You set me down in this open valley. And now you ask me, a finite and infinite question. You have purpose for putting your hands on me, bringing me here and setting me down in this decayed valley. Let me give your question back to you:"

(1) Thou who made water wet, streams and rivers to run, ice to freeze and snowflakes to blanket the earth in the winter - Thou knowest.

(2) Thou who made the microscopic paramecium and the howling elephants - Thou knowest.

(3) Thou who has taken the unseeable atom and broken it down into protons, neutrons, and mesatrons — Thou knowest.

(4) Thou who planted the towering pines, the spreading junipers, the mighty oaks and the beautiful ash trees without a seed — Thou knowest.

(5) Thou who has taken green grass and carpeted the earth and tacked it down with lilies, roses — Thou knowest.

The Lord had the preacher where He wanted him and could use him. Ezekiel had come to the point of relying upon the knowledge of God — O Lord God, Thou knowest. Ezekiel would have had a problem preaching in what appeared to be a hopeless situation. But, the Lord said, "Prophesy unto these bones and tell them, O ye dry bones, hear the Word of the Lord." That must have been something! Can you imagine bones, dry bones hearing?

The Lord told Ezekiel to preach. God, Himself, told the bones that He would cause breath to enter into them, and they shall live; and He would cause muscles, skin and flesh to cover them, and they shall live and know He is God. That made Ezekiel's work a bit more bearable; we have Divine Intervention and help.

The preaching started dry bones to moving. A scattered foot found its way to the right leg. A far removed backbone skipped across the valley and found the proper hand. A misplaced toe made its way to the proper foot. And a long forgotten eye made its way to the right socket. What a mighty rumbling in the open valley. Ezekiel was encouraged by the sight. Listen at him shouting, "O ye dry bones, hear the Word of the Lord." Then, no more shaking, no more rattling, no more bones—just bodies laying out everywhere. Lord, I have done what you told me to do, but they aren't breathing. I can't handle this breath! What must I do now? This breath business is in your realm of operation. I can't argue with your track record. Your Genesis account is sufficient for me in Chapter 6:6—"Then the Lord God formed man of dirt from the ground, and breathed into his nostrils the breath of life; and man became a living being."

The Lord said, "I have another sermon for you to preach. Don't bother the bones, preach to the breath, Son of man;" say to the breath, "Thus saith the Lord God, come from the four winds, O breathe and breathe on these slain that they may come to life." Wind and spirit, breath and spirit are synonymous terms in Greek.

The bones had come together, muscles formed and skin covered flesh. All they needed now was to live. They needed breath - they needed Spirit. I am sure that many of these congregations of dry bones across America need breath to flow upon them. Many of us who preach are guilty of creating valleys of dry bones. Be as intellectual as you can be, but never forget to say, "Thus saith the Lord." You need to allow the spirit to infiltrate your intellect and give your whole self to His Divine Proclamation.

Ezekiel did not hesitate to preach to the wind. The wind began to blow and these slain bones stood up an exceedingly great army.

My brothers and sisters, I stand to tell you that this grand old Convention can live. We can live because resurrection power is within us. The wind has blown across the nation in Prichard, Alabama; Pasco, Washington; Newark, New Jersey; Philadelphia, Pennsylvania; San Antonio, Texas; Ville Platte, Louisiana; Biloxi, Mississippi; Clewiston, Florida. We have resurrection power, because the wind has blown.

> "What a wonderful change in my life has been wrought
> Since Jesus came into my heart."

Presidential Recommendations
The National Baptist Convention of America

1. That this convention, all of its auxiliaries and Boards would be audited by a reputable certified public accounting firm.

2. That during our mid-winter Board meeting, we would program four seminars:

a. Prayer: Dr. Harry Blake, Shreveport, Louisiana
b. Economic Development: Dr. A. L. Bowman, Denver, Colorado
c. Developing a Strong Sunday School: Rev. Lonnie Dawson
d. Taxes and Investments: Dr. West Kellogg III, Inglewood, California

3. That the National Baptist Youth Convention should meet during the week of the National Baptist congress. This change effective in 1987.

4. That a pragmatic, illustrative, easily understood and doctrinally sound manual for youths would be written and published. We need to have uniformity and purpose in what we teach our youth nationally. Dr. Hayward Wiggins will head this project.

5. That the Young Men for Christ would become an auxiliary to the National Baptist Brotherhood Union and share at least two (2) joint sessions.

6. That Dr. Marvin C. Griffin would author a book on the History of the National Baptist Convention of America. He will be compensated for this work. The Convention will own the publishing rights. Proceeds beyond the cost of publication will be distributed to the boards of our Convention.

7. That Dr. Samuel Gilbert would assimilate and edit two (2) books of sermons to be published by this convention. Preachers of the Past: Drs. P. S. Wilkinson, D. Manning Jackson, J. T. Stewart, J. P. Reader, A. A. Lucus, C. D. Pettiway, E. H. Branch, Earl A. Pleasant, Sr., John Thurston William Downs, M. M. Britt, E. F. Leadbetter, J. F. Seargant, Sr., M. L. Price, G. Gooins Daniels, Rufus Daniels, and J. C. Sams. Preachers of the Present: Drs. Robert H. Wilson, S. M. Lockridge, N. Samuel Jones, S. M. Wright, Isadore Edwards, Samuel Gilbert, W. N. Daniels, Wallace Hartsfield, Sr., Marvin C. Griffin, John W. Williams, Hayward Wiggins, Mac Charles Jones, W. A. Johnson, and Stephen Thurston. Proceeds beyond publication will go to the boards. The Convention will own the publishing rights. Dr. Gilbert will be compensated for his efforts.

8. That Thursday nights would be rotated between the Foreign Mission, Home Mission, and Benevolent boards. Friday nights would be designated education, social justice, and evangelism with the Evangelical Board, Social Justice Commission, and the Education Board rotating years.

9. That we would develop a plan for monthly financial support for our Convention. Under this plan, churches would send into the office of the Convention their budgeted amount. You would be immediately receipted. A quarterly newsletter would be sent to all participating churches and pastors.

a. All boards would receive an appropriated pro-share of a percentage of the quarterly gross income. The Budget Director and the Executive Board would develop a formula to be adopted by this convention.

b. A second percent would be placed on short-term interest-bearing investments.

c. A third percent would be used for administrative expenses.

10. That we give $50,000.00 to Bishop College this convention year. A special effort to be culminated at our mid-winter board session. Bishop College is on its way up, we need to get it up. I am appointing a special committee with Dr. Melvin Wade of California as chairman.

11. That Rev. Isadore Edwards would become our Public Relations chairman.

12. That Dr. W. N. Daniels of Chicago would become our Budget Director.

13. I recommend that every church that does not have life insurance on its pastor would do so. We are in a position to insure any preacher up to 75 years of age without a physical examination, up to $25,000.00 guaranteed insurance by a reputable insurance company.

14. That we meet in a joint session during our 1988 Annual Session with National Baptist Convention U.S.A., Inc. It is our intent to fill the Cotton Bowl in Dallas, Texas on that Thursday night. We will meet in Fort Worth and National Baptist Convention U.S.A., Inc. will meet in Dallas and that Dr. Albert E. Chew would be host.

Annual Address of Dr. E. E. Jones
President of the National Baptist Convention of America
In Session at Cleveland, Ohio, September 11, 1986

A Charge to Keep I Have

Vice-Presidents Lockridge, Chew and Hartsfield, Distinguished leaders of all the Auxiliary Bodies charging and challenging leaders of Boards, Commissions and Committees, Messengers to the 106th Annual Session of the National Baptist Convention of America, my brothers and sisters and others present, greetings in the precious name of our wonderful Lord and Saviour, Jesus Christ! I thank God for you and remember you in my prayers.

These twelve months have flown by with lightning speed. It seems only yesterday that we were gathering in my city, Shreveport, Louisiana to begin the 105th Annual Session. According to schedule we are here in the city of Cleveland, in the state of Ohio.

Cleveland, where the Stokes brothers made history, one the Mayor, the other a U. S. Representative.

Cleveland, where George Forbes heads the City Council.

Cleveland, where the waters of Lake Erie kiss the soils of Ohio.

Cleveland, where the Cleveland Indians swing a big bat.

Cleveland, where Jim Brown set football history with the Cleveland Browns.

Cleveland, where my long-time friend, Bill Downs took flight to heaven.

Our thanks go forth to Dr. A. Charles Bowie, and the great East Mount Zion Baptist Church, the Dr. Joseph Solomon Sutton, and the caring Sardis Baptist Church, the clergy of this city and state, elected officials and the cumulative lot of helpers who have made our entertainment possible, I assure you we are grateful. From the bottoms of our hearts, we say, "Thank you and God bless you."

Last year, you bestowed upon me the highest honor this convention has to offer. I have not taken that bestowal lightly, because I believe two things deep down in my heart: First, that God ordered it so, and second, you put your trust in me to do my best in leading this historic Convention to higher heights. I have striven hard not to fail the Lord, nor to fail you. You have placed me in a very precarious position, as President. The honors are many but for every honor there are many problems. The prestige is unbelievable, but the pressures are even more unbelievable. The office makes it possible to fellowship with people in high places and at the same time it positions me to be thrown at by my fellow peers. It is a high place being President and it is a hot place. I knew and now I am thoroughly convinced that being President of anything is not a coward's place. Friends and foes alike must know that. Often friends feel a certain place of prominence from everyday experiences and feel that they should spill over into the "Kingdom's agenda" with personal privileges. . . not so! Foes must not get trapped in meekness and mistake it for weakness. You and I alike must remember that this is not a work for special interest groups; it is not a political assignment; it is not for E. Edward Jones; it is the Lord's work and this demands that it be done decently and in order. Last but not least, being the President is very lonely. Nothing is as it was and nothing is quite as it seems. My one realization is, I have a charge to keep and keep it I must. I feel good about keeping my charge in this year.

The Lord has used my mind, energy and gifts in striving to pull us together to do what we could never do apart. Therefore, I have come to report to you my stewardship as President. Before I do that, let me express to you the splendor of the Galilee Church family. They have gladly and willingly shared me with this nation and the world. They have rejoiced with me in every victory; wept with me in every sorrow; encouraged me in every defeat; and prayed for me in every undertaking. They have convinced me that God has joined us together. Now, I would remind you brethren those whom God has joined together, let not man put asunder. Galilee is a great church, if not the greatest church in America. I love them dearly and they return that love to me manifold. I thank God for that pulpit.

Let me proceed with my report. My plan this past year was to visit the areas where we once have been strong, but are now weak. I have done that. It has been my joy to share with the leaders of our churches in New York. Thank you, Dr. Deen, for making it possible to share with you and the brethren of New York State; Dr. Joshua Groves and the brethren of Pennsylvania; President Wilson and the brethren of Maryland as well as the brethren of New Jersey. It was a cold snowy night in New York, but we had a hot time in the Lord. Thank you, D. I. Joseph Williams, for inviting me to Virginia for one of my two visits to that state. We held a number of conferences explaining the work of N.B.C.A.

As President, I have spoken at a number of institutions of higher learning including the following: Virginia Union Seminary in Richmond, Virginia; Florida Memorial College of Miami, Florida;

Benedict College in Columbia, South Carolina; Bishop College in Dallas, Texas; and Union Bible College in Houston, Texas. At the latter, the L.L.D degree was conferred on me at the same commencement service, the D.D. degree was conferred by Guadalupe College of Texas. Now I am four times a doctor. I have had one main purpose in each of these speaking engagements and that was to represent Christ. We know full well that if He is represented, our Convention will be represented. We are about the work of the Kingdom's agenda.

Because of you, I was the guest preacher for the National Baptist Convention U.S.A., Inc., in the Bahamas in January, 1986. I was more than pleased to have accompanying me, Vice-President and Sister Hartsfield, Moderator Howard Robinson and his wife of Seattle, Washington, Pastor and Sister Brooks of Nashville, Tennessee, and our very capable Corresponding Secretary, Dr. Stephen Thurston of Chicago, Illinois. We gave it our best shot and the Lord blessed mightily! The road led to Washington, D. C. for the Annual President's Prayer Breakfast. I felt a great need to attend this meeting because of our President and our nation's need for prayer.

The State Convention of our structure honor me in sharing their podiums with me. We had a spiritual ball with the General Baptist State Convention of Ohio. All three national bodies are represented in this convention. Dr. Newman, the state President, Sister Ester Burton, our brethren and all of the Ohioan's treated me royally. It was my good pleasure to share with the brethren of the Missionary General Baptist State Convention of Texas, where Dr. Robert Rowe is President and Dr. S. M. Wright is Executive Vice-President. That convention gives the appearance of the National Baptist Convention. Our First Vice-President, Dr. S. M. Lockridge gave me an invitation to attend the great California Baptist State Convention. Texas needs to watch out! California is inching along. The hospitality of California was superb. I felt highly honored to preach in the Progressive Missionary and Educational Convention of Florida. Both Texas and California had better watch out! In Florida, they attend the convention two on a mule. I recently returned to Florida to inaugurate the new President, Dr. H. T. Rhim of Jacksonville, Florida. I predict great success for the Progressive Missionary and Educational Convention of Florida under the leadership of this fine preacher. A month ago, I was the guest in my home state of one of the best conventions in our structure, the Louisiana Home and Foreign Mission Convention of Louisiana where the Dr. Freddie H. Dunn is President. No one has treated me any better. In fact, it might be a good idea for Dr. Dunn to hold seminars on how to treat the President.

I am emerging as a pretty good banquet preacher, not speaker. On Monday night of this week, I spoke for Dr. T. J. Jemison's Presidential Banquet in Kansas City, Missouri. I just can't seem to keep the preacher down in me. In Lufkin, Texas, I felt the same way at the American Baptist Convention's Congress headed by Dr. Mills. It was no different down in Austin, Texas, with Dr. George Clark and the St. John District. It seemed more apparent at the St. John Landmark Association in Fort Worth, Texas with Moderator Sanders. Of course, I would not have acted up in Houston, Texas for the Gethsemane Baptist Church Banquet if Dr. Hayward Wiggins had not been hamming it up. Hayward feels that you have to blow at every stop. I made a new friend and a good friend in Dr. Booker of Houston. He is a success story all in his own right. In addition to good food, I have come away with coats, hats, other items and some fairly good donations, sometimes not so good. However, I am thankful.

The number of churches visited are not too many, because I have a church that requires a little of my time. You need to know that I try to do my best there, every time I get up. Galilee never knows when it has done enough for its pastor. And, of course, please be reminded of the finest State Convention in this nation, the Baptist Missionary and Educational State Convention of Louisiana. They are very tolerant of me. I do not know what I would do in our state without Dr. C. L. Pennywell. He literally runs it, but never does he do so without my O. K. I need that convention to know that I love them more than words can express.

So much for my traveling and speaking. What about us as a Convention? You are doing a good job of revealing what can actually be done. I am thankful but I am not nearly satisfied. During our Annual Session last year, we raised $511,000.00 from all sources. In our Mid-Winter Board, we raised $164,000.00 from all sources. In our Summer Board, we raised nearly $50,000.00 in New Orleans, $26,000.00 of that was a donation from the National Congress.

Your Convention during this last year has contributed about $13,000.00 to Dr. Jesse Jackson and the Rainbow Coalition, approximately $9,000.00 to the NAACP; $10,000.00 to the flood victims of Mississippi; more than $57,000.00 to Bishop College; gave the Foreign Mission Board $3,000.00 for an emergency trip to Africa that the Secretary-Treasurer had to make; loaned Cornerstone Magazine $6,000.00 to keep the magazine afloat, hired two persons to staff the office for a total of $1,100.00 a month, retained a lawyer for the Convention, Dr. Arthur Thompson, a Baptist who is a trustee, a church and Sunday School attending attorney. All boards have been funded at a new level that is still too low to do the kind of work we need to be doing.

We have come to Cleveland with $100,000.00 in the Million Dollar Fund. Not bad, but not good. We should be started with the second million dollars now. My great disappointment is in the leaders of our Convention who find it hard to follow. At this point, we must be merciful: "Father, forgive them, for they know not what they do."

Because of some strenuous recommendations I made last year, some of our auxiliary bodies are a little confused. Don't panic! I mixed you up and I intend to straighten you out organizationally. Keep doing what you are doing until we get to that point. However, all auxiliary bodies and boards need to know that the audit is for real. This year, the Parent Body has been audited. Judgment suggests, if I audit myself, I sure do intent to audit everybody else. Don't be fearful. You will be happy to let the convention know just how you have been implementing the Kingdom's Agenda.

Our thanks to Dr. Sams who rests with the fathers for the purchase of land in Deland, Florida. We do not have an orange grove any longer. Several freezes have killed what trees we did have. But, we do have the land and its value is escalating. We have had several offers for sale of the property. The offers are getting more and more attractive. Yet to be decided, however, is whether or not we sell. Before a decision is final we will discuss, pro and con, the merits of selling.

Mass Communications Connect The World

What a great time to be alive! The world is brought into our living rooms via satellite television, making the most distant places close. The day of the "pony express" is long gone. While a disaster is happening in the Cameroons, it is being telecasted simultaneously in Cleveland. What a great time to be alive!

While we glory in technical advances, we also become international mourners. When the Challenger exploded in mid-air last spring, the entire world mourned. The exploding of the nuclear reactor in Chernobyl, Russia was another cause of world concern. Radioactive particles were blown over portions of the Eastern and Western hemispheres. It is not a matter of whether we are of the Free World or of the Communist bloc, people are people. Our suffering is no longer isolated. The acid fall-out in Cameroons, Africa, took its toll on us. There is something of a universal suffering when one nation experiences problems. Sometimes, the question should be raised: Is this really a good time to be alive?

The Christian acknowledges that God destines us for a particular era. 'Tis within that span of time we must busy ourselves in the implementing of the "Kingdom's Agenda." Yea, even in the midst of suffering, we are called upon to demonstrate the love of Jesus Christ.

Everything God has made is good. The same media that causes us to weep and sympathize; to get ecstatic during sports contests; to be patriotic in victories, should also be used to glorify God who made it all possible. God has given to this Convention some of the brightest minds in this nation. No longer can we remain hidden and relegate ourselves to apathy. 'Tis not a matter of escalating ourselves, the fact remains: "I, if I be lifted up from the earth, will draw all men unto me."

The constant recurring acts of terrorism remind us that our Christian work is not ended. Sin is still on the rampage and sinners are still lost. We cannot forget our real purpose. We cannot forget our strategy: "Go ye therefore, into all the world, and preach the gospel..."

Crime Continues to Rise

Research reveals that in the single year of 1968, more people were beaten or murdered on the streets of America than were killed or wounded in the seven and one-half years of the Vietnam War. Annually, about one million Americans are victims of reported violent crime. Between 1820 and 1945, it is estimated that 58 million people died at the hands of fellow human beings.

Examination of the Uniform Crime Reports (UCR) prepared annually by the National Crime Survey (NCS) indicates that blacks, constituting approximately 12% of the nation's population, have accumulated 50-to-60 percent of the arrests for forcible rape, close to 60 percent of the arrests for robbery, and between 40-to-50 percent of the arrests for aggravated assault. Relative to whites, blacks sustained criminal homicide rates that were between seven and thirteen times greater, forcible rape rates about seven times greater, robbery rates that were 10-to-17 times higher, and aggravated assault between four and seven times greater. Over the span of the decade, whites exhibited more pronounced increase in arrest rates than did blacks for forcible rape, robbery and aggravated assault.

The white rate of criminal homicide increased substantially while the black rate decreased slightly.

How can the church be silent in turmoil? Institutions and self-help programs are prevalent across this nation. Much good is coming from these sources. This is not to be denied, however, there is a paramount need for the church to address its major enemy: Sin and Satan.

Satan is doing a job on us. His attack on the family is quite obvious. The black family is deteriorating as divorce rates become alarming. There is a move to disenfranchise black culture and lifestyle. Some of us are embarrassed by our culture. Shame on us! The rare treasures of the past must be preserved for future generations. Certain factors are designed for the deterioration of the black family. One such factor, the Graham-Rudman Act, has great impact on social programs. The present administration is advancing strong conservative policies directed toward subverting black participation in the mainstream of America. Just recently, the High Court stayed affirmative action. Yet more discouraging is the exploiting of black voters. Many politicians want our vote to ensure victory, but we are tired of being taken. We must have some accounting for politician's stewardship; black politicians included. If you are in one of these areas where it is certain you can be elected, you must produce or be replaced.

Unemployment is staggering...

1984	15% Black	6% White
	Ages 20-24	28.3% Black men
		24% Black women
	Ages 25-29	12.7% Black men
		15.8% Black women
1985	15.1% Black	6.2% White

The black family is being disrupted by teen pregnancies. . .

1980	57% of babies born to teenagers under 17 were born to black teenagers.
1985	58% of all babies born were born to unwed mothers. 45% teenage mothers are likely to become grandmothers at age 40. Most likely these teens will not get married.

The black family is gullible for all vice. The young people of today must be taught and trained to put a premium on family life. The church must continue in its role to be a stimulant for youngsters who have no hope at home. The church must exhibit a "sweet spirit" that is far superior to drugs and alcohol. The music of the church must be heavenly. We have a charge to keep. We have no other choice.

This Convention has a Charge to Keep

I do want to be as disturbing as I can possibly be. God is not satisfied with the stewardship of His people. Many are caught up in the glory of selfishness. Superficially, you call the name of the Lord, because you remember this is supposed to be a church meeting. It doesn't make any difference if the Lord's real causes are not addressed. God is not addicted to mediocrity. He expects our best.

Our causes must be redefined. Our mental horizons must be expanded. The war is in the heart of battle and there is the possibility of some casualties. The cause of Christ is not for sale; not in this convention. I do not intend to engage in battle on my own. I remember He said, "Stand still, and I will fight your battle." Of course, He didn't say if someone steps on your feet let him stay there. As the General of this mighty host, I await orders from the Commander-in-Chief.

Our auxiliaries must not get bogged down in the morass of yesterday's achievements. Yesterday is past; soon today will be yesterday; so you must grip today and gaze at tomorrow. I call upon you to do more than to scheme to raise money. Why? Because the problems are with us. The problems are in this world. "In this world you shall have tribulations." There is a need to do some Bible searching to find out how to soundly combat our most formidable foe, Satan. Wade into the ocean of knowledge the Lord has in His Word. Dig deep into His eternal resources. With the high rate of pregnancies among our teenagers; dope flowing like the Mississippi River; crime crashing into every community (remember a few days ago in Edmond, Oklahoma), poverty and starvation on every hand, child abuse, wife abuse, single parent dilemmas, divorce, world problems (hijacking, etc.) and national problems, it is time to get Jonah out of the belly of the fish. A good National Baptist Convention starts at the level of the local church. We can provide some inspiration and general information at the National level, but the good job must be done at home, not here. You've got a charge to keep!

The men of our churches must be inspired to go back, dig into the Word and spend some time with the little boys who are growing up in homes without a father image. There are far too many boys, men, and I understand some preachers who are switching more than these ladies. The Brotherhood must meet the problems of homosexuality with biblical solutions.

Brethren, you stay with the Word. Get into it! Rejoice in His goodness. Don't be guilty of trying to pastor. Read the Word for yourself and see what your duties are. When you see what to do, do it! The church, like the home, needs some inspired men. Be on fire! You have a charge to keep.

Brother pastors and preachers, the Lord calls you to service. Stop striving to be big. Big folks don't want to listen to anybody. How in the world can you serve (be a servant) being high-minded? Come on down to reality and let's serve our fellow man and thus serve God.

Our ministry touches base with so many varied ministries. I hasten to say to you, visit your sick, minister to the broken-hearted, guide your office staff, get involved in civic matters that will help your people to enjoy the more abundant life, but most important, preach!

Paul said to Timothy as he faced Nero's chopping block, "I charge *thee* therefore before God, and the Lord Jesus Christ, who shall judge the quick and the dead at His appearing and His kingdom; preach the Word; be constant in season, out of season; reprove, rebuke, exhort with all long-suffering and doctrine. For the time will come when they will not endure sound doctrine; but after their own lusts shall they heap to themselves teachers, having itching ears; And they shall turn away *their* ears from the truth, and shall be turned into fables. But watch thou in all things, endure afflictions, do the work of an evangelist, make full proof of thy ministry."

In a cold cell in Rome, the Saint Paul knows that his time is running out. Whispers are being passed on throughout the jail house that Paul will be executed today. He glances out the side of his cell and sees the men hurrying here and there, making preparation for this execution. His sensitive ears hear the grinding of Nero's ax. He should be frightened, but he is not. He knows in whom he believes and that He is able to keep that which He has committed unto this day. Prior to his execution day, he writes his young son, Timothy.

"Listen, Timothy; you have a charge to keep. It must be in order now because it is not me you have to please. I won't be around anyway. But it is to be done before the Lord and His Son, Jesus Christ. He is watching. Now don't forget that He is watching because He is going to do some judging between the quick and the dead. I just want to remind you of one fact: 'Preach the Word'."

Preach the Word — it is power. . .

Preach the Word — don't get too wrapped up in *Newsweek* and *Ebony*.

Preach the Word — it will straighten out dope pushers, pimps, and prostitutes.

Preach the Word — if I never, never see you any more.

Preach the Word and don't forget now, men won't hear. Don't worry about that, just preach.

What I am saying to you is preach the Word in season and out of season. The time will come when they will not want to hear sound doctrine. They are going to be listening for a preacher that won't rock the boat. They are looking for a preacher who will shut up because he is afraid that if he speaks out they will cut down or cut out his anniversary. They are going to be looking for someone with some "praying clothes."

Preach the Word: They are seeking someone with itching ears. Some of these fellows are going to be in big churches, but they have personal interests. They want to know what the crowd wants to hear, not what the Lord has to say. They will sit up in your congregation and look out of the window. They will get mad with you because you rebuke them and get ice cold and won't say "Amen." They may even get up and walk out in the middle of your sermon, but your charge is to preach!

Preach until you feel like you are in Heaven. . .

Preach until it seems like there is angelic company. . .

Preach until haters come to love, until the spiritually blind receive their sight. . .

You've got a charge to keep. . .

Know what you are preaching — Jesus!